THE NATIONAL CONSUMER COUNCIL

Consuming Secrets

How Official Secrecy Affects Everyday Life in Britain

Edited by

Rosemary Delbridge
and Martin Smith

Foreword by
Harold Evans

BURNETT BOOKS
London

First Published 1982 by
Burnett Books Limited

Produced and Distributed by
The Hutchinson Publishing Group
17–21 Conway Street
London W1P 6BS

British Library Cataloguing in Publication Data
Consuming secrets: how official secrecy affects
    everyday life in Britain.
    1. Official secrets—Great Britain
    I. Delbridge, Rosemary   II. Smith, Martin
    III. National Consumer Council
    323.44'5   JN329.S4

ISBN 0–09–147590–2
ISBN 0–09–147591–0 Pbk

HARINGEY LIBRARIES

THIS BOOK MUST BE RETURNED ON OR BEFORE
THE LAST DATE MARKED BELOW.

To:

Contents

Editors' Note and Acknowledgements

Most of the material used in this book reflects English experience. Its commentary is nevertheless applicable to Britain as a whole. One important qualification should be noted. The laws and administrative arrangements of Scotland differ from those of England in some respects. This is particularly relevant to chapters four and five. A Scottish perspective on information issues can be found in *Rare Access: A Report on Access to Information in Scotland*, available from the Scottish Consumer Council.

Many people have offered encouragement, advice and generous assistance during the preparation of this book. Particular thanks are due to James Michael, James Smith and Liz Dunbar. Responsibility for the book's failings, however, rests solely with the editors.

Consuming Secrets is dedicated to the memory of Rosemary Delbridge, who died aged thirty-two as the book went to press, and without whom it would not exist.

Contributors

Harold Evans is editor of *The Times* and was formerly editor of the *Sunday Times*.

Rosemary Delbridge was, until her death in 1981, Parliamentary Officer of the National Consumer Council.

Martin Smith is a research officer at the National Consumer Council.

Stuart Weir is the assistant editor of *New Society* and was the founding editor of Shelter's *Roof* magazine.

Peter Newell was for three years deputy editor of *The Times Educational Supplement*, and since 1977 has worked for the Advisory Centre for Education. His publications include *A Last Resort? Corporal Punishment in Schools*.

Maurice Frankel works for the Public Interest Research Centre. He was co-editor of the journal *Social Audit* and his publications include *The Social Audit Pollution Handbook*.

Peter Stringer is Professor of Social Psychology at the University of Nijmegen in the Netherlands. His publications include *Planning and Participation in Practice* and *Public Participation in Local Services*.

Mick Hamer is a freelance journalist specialising in transport. He writes regularly for a variety of publications including *New Scientist* and *Municipal Journal*.

Peter Sand is Head of Research at the Consumers' Association and a member of the Government Advisory Committee on Electrical Safety.

Joyce Epstein worked as a social psychologist at American and Canadian universities before becoming a research consultant to the Consumers' Association in 1978.

Melanie Phillips is a leader writer for the *Guardian* and was Reporter of the Year for 1979.

Frances Williams works on the economics staff of *The Times*. Her publications include *Why the Poor Pay More* (editor).

Foreword

The British have learned to be suspicious of young men bearing theodolites and surveying poles. It is so very often the first sign that somebody somewhere is planning a nasty surprise: the demolition of half the High Street, the construction of a motorway across the common, or a bright new nuclear power station, perhaps on the estuary. In a well ordered world we would know about such things in time to make a polite point or two before it was too late. In Britain, the flow of information is so sluggish and erratic that the affected citizen is often one of the last to know; and there are some things which impinge on our lives which it is ordained we should not know at all. There are at least ninety-five subjects on which MPs cannot expect answers to questions, innumerable statutes which ban publication of this or that, the law of confidence which spreads like creeping buttercup through the English legal garden, suffocating administrative rules, and a style of paternalism which all combine to provide a quiet life for those in authority. If we were at all unstable we would be a nation of paranoiacs; in fact, the blockages to the free flow of information are too widespread and deeprooted to be the product of any conspiracy. Evidence there certainly is from time to time of a stealth and obstinacy which amounts to plotting against the public but there is more muddle than melodrama, more inertia than intrigue.

It is one great virtue of this book that it keeps its voice down. It is another that it describes the restrictions on information at a practical, human level. It reports on the ebb and flow of national and local practice as it affects welfare benefits and the language by which they may be claimed, shoddy paints, housing schemes, juggernaut lorries, poisoned rivers, how children are graded in school, and so on. In the most valuably concise Chapter Three it compares our custom and practice with the United States, Sweden, Canada and Australia. The essays are fair to the point of understatement. They recognise that there is sometimes a case for confidence. They are sensitive about personal privacy. They are aware of the risks of industrial espionage, of inhibiting frank discussions and of the weak objections about ministerial responsibility and expense. This is an attitude of patient enquiry for truth which one commends to the opponents of openness on the Bench and in Whitehall and Westminster who still tend to caricature it as a demand for Government in a goldfish bowl. But when all the quiet voices of this book are put together the effect is overwhelming. Why should we tolerate secrecy over figures purporting to justify road-widening, over food additives, hygiene on passenger liners, the safety records of cars as recorded by road accident statistics, the honesty of garages, the damage caused by heavy lorries, the full details of lead pollution, the carbon monoxide level of cigarettes, the incidence of hypothermia among old people, and the connection between atomic testing and leukaemia? Does it not remain absurd, and demeaning, that on some of these subjects we can learn more about our affairs in Washington than we can in London because British firms trading with the United States have to comply with the American regulations which insist on the publication of more information? Of course, nobody pretends, least of all the authors of this book, that an age of sweet reason will dawn if authorities have to divulge more. It is well, for a start, for us in the press to recognise that if ever the citizen does acquire rights similar to the American citizen it will be the press which must conscientiously exercise them on his behalf – and that the creation of understanding is a more complex task than printing information. We will still make big mistakes, we will still have a lot of arguments. But one cannot pretend that secrecy has been the handmaiden of achievement. And there is a further unanswerable argument for more openness which goes beyond mere efficiency: secrecy strikes at the roots of democratic society. It produces fear instead of trust. It excites hostility instead of cooperation. It repels the idea of tolerance for authorities coping with complex problems. It produces conflict instead of cohesion.

The National Consumer Council is to be commended for its imagination in producing this book. May there soon be a second edition celebrating the progress which this volume will inspire.

HAROLD EVANS

Introduction

Rosemary Delbridge

Official Secrets – the phrase immediately conjures up an image of spies, security, and surveillance. This book is about none of these. It is about official secrecy as it operates where you least expect and where it has the most immediate impact: when you send your child to school, pay an electricity bill or lose your local train service. Freedom of information is a *consumer* issue.

Informed consumer choice based on proper information is now an accepted principle for the purchase of a washing machine. But the National Consumer Council has always argued that the four basic tenets of the consumer movement – choice, representation, means of redress and information – are as pertinent to the public sector as they are to the private sector.

And access to information is the lynch-pin. The consumer case is a simple one: within government there is a great deal of information which would be valuable to consumers if it was publicly available, and whose collection has been paid for by consumers through taxation and rating. Consumers should have a *right* to such information unless there are good reasons (such as national security, trade secrets, and personal privacy) against its release.

There is a more fundamental – yet equally simple – argument. Open government is likely to be more honest and efficient than government conducted behind closed doors, and in this way the consumer gets better value for money as a tax-payer. Access to official information is also a citizen's best insurance policy to guarantee that government is conducted in the public interest.

Hence the National Consumer Council's decision to illustrate the consumer interest in access to official information – an aspect frequently absent from the acrimonious disputes that occasionally erupt into public debate on this subject. The evidence presented in the following chapters makes it quite clear that one of the most striking features of secrecy in Britain today is not how sinister it is but how absurd.

If the government collects data on the defects of motor cars, which it does, why is that information not publicly accessible? If the government knows the toxic content of all brands of cigarettes, why should this information remain secret? And is it the *law* that preempts the release of such information which to the most jaundiced eye could not be seen as a threat to our national security?

In Britain, as a result of the wording of Section 2 of the Official Secrets Act 1911, information is secret unless the government – at its discretion – decides that it should be released. (See Chapter Two). But the evidence presented in this book suggests that it is far too simplistic to see Section 2 as the sole cause of the problem. Ten years ago Professor Wade, then Professor of English Law at Oxford, told the Franks Committee:

The law as it now stands shows a complete failure to understand that accessibility of information about the government of the country is of vital importance in a democracy. It is so crude, and so excessively severe, that it is rendered tolerable in practice only by the Attorney General's tight control of prosecutions. It also has the insidious effect of conditioning ministers and civil servants to believe that unauthorised disclosure of any official information ought to be a crime. . . . It lowers the reputation of the public service, since it is thought to be used for covering up mistakes, even when this is not true. It has aggravated the secretiveness for which British administration has a bad name with its best informed critics, from the Fulton Committee to Mr Crossman. It has become one of the great vested interests of government. It is a classic example of bad law creating bad practice.[1]

Bad law creates bad practice – official secrecy leads to unofficial secrecy. There is no doubt that both government departments and local authorities are making more information available than ever before – every chapter in this book highlights this progress. But it is equally clear that in many circumstances information is withheld not because it is perceived to be illegal to release it – but because it would be embarrassing, time-consuming, or politically awkward to do so, or 'too complex' for the potential recipient to deal with. The American lawyer James Michael has pointed out:

No one who exercises authority is particularly keen to explain the true reasons for his decisions, or to submit to critical questioning about them. Such an inquiry is all too likely to expose the extent to which guesswork, prejudice, and the simple imitation of precedents can influence important decisions. And an informed observer might conclude that mistakes are being made by those in charge of things.[2]

Consumers need access to two quite different kinds of information. First, as members of the wider community they need to know the factual basis on which policy decisions about gas pricing, new motorways, or food additives are made. Secondly, they need information as individuals: the basis on which they have been refused a council house, or why, if they are disabled, they are not entitled to certain benefits.

How can this be achieved? Repealing Section 2 is not the panacea. What the evidence in this book suggests is that just as important as legal reform is change of attitude from ministers, their officials and Parliament. The National Consumer Council commissioned the authors of the various chapters to illustrate from their experience the extent and the impact of official secrecy on consumers. Although obviously the views expressed in each chapter are those of the authors rather than official National Consumer Council policy, we are now convinced that there is a need for Professor Wade's 'Bad Law' to be repealed, but also that 'Bad Practice' can and must be improved since such statutory reform seems unlikely to take place in the foreseeable future. The Council believes that this book is a vital contribution to a debate that has got lost in the rarefied air of political science, constitutional hyperbole and treason trials. Spies, Security and Surveillance are proper concerns for those who attempt to analyse the nature of official secrecy in Great Britain. But so are Gobbledegook, Gas Bills and Government Guile.

REFERENCES

1 *Departmental Committee on Section 2 of the Official Secrets Act 1911* (Chairman: Lord Franks), Cmnd 5104, HMSO, 1972, vol. 2, written evidence submitted to the Committee, pp. 411–12.
2 Michael, James, 'The Politics of Secrecy/The Secrecy of Politics', *Social Audit*, vol. 1, no. 1, Summer 1973, p. 53.

The Secrecy Debate in Britain 2
Rosemary Delbridge and Martin Smith

What is the Official Secrets Act? What kind of information falls within its orbit? This chapter traces the history of our official secrecy legislation and the attempts that have been made to change it. It deals briefly with other kinds of official and quasi-official information not directly controlled by the Act – material originating in or held by local government and the nationalised industries – and looks at the context of the secrecy debate in Britain since the 1960s and the problems presented by attempts to replace the existing legislative framework.

There are two distinct approaches to changing the ground rules on official secrecy in Britain. One seeks to liberalise, rationalise or otherwise alter the current criminal law on disclosure; the other, to follow several countries[1] in establishing a *fundamental right to know*, exceptions to which must be closely specified and subject to some form of independent check.

This second approach – 'open government' – is in principle the easier to understand; but in practice the two debates have often overlapped. This complex interpenetration of essentially rather different issues helps to explain the confused and contradictory approaches of successive governments to secrecy reform.

This chapter is concerned with the legal status of information originating in central government – information, that is, which falls within the orbit of the Official Secrets Act – and with proposals to change the law. It also deals briefly with other kinds of official and quasi-official information not directly controlled by the Act, material originating in or held by local government and the nationalised industries.

The Official Secrets Act

The current law on secrecy is laid down in the Official Secrets Act of 1911.[2] This replaced an earlier statute of 1889; and has itself been affected by further Acts of 1920 and 1939 – in fact, since these measures have not been consolidated, it is strictly proper to talk of the Official Secrets Acts in the plural, although these later measures are of relatively little significance.

The context in which the 1911 Act was passed is important. It was presented to the public and to Parliament as an emergency defence against foreign espionage. The Agadir crisis, and reports of sinister strangers hanging around bases and dockyards, produced a sense of imminent danger in which the Act passed through both Houses by massive majorities, and almost without debate.

The Act's scope in practice has been far greater than the government of the day imagined; and it has often been suggested that its confusions and all-embracing character are the result of the urgent speed with which it was drafted. The Franks Committee, however, concluded that it was meant to do exactly what it does do: to function as a 'general check against civil service leaks of all kinds'.[3] It is certainly true that leaks and scandals just as embarrassing as the recent crop – and equally unconnected with national security – were occurring in the years before 1911.

The most important parts of the Official Secrets Act are its first two sections. Section 1 is concerned specifically with espionage: it applies only to military and naval information, and although a certain amount of controversy exists over its terms (mainly to do with the way in which it places the burden of proof on the accused), it is not very relevant to this discussion.

Section 2 lays down a number of *criminal* offences, centred on two broad categories: the unauthorised communication of official information, and its unauthorised receipt. We can roughly define 'official information' as *any* data which someone possesses through their position as a Crown servant, a government contractor, or a contractor's employee.

It is immediately clear that 'official information' includes a vast range of material with no possible bearing on national security, or – the other important target of the Act – on corruption, theft, and so on. And this is the first major objection to Section 2: its monolithic inclusiveness, drawing no distinction between treason, corruption, and public-interest journalism, establishes no scale to relate the punishment to the deed. In theory, if not necessarily in application, precisely the same offence has been committed if you sell technical secrets to the Chinese, or if (as in 1972 and again in 1979) you print in a British newspaper details of a discussion document on possible rail closures.

This example raises a second feature of Section 2 which journalists tend to find particularly objectionable. In 1972 the editor of the *Sunday Times* was told by the police – quite correctly – that the simple receipt of information on suggested rail closures in itself constituted a breach of the Act. As the Franks Report pointed out in a general observation on Section 2, 'it is immaterial whether the recipient subsequently passes on the information or makes any other use of it'.[4]

Now it is certainly arguable that it should not be an offence to receive passively information, and do nothing more: that the responsibility should rest solely with the person who communicated it. (It does have to be shown that the recipient could reasonably have known that the information was protected.) But whether or not the material is passed on by the receiver – it might, for example, be published – there is some doubt about the extent of culpability.

A key concept in Section 2 is *authorisation*. The day-to-day business of the Civil Service is only possible on the assumption of *implicit* authority to communicate a wide range of information which, simply because it is government information, technically falls within the Act. This notion of authorisation is very elastic in practice. But it is certainly not always easy for someone who receives official information to judge whether it has been properly communicated.

This question of uncertainty is fundamental. In a strict sense, Section 2 of the Official Secrets Act must be breached thousands of times a day – every time, for instance, that a civil servant talks about his day over dinner. Of course, the Act never has been and never could be interpreted in this way, but how is an editor to judge whether a particular piece of information is likely to lead to prosecution? There is a suspicion that what most annoys the government of the day is more likely to be prosecuted, and it was stated in evidence to the Franks Committee that the threat of Section 2 has on occasion been used to prevent publication.[5] Whether or not made explicit, the threat is always there. And in recent years, there has been an increasing public perception, justified or not, of randomness and government self-interest in the application of the Act.

No prosecution under the Official Secrets Act can be brought without the consent of the Attorney General (in Scotland, the Lord Advocate). This consent has certainly not been easily obtained: between 1945 and 1971, only twenty-three prosecutions were launched under Section 2, most of these quite uncontroversial.[6] It can be argued, though, that, as a politician, the Attorney General is not the right person to make these decisions. Many leaks result in an embarrassment which is purely party-political rather than a matter of security. On the other hand – and this was the position taken by the Franks Committee – perhaps politically sensitive decisions on prosecution *should* be taken by a politician rather than by a lawyer.

To sum up: Section 2 of the Official Secrets Act, by its looseness of reference, means that civil servants and investigative journalists may frequently be in technical breach of the law, since anything not permitted is forbidden. Compare it with Alice in Wonderland: all the players are under permanent sentence of execution, permanently postponed – except that the axe does occasionally and unpredictably fall.

However, since Section 2 is open to such wide variations in interpretation, it has not prevented a considerable increase in access to information over the last twenty years. Administrative decisions like the publishing, since 1962, of planning inspectors' reports; political innovations like the green papers; and the general shift towards greater openness of debate fostered by the growth of pressure groups – all these factors have created a considerable change of atmosphere without any change in the law.

The Debate on Secrecy

There was little public discussion of these issues between 1911 and 1968 except for the 1965 report by a joint working party of JUSTICE (the British section of the International Commission of Jurists) and the British Committee of the International Press Institute. Chaired by Sir Hartley Shawcross, the working party deplored the fact that 'information which is not prejudicial to the national interest or to legitimate private interests, and relates solely to the efficiency or integrity of a Government department or public authority'[7] was (and is) protected from disclosure by the criminal law.

This report produced comparatively little interest, and no action. But in 1968, the Fulton Committee on the Civil Service stated that 'the administrative processs is surrounded by too much secrecy' and that 'the public interest would be better served if there was a greater amount of openness'.[8] It recommended a wide-ranging review of the law and current practice.

The Labour government reacted defensively. Its white paper,

Information and the Public Interest, emphasised that the flow of information from government departments was increasing; and that Section 2, since it applies only to *unauthorised* disclosure, was not itself a barrier to greater authorised openness.[9] This is of course true, but as an argument it may be stood on its head: the ambiguity of the concept of authorisation forms one of the strongest arguments for the reform of the law.

The Conservative election manifesto of 1970 responded to the Fulton report by promising to eliminate unnecessary secrecy in government and to review the operation of the Act. To this end, in April 1971 the new government set up the Franks Committee 'to review the operation of Section 2 of the Official Secrets Act of 1911, and to make recommendations.' It is important to note that these terms of reference were much narrower than those recommended by Fulton: an inquiry 'to make recommendations for getting rid of unnecessary secrecy in this country not least in policy-making and in administration.' With evident regret, the Franks Committee decided that its brief precluded the consideration of freedom of information proposals.

The Franks Committee's verdict on Section 2 was unambiguous. Section 2 is 'a mess. Its scope is enormously wide. Any law which impinges on the freedom of information in a democracy should be far more tightly drawn.'[10] The Committee proposed that Section 1 of the Act be replaced by an Espionage Act, and Section 2 by an Official Information Act.

This Act, it was suggested, should be limited in its operation to six categories of official information. These were: a) defence and national security; b) foreign relations; c) currency and the reserves; d) information likely to impede the law or assist crime; e) Cabinet documents on whatever subject; and f) information given to the government by private individuals or concerns – whether or not explicitly given in confidence.[11]

In relation to the first three of these categories, the Franks report introduced the important principle that the information concerned *must* have been officially classified as secret – and that the court must be satisfied that this classification was correct.[12] It recommended the 'hiving off' of the offence of corruption to an extended Prevention of Corruption Act, since official secrecy is not the prime issue involved.[13]

Franks also recommended that the mere *receipt* of information by a private citizen should no longer be an offence, though its further communication would be (provided always that the accused could be shown to have had reasonable grounds for knowing that the information was secret). The report laid out at some length the responsibilities of different categories of people – Crown office-holders, contractors, private individuals, and so on – what would constitute a defence in each case, and what the prosecution would have to show.

Presented in September 1972, the Franks report generated considerable interest – partly as a result of the *Sunday Telegraph/* Biafra trial of the previous year, in which the defendants were acquitted and the judge spoke sharply of 'pensioning off' Section 2.[14] There was praise for the high quality of the Franks Committee's work; its conclusions, however, became a sort of no man's land between entrenched positions.

The Conservative government which had called for the report rejected it as too radical. They accepted the principle of a new, rationalised Act, but argued that it was not possible to determine in advance precisely what kinds of information would constitute a threat to national security. Like the previous Labour government, once in office the Conservatives came down in favour of an inclusive law, liberally interpreted in practice: in effect, an administrative solution.

On the other hand, many journalists and other commentators found Franks too conservative. In particular, it was regretted that Franks had not accepted the 'public interest' principle – that, in the words of JUSTICE's 1965 report, 'it should be a valid defence . . . to show that the national interest or legitimate private interests . . . were not likely to be harmed and that the information was passed and received in good faith and in the public interest.'[15]

However, the growing freedom of information lobby had a much wider criticism of the Franks report. It saw the isolated reform of Section 2 as irrelevant to the main issue: to reverse the whole basis of secrecy law to establish a fundamental right to know. On this principle, no longer could everything be forbidden that was not permitted; everything would be permitted, and even enforced, which was not forbidden.

Some years, and a change of government, followed before any action was taken on the Franks report (apart from a Cabinet committee to consider the matter). In the second general election of 1974, the Labour party manifesto specifically promised 'to replace the Official Secrets Act by a measure to put the burden on the public authorities to justify withholding information' – the freedom of information principle. But not until November 1976 did the Labour Home Secretary deliver a statement of intent – and this only on the more limited issue of Section 2.[16]

This statement accepted the Franks proposals, with three major changes. Two of these went further than Franks. The government intended to remove the Committee's third category of criminally actionable material, relating to currency and the reserves; and also to limit the protection of Cabinet documents to those covered by the other Franks categories. Thus the six categories would be reduced to four.

However, the Labour government also planned a major *extension* of the recommended classification 'Defence – Confidential' (concerned with weapons and military equipment). This would now cover: 'certain areas of defence policy and strategy and of international relations where unauthorised disclosure would be prejudicial to British interests, to relations with a foreign government, or to the safety of British citizens.'

Had this widely drafted proposal been law at the time, it would very probably have changed the verdict in the *Sunday Telegraph* trial, where the information published was clearly damaging to relations with the Nigerian government.

But, as the history of the issue might lead one to expect, it was nearly another two years before the government's intentions got as far as a white paper. And during this time, the pressure for a right of access increased dramatically. The All Party Committee on Freedom of Information was formed in 1976, and published a draft Bill on Freedom of Information and Privacy – in effect, an attempt at a double strengthening of the private citizen's rights vis à vis the state which would limit the flow of information in one direction and encourage it in the other.

By the time the government got round to issuing its white paper, *Reform of Section 2 of the Official Secrets Act 1911* in July 1978,[17] many people saw it as too little too late. The debate had moved on into the area of 'open government'. It was even argued that the rationalisation of Section 2 by itself would actually worsen the situation: it would leave a vacuum in the huge middle ground between protected information and run of the mill information which the government was happy to release.

Only a Freedom of Information Act would fill this vacuum; and as it happened Clement Freud MP, who had won first place in the private member's ballot, announced at the end of 1978 that he would introduce an Official Information Bill incorporating a public right of access. This Bill (drafted by the now defunct Outer Circle

Policy Unit) would at once have replaced Section 2 and have established a fundamental right to know in all areas not specifically protected.

Though falling short in some respects of proposals for full 'open government', the Bill attracted considerable public and backbench support. Once again, a secrets trial helped to focus interest; the 'ABC' trial was widely perceived as making a mockery of the current law. Despite the coolness of both front benches, Freud's Bill obtained an unopposed Second Reading and went to a sympathetic Commons standing committee. It was widely expected that an unhappy government would starve the Bill of parliamentary time at the Report stage; but before the crunch came, Parliament was dissolved for the May 1979 election which produced a Conservative victory.

Before its fall, the Labour government had been moved to issue two new documents on the subject. *Disclosure of Official Information: A Report On Overseas Practice*[18] reviewed the situation in nine countries which either had, or were actively considering, some form of public access legislation. A green paper, *Open Government*,[19] was an explicit rejoinder to the Freud Bill: it again rejected the case for a statutory right of access in favour of a voluntary code of practice.

Earlier, in July 1977, the Callaghan administration had introduced the basis for such a voluntary approach in the form of 'the Croham directive'. This memorandum was circulated with prime ministerial authority by Sir Douglas Allen, then head of the Home Civil Service and subsequently ennobled as Lord Croham, to fifty-one heads of department in Whitehall. It called for more departmental policy papers to be made available to the public. The directive was intended, in its own words, 'to mark a real change of policy'.

In the past it has normally been assumed that background material relating to policy studies and reports would not be published unless the responsible minister or ministers decided otherwise. Henceforth the working assumption should be that such material will be published unless they decide that should not be.[20]

Furthermore, the directive instructed departments to keep a record of material released under its provisions.

In 1980 *The Times* carried out an audit of documents made public as a consequence of the directive and concluded that far from marking 'a real change of policy', the directive's instructions had been largely ignored. In mitigation, it was claimed in Whitehall that the enthusiastic pursuit of the directive's aims would have been too costly in money and manpower.

The new Conservative government, like its predecessor, was firmly opposed to a right of access; and even to a more liberal code of Civil Service practice. One of its first acts was to suspend work on the Croham directive as an economy measure. It was, however, committed to repealing Section 2; and acted with unprecedented swiftness. But its proposed replacement, the Protection of Official Information Bill (introduced in late 1979), was widely seen as worse than Section 2 itself.

It is still unclear whether the draconian elements of this Bill were intentional, or the result of poor drafting. Introducing its Second Reading in the Lords, Lord Hailsham described it as 'more liberal' and 'more intelligible' than Section 2, 'and even capable of enforcement'.[21] But critics had four major objections.

The new Bill proposed to apply criminal sanctions to a very wide range of information – including, like Section 2, some which had no capacity to injure national or private interests. In fact, the category of 'official information' would be extended to material not generally thought to be covered even by Section 2. The Bill rejected the Franks Committee's recommendation that only properly classified information should be protected. Proof of damage to national security would be established merely by a minister's certificate to that effect. And finally, the grounds of defence against a charge of improper disclosure would be severely limited.

Opposition to the Bill – especially to its potentially drastic effect on journalists – was just beginning to limber up when the Blunt case provided a fortuitous demonstration of the argument. It was realised that, had the new Bill been law, it would have prevented all public discussion of Sir Anthony Blunt's treason. The government bowed to the inevitable and immediately withdrew its Bill; it is thought unlikely that any substitute measure will be introduced before 1983.

The proponents of a public right of access have vainly persisted with further draft Bills on the lines of Freud. The most recent, another private member's Bill introduced by Frank Hooley MP, was in February 1981 when the government used a procedural device to prevent it from completing its Second Reading.

The Issues behind the Arguments

One thing which is very clear from this brief historical sketch is that the issues of secrecy and access have never been systematically debated in this country. Proposed reform has constantly been subject to jolts and interruptions from outside events: changes of government, fortuitous scandals and *causes célèbres*. Government policy has not kept pace with the development of public feeling. Also, government views have no doubt been importantly affected by Civil Service advice – to which, currently, there is no access. And although both saw the relevance of the issue, neither the Franks Committee nor the Royal Commission on the Constitution (which reported in 1975) was able to look directly at 'open government'.

The central argument against a public right of access – stated, for example, in the *Open Government* green paper – is constitutional. It is claimed that freedom of information is incompatible with the principles of ministerial responsibility and the anonymous civil servant. This argument is considerably weakened by open government legislation drafted (though at the time of writing not yet enacted) in Canada, a country with a Westminster-style constitution.[22]

In fact, back in 1968 the Fulton report argued that these principles were 'no longer tenable'; that administration suffers from the sacred myth that ministers can be aware of everything that is happening in their department. It concluded that 'the concept of anonymity should be modified and civil servants, as professional administrators, should be able to go further . . . in explaining what their departments are doing.'[23] Many practical developments in this direction have taken place since then; but it may be said that, without statutory backing, these changes are still subject to the unchallengeable whim of the administrators.

It is undeniable that, within the current legal framework, a change in the hearts and minds of the Civil Service could go a very long way toward open government. After all, the big scandals are perhaps ultimately less important than the day-to-day cloak of silence which surrounds areas like housing, transport, energy, welfare benefits – the areas covered in this book. However, even if a drastic change of atmosphere could somehow miraculously be effected, the public would still need some means of discovering what information is there to be asked for. The establishment of public registers of information held would be by no means the least important feature of open access legislation. Also, reform through administrative fiat is subject to no independent appeal or check.

In 1978, a second JUSTICE report, *Freedom of Information*,[24] proposed just such an administrative shift: a code of practice for voluntary disclosure, backed up by an appeal to the Parliamentary Commissioner for Administration (the Ombudsman). JUSTICE argued that 'there are no rigid formulae' for disclosure, and that legislation is therefore inappropriate. Most other proponents of public access disagree. They say, firstly, that effective access *does* mean a major change in the relationship between government and public, and therefore *ought* to be decided by Parliament; and secondly, that the Ombudsman has no power to enforce his decisions, and that a new statutory appeal mechanism is therefore essential.

Almost everyone is agreed that Section 2 of the Official Secrets Act is wholly unsatisfactory. Not only is it negative in its effects on public life; it is also bad law. However, its replacement has proved to be a matter of some difficulty – not just for the practical and contingent reasons referred to above, but also because it cannot really be separated from the issue of 'open government'.

The two questions are distinct but related. Any replacement of Section 2 which retains the principle of a general or 'catch-all' prohibition will necessarily militate against public access. Any replacement which takes the opposite road, and strictly limits prohibited categories, must cry out for a Freedom of Information Act to deal with the vacuum which will then surround all other official information.

It is in any case unlikely that Section 2 could be replaced with legislation which would eliminate all scandal and controversy. As many have pointed out, it is not possible to define in advance all possible threats to national security; and there is never going to be a universal consensus over what should or should not be publicly known. The 'ABC' trial raised the very difficult issue of the journalist who assembles and synthesises scraps of information which are already separately and publicly available (a major activity, as the defence pointed out, of all intelligence organisations).

But none of this is an argument for leaving Section 2 as it is. Nor is it an argument for taking the path of the Conservative government in 1979 of drafting legislation which is unambiguous by virtue of its severity. Section 2 is clearly inappropriate to current public feeling; most importantly, perhaps, because of the 'safety first' atmosphere created by the burden of interpretation which it places on individual civil servants.

Local Government

The Official Secrets Acts do not apply to local government. There might be circumstances in which a local government employee passed on classified information which came from central government; but no prosecutions of this kind are known.

Within local authorities, the kinds of information available are unlikely to cause major damage to the public interest if disclosed; it is much more likely that the interests of private individuals or firms would be affected. Information is therefore protected by internal discipline and in some cases by statute; but it is clear that local government secrecy extends much further than is necessary for this protection. As with central government, it is not even possible to say exactly what or how much is kept secret.

But there are several statutory public rights of access, covering audits, various types of documents, meetings, and the powers of the 'local ombudsman'. And central government has encouraged local authorities to interpret these rights generously.

Audits Any elector or ratepayer is entitled to examine their authority's accounts and supporting documents during the seven days before the annual audit. They may use an accountant to help them do this; they may then lodge an objection to the accounts when the audit takes place. (This right is established by the Local Government Act of 1933, amended by section 159 of the Local Government Act 1972.)

Access to Documents There are two major rights here, and a hodge-podge of piecemeal entitlements. Section 228 of the Local Government Act 1972 states that any elector may inspect and make copies of *minutes, orders for payment*, and *statements of account*; while the Town and Country Planning Act 1971, section 34, provides that *planning applications* must be recorded in a register open to public inspection, and that anyone affected by a particular application may see the relevant file and plan, and object to the granting of the application.

Several other rights of access exist by accident, as it were, in quite separate statutes. For example, the public may examine records of councillors' expenses (Local Government [Allowances] Regulations 1974). Under section 32 of the 1936 Public Health

Act, plans of sewers may be studied; and under section 238, registers of common lodging houses are open to inspection.

Many documents relating to property may be inspected only by 'interested persons', that is, those with a direct property interest. This applies to clearance and compulsory purchase orders. Some other rights of access, without this limitation, clearly are intended in the same way: for instance, the Land Charges Act of 1972 established a register of various details of land use – but although anyone may consult it, enquiries must be made about individual properties rather than groups or areas.

Admission to Meetings   Section 1 of the appropriately named Public Bodies (Admission to Meetings) Act 1960, laid down the principle that council meetings should be open to the public; and this was extended by section 100 of the 1972 Local Government Act to council committees. But the public and the press may be excluded from all or part of a meeting on grounds of confidentiality without even knowing what is to be discussed.

Local Ombudsmen   The Local Commissioners (established in 1974) are empowered to investigate complaints from the public – filtered through councillors – of maladministration by delay, neglect, incompetence or prejudice. They can examine all relevant papers, and issue public reports. (But they cannot consider the rights or wrongs of a *decision*, only whether it has been properly arrived at. They have no powers to enforce their verdict.)

Reporting on the conduct of local government in 1974, the Redcliffe-Maude Committee[25] stressed the importance of maximum openness as an essential safeguard for probity and public confidence. Both before and since, the Department of the Environment (DoE) has urged local authorities in this direction – for example, to make positive efforts rather than minimal gestures towards informing the public about development plans. DoE Circular 45/75 encouraged the widest interpretation of the law in relation to documents and public attendance (which it felt should apply also to sub-committees); it stressed the importance of a good relationship with the press.[26]

There are, however, some areas of local government information where disclosure could lead to unfair gain or advantage – for example in relation to commercial development decisions; or to a breach of personal privacy – for example, the great quantities of personal data held by education, housing, and social service departments. Very few authorities have developed a coherent view of the balance between public and private interest in these matters.

One important issue concerns the individual's right to inspect and correct files about himself – a right acknowledged by very few authorities.[27] Another difficult and controversial area is the role of elected councillors: what sorts of information should be available to them, and on what terms?

Council Employees There is some information which council employees are forbidden by statute to disseminate. Some of these measures (like the 1974 Rehabilitation of Offenders Act) protect individual privacy. Others are more questionable. Trading standards officers may not generally disclose information acquired through investigating companies; the same is true of much information obtained by environmental health officers inspecting factories or other commercial premises.

The point has been well illustrated in the course of work conducted by the Scottish Consumer Council (SCC). In response to an enquiry from the SCC, the Consumer Protection Department of Strathclyde Regional Council expressed concern at the inhibiting effects of those Acts, the Trade Descriptions Act 1968 being the most important, which restrict the disclosure of information by their own inspectors. (The Department carried out 3,265 inspections under this Act alone in 1979–80.)

The Department interprets the law to mean that an inspector engaged in an investigation under the Trade Descriptions Act who obtains information about some offence or other matter which in his view ought to be looked at by some other enforcement agency, for example the Environmental Health Department, will, if he passes on that information, be in breach of the Act. Similarly, if a citizen makes a complaint to the Department and the Department starts to investigate the circumstances of that complaint under the Trades Descriptions Act, it cannot then pass on to the complainer such information as is unearthed to do, for example, with the trader's response to the investigation or with any tests made for the Department on the goods in question. In the absence of any test of possible commercial damage, it seems that businesses are over-protected at the expense of the public.[28]

Besides such statutory measures, all council employees are bound by the National Joint Council conditions of service, which stipulate that:

No officer shall communicate to the public the proceedings of any com-

mittee meeting, etc., nor the contents of any document relating to the
authority unless required by law or expressly authorised to do so.[29]

The general opinion of local authorities has been that internal
discipline provides adequate safeguards against improper disclosure: as the then Association of Municipal Councils told the Franks
Committee in 1971, 'in view of the lack of any sanction such as
Section 2 . . . it is noteworthy how little the unauthorised disclosure of documents takes place.' The Association did not, and its
successors do not, envisage the introduction of criminal sanctions
– though Franks did not rule this out.[30]

To an outside observer, it may seem that leaks in local government are actually quite frequent; and sackings do occasionally
occur. An official in the Kilmarnock and Loudon planning department was sacked after he wrote to the local paper criticising
town centre redevelopment plans; an industrial tribunal ruled
against the council, and ordered compensation but not
reinstatement.[31]

Councillors   The position of councillors *vis à vis* authorities
over information is ambiguous. Sometimes, the individual councillor figures as the aggrieved party being denied access; sometimes as the leaker; sometimes, individually or collectively, as the
refuser of access to others. Council procedures are generally un-
specific over councillors' rights of access. Most councils attempt
some form of prohibition of leaks – perhaps more honoured in
the breach than the observance. Sanctions, at worst, will consist
of the withdrawal of the party whip.

The Department of the Environment's model standing orders
suggest that councillors should be able to inspect documents *only
in the pursuit of their duties*. And the right of an authority to
withhold information has been established in court (R v. Barnes
Borough Council *ex parte* Conlon (1938) 3 All E.R. 226, citing
earlier cases). Some hard fought disputes have taken place on this
issue: for instance, over the Inner London Education Authority's
persistent refusal to give Putney councillor Leonard Harris the
names and addresses of school governors in ILEA area 10. It was
acknowledged that this list existed and was not marked confidential; but the Authority argued that it would have to obtain the
consent of each individual governor and that this would be too
expensive.[32] More frequently, councillors are given information
only on condition of strict confidence.

There is little consistency over information access in local government. Apart from the statutory rights outlined above, a great deal depends on the discretion of authorities: there are wide variations in, for example, the amount of committee business conducted *in camera*, or the extent and outgoingness of the public information programme. Both within and between authorities, there is a sense of arbitrariness in what is and is not available (see Chapter Seven).

With respect to the presentation of statistical data, this unevenness has been largely corrected by the information provisions of the 1980 Local Government, Planning and Land Act. The effect of these provisions and of their associated codes of practice is to oblige local authorities to publish certain statistical data in codified form. This will help those who seek to make comparative analyses of local government expenditure. Three main categories of information are involved: regular management information about day-to-day performance; information distributed with rate demands; and annual reports. This reform will undoubtedly open up some previously closed recesses of local government decision-taking, but will not have a fundamental impact.

There are different views as to whether local government is more, or less, secretive than central government. Present arrangements in local government generally approximate to those in central government in that officials release what they choose to release on a discretionary basis. However, the officials themselves are more accessible in local than in central government, not least to elected representatives. Nevertheless, the situation at local level still fails to reflect the thinking (no doubt motivated by a degree of self-interest) of the London Government Public Relations Association which declared in 1974 that:

The cost of local government is borne by the people and they therefore have a right to adequate and timely information about their council's problems, work, and services. The duty of providing this information service should be enshrined in Acts of Parliament and should be mandatory.[33]

Nationalised Industries

The range of bodies under some form of public ownership and/or control is very wide indeed. Their performance has a direct and daily impact on the lives of everyone. This section is concerned primarily with the major fuel, power and transport industries: with the legal and other constraints on disclosure, and with the mechanisms that exist to inform the public about their activities – chiefly, the nationalised industry consumer councils.

The terms of Section 2 of the Official Secrets Act allow for a certain ambiguity about the status of nationalised industries. This applies both to the *information* available, and to the *individuals* concerned. Though there has never been a test case to establish this, it is generally felt that employees of nationalised industries are not holders of office under the Crown. However, through their employment, some of them come into contact with secret or confidential official information. Members of the boards of nationalised industries, on the other hand, may well be regarded as Crown office-holders, though the old Gas Council said in evidence to the Franks Committee that it had been advised otherwise.[34]

There is clearly room for uncertainty; and what is more, it is often hard to judge the precise status of information held by nationalised industries. Some of it originates in central government. Other material may be generated within the industry, but later be given a government classification – with or without the industry's employees being informed. The crucial national role of these industries unavoidably leads to interpenetration between commercial information and official information.

Since there are no recorded instances of prosecution under Section 2 in this area, these may be regarded as purely technical difficulties. Thus, the old British Railways Board told the Franks Committee that 'the continuance of legislation along the lines of Section 2 probably has no bearing on either the conduct of their business, or their relationship with Ministers of Government Departments.'[35] It seems clear that nationalised industries, like private businesses, rely mainly upon internal discipline to maintain confidentiality. Penalties and procedures vary from industry to industry; but essentially, the protection of confidentiality is regarded as a condition of employment.

However, some nationalised industries – on government advice – do invite or require staff in sensitive areas to sign a declaration that they have read and understood the Official Secrets Act. In evidence to the Franks Committee, the Electricity Council said:

The Department of Trade and Industry and its predecessors in seeking to protect this information have drawn to the attention of the Council the Official Secrets Act and in particular Section 2 . . . and have asked the Council and the Generating Board to ensure that staff who have access to Government information classified confidential . . . should sign a declaration form on which is printed Section 2 of the Official Secrets Act 1911 (as amended) and Section 1 (2) of the Official Secrets Act 1920.[36]

This declaration is one of a set of variants on that signed by civil servants; other versions exist for government contractors, advisers, and so on. In its original form, the Electricity Council declaration seemed to go beyond even the wide terms of Section 2, and to apply, for instance, to information generated within the industry itself. It has since been re-drafted; but it remains the case that signing it *has no legal force* – it is a purely symbolic act. Employees of nationalised industries are legally liable under Section 2 in precisely the same way as other private citizens; and no further.

This interpretation is supported by the fact that two public corporations *do* have special status under the Official Secrets Act. Legislation lays down that all employees of the Post Office and of the United Kingdom Atomic Energy Authority are, for the purposes of Section 2, Crown office-holders. This strongly implies that employees of other nationalised industries do not have this status.

There is, however, a difference between public and private industry, of which the occasional signing of declarations of secrecy is a symbol. Nationalised industries are of national importance; they often have a visibly quasi-official role, and thus a quasi-official awareness of their status and responsibilities. This awareness has certainly not prevented a steady stream of leaks – for example, about proposed cuts by British Rail, proposed pit closures by the Coal Board, and proposed redundancies by British Steel. But it may well be a factor in the extreme secretiveness often displayed by nationalised industries.

Much general information is of course made available to the public by nationalised industries: timetables, tariffs, servicing facilities and so on. Annual reports contain more detailed statements of finance and of general policy. The amount and kind of information varies between industries, especially in proportion to the extent of their sales to the public – the National Coal Board, for example, sells mainly to Approved Coal Merchants, and thus has less direct contact with the general public than the gas or electricity industries.

Apart from this kind of information – necessary to the functioning of the industry itself – there is very little voluntary disclosure. The ethos of 'confidentiality' is omnipresent in the nationalised industries; and few senior personnel accept that their public ownership status implies any special obligation to openness. Sir Denis Rooke, chairman of the British Gas Corporation, has said:

> I would point out that the Corporation, while a Statutory Corporation, is not expending *public money* in the normally accepted sense of that term and (that) no special onus for disclosure arises on that account. The Corporation is a trading body and derives its income from its customers like any private company.[37]

This appears to be the general attitude of nationalised industries.

Little is known about the procedures by which nationalised industries classify documents as confidential. Charles Medawar of the Public Interest Research Centre has examined the indexes of the Electricity Council and Central Electricity Generating Board libraries, and discovered no less than eleven different security or privacy markings, excluding personnel information; he believes that at least fourteen such markings are used by the industry, on a basis of 'apparent arbitrariness' – and in comparison with a mere six classifications used in central government.[38]

This is the information which is withheld, not only from the public at large, but generally also from the nationalised industry consumer councils. Examples of titles listed by Medawar show clearly that some of the material is of public interest and importance: *An Investigation Into Electricaire Fan Failures (1975). Confidential. The Electricity, Gas, Oil and Solid Fuel Industries: An Industrial Image Survey (1973). Confidential. Fluorescent Light: A Review of its Effects on Users (1971). Confidential.*

The old House of Commons Select Committee on Nationalised Industries (SCNI) was set up in 1956 to 'examine the Report and Accounts of the industries' and 'inform Parliament'. But its terms of reference very quickly became widened: as early as November 1956, a spokesman gave as examples of its objects of inquiry, techniques of managerial efficiency; the recruitment and training of staff; and relations with the public and with other industries. In 1966 the Committee was enlarged, and authorised to appoint sub-committees with important powers. In 1979 a completely new structure of fourteen departmental 'shadowing' select committees was initiated and the SCNI dismantled.

The SCNI took its job very seriously, and in its first twenty years presented twenty-five weighty and thorough reports to the House of Commons, mostly concerned each with an individual industry, some with more general topics like *Ministerial Control* (1968) and *Relations with the Public* (1971). These hugely detailed investigations had little impact on Parliament; they were seldom debated. Journalists, however, were grateful for this rare opportunity to get information on nationalised industries; and some individual executives of industries also welcomed them. But the overall reaction of the nationalised industries was defensive and dismissive, and there is little evidence that many criticisms were taken to heart. It may also be doubted whether the SCNI really penetrated the secrecy of the industries, any more than other select committees have managed to do with the Civil Service.[39] The work of the now defunct SCNI has been distributed among the new departmental committees, chiefly the Treasury, Trade and Industry and Energy watchdogs. Standing orders do provide for members of the new committees to regroup across departmental lines to consider any matter concerned with two or more nationalised industries, though at the time of writing this power has not been used.

The communications, fuel and transport industries are also 'shadowed' by consumer councils which have developed on an *ad hoc* basis since 1946, and which vary greatly in structure and powers. Some are statutory, some are not.[40] These nationalised industry consumer councils (NICCs) are not the product of any coherent strategy: they have 'just growed'. But they are, or could be, important vehicles of consumer representation in what are essentially monopolies. Their effectiveness is determined not only by their own energy and resources and by the restricted nature of the powers bestowed on them, but also by the flow and quality of the information they receive.

Some nationalised industries, or parts of them, have a statutory obligation to supply information to their consumer councils. Area electricity boards – though not the Electricity Council or the Central Electricity Generating Board – must inform the appropriate area consultative councils of their 'general plans and arrangements' under the Electricity Act of 1947: a wording which has been described as so 'loose and timid' that access to specific information can still be extremely difficult.[41] British Gas has a duty to inform the National Gas Consumers' Council of its plans and arrangements in relation to gas supply, and especially about proposed changes of tariff; the Post Office must generally consult the Post Office Users' National Council before making any major changes in its services. British Rail must notify the relevant Transport Users' Consultative Committee at least six weeks before closing stations or lines. (The chapters on Energy and Transport discuss these obligations more fully.)

There are many inadequacies here. Transport Users' Consultative Committees, for example, have no enforceable right to the financial information which is used to justify line and station closures. Thus, for example, the Kings Lynn-Hunstanton service was closed in 1969 on the basis of British Rail figures which afterwards turned out to be misleading. The Post Office Users' National Council has complained that notification of postage rate increases has been received too late. An attempt by the Domestic Coal Consumers' Council to establish a clear right to be informed and consulted by the National Coal Board on matters bearing directly on domestic coal prices by means of an amendment to the Coal Industry Bill, failed in 1980.

In 1979, the Select Committee on Nationalised Industries published *Consumers and the Nationalised Industries* which proposed to extend and regularise the NICCs' rights to information.[42] It also proposed to extend to all NICCs the right to representation on industry boards, a right which already exists in the electricity industry, where consultative council chairmen are ex-officio part-time members of their area boards.

If acted on (they have not been), these proposals would have had an undoubted impact. But the recommended rights to information are still vague enough to depend on the good will of the industries. Also, representation on boards is subject to confidentiality: it does not establish that the information received by NICC chairmen will be available either to the public or even to the rest of the consumer council.

In general NICCs, and hence the general public, are dependent for adequate information on the generosity of the industry. There is no *right* of access to *any* information held by *any* nationalised industry: statistics, policy option drafts, or performance records. Thus British Rail supplies the Central Transport Consultative Committee with regular breakdowns of its complaints data – but only on an 'in confidence' basis. Thus British Gas carries out its own investigations into gas explosions – but the reports are not made publicly available even to the victims. There is thus no way of challenging the findings; and no way for gas consumers' representatives or the public to make an independent judgement on the industry's safety record.[43]

Without adequate access to information, NICCs cannot be totally effective. It is also, arguably, a matter of wider public concern that crucial nationalised industries are so little open to scrutiny – not only by NICCs, but by journalists and other interested individuals. The nationalised industries might also consider whether greater openness would not be to their own advantage. In 1976 the National Consumer Council argued that this would be the case:

At present, the boards of nationalised industries are "leaned on" heavily and frequently by their supervising government departments on prices and . . . other questions of political importance. But it is all (or mostly) done behind closed doors. The pressure from the department would in many ways be easier to bear if it were fully in the public eye and subject to explicit consideration by Parliament.[44]

REFERENCES

1 The international context of the secrecy debate is summarised in Chapter Three.
2 But see also the Appendix.
3 *Departmental Committee on Section 2 of the Official Secrets Act 1911* (Chairman: Lord Franks), Cmnd 5104, HMSO, 1972, vol. 1, report of the Committee, appendix III, p. 123.
4 *Ibid.*, p. 15.
5 *Ibid.*, vol. 2, pp. 267–70 (written evidence submitted to the Committee by the Institute of Journalists).
6 *Ibid.*, vol. 1, appendix II. See also Williams, David, *Not in the Public Interest*, Hutchinson, 1965.
7 Quoted in Wraith, Ronald, *Open Government: The British Interpretation*, Royal Institute of Public Administration, 1977, pp. 34 5. The report itself is now out of print.
8 *The Civil Service* (Chairman: Lord Fulton), HMSO, 1968, vol. 1, report of the Committee, p. 91.
9 *Information and the Public Interest*, Cmnd 4089, HMSO, 1969.
10 *Departmental Committee on Section 2 of the Official Secrets Act 1911* (Chairman: Lord Franks), Cmnd 5104, HMSO, 1972, vol. 1, report of the Committee, appendix III, p. 37.
11 *Ibid.*, pp. 47–76.
12 *Ibid.*, p. 56.

13 *Ibid.*, p. 75.
14 The trial is described in detail in Aitken, Jonathan, *Officially Secret*, Weidenfeld & Nicolson, 1971.
15 Quoted in Wraith, Ronald, *op. cit.*, p. 63.
16 *Hansard* (House of Commons), 22 November 1976.
17 *Reform of Section 2 of the Official Secrets Act 1911*, Cmnd 7285, HMSO, 1978.
18 *Disclosure of Official Information: A Report on Overseas Practice*, Civil Service Department, HMSO, 1979.
19 *Open Government*, Cmnd 7520, HMSO, 1979.
20 Quoted in Bennett, C. and Hennessy, P., *A Consumer's Guide to Open Government: Techniques for Penetrating Whitehall*, Outer Circle Policy Unit, 1980, p. 19.
21 *Hansard* (House of Lords), 5 November 1979.
22 See also Chapter Three.
23 *The Civil Service* (Chairman: Lord Fulton), HMSO, 1968, vol. 1, report of the Committee, p. 93.
24 *Freedom of Information*, JUSTICE (British section of the International Commission of Jurists), 1978.
25 *Conduct in Local Government* (Report of the Redcliffe-Maud Committee), Cmnd 5636, HMSO, 1974.
26 Department of the Environment, *Publicity for the Work of Local Authorities*, Circular 45/75, paras. 3, 9 and 16.
27 See also Chapters Four and Five.
28 Scottish Consumer Council, *Rare Access: A Report on Access to Information in Scotland* (provisional title), Spring 1982.
29 National Joint Council for Local Authorities, *Scheme of Conditions of Service for Administrative, Professional, Technical and Clerical Services*, section 7, para. 72.
30 *Departmental Committee on Section 2 of the Official Secrets Act 1911* (chairman: Lord Franks), vol. 2 (written evidence submitted to the Committee), HMSO, 1972, p. 222.
31 Michael, James, *The Politics of Secrecy*, National Council for Civil Liberties, 1979, p. 14. Leaking and 'whistleblowing' by public servants raises important issues: see Beardshaw, Virginia,[1] *Conscientious Objectors at Work*[1], Social Audit, 1981.
32 *Municipal Journal*, 7 March 1980, pp. 285–6.
33 London Government Public Relations Association, *The Right to be Informed*, LGPRA, 1974.
34 *Departmental Committee on Section 2 of the Official Secrets Act 1911* (Chairman: Lord Franks), Cmnd 5104, vol. 2 p. 195 (written evidence submitted to the Committee).
35 *Ibid.*, p. 179.
36 *Ibid.*, p. 187.
37 Quoted in Chick, Linda and Farrar, Anthony, *On Gas Explosions*, British Safety Council, 1980, p. 18.

38 Medawar, Charles, *Consumers of Power: Measuring and Improving the Performance of the LEB*, Social Audit Ltd, 1980, p. 20.
39 Wraith, Ronald, *op. cit.*, pp. 45–7.
40 The structure, status and powers of the nationalised industries consumer councils are most fully described in the Second Report from the Select Committee on Nationalised Industries 1978–9, *Consumers and the Nationalised Industries: Pre-legislative Hearings*, HMSO, 1979.
41 See also pp. 214–20.
42 Second Report from the Select Committee on Nationalised Industries 1978–9, *op. cit.*
43 See also pp. 229–30.
44 National Consumer Council, *Consumers and the Nationalised Industries*, HMSO, 1976, p. 83.

Freedom of Information –
The Overseas Experience 3
Rosemary Delbridge and Martin Smith

A number of countries around the world, with a wide range of democratic political systems, have introduced Freedom of Information legislation. Using four examples – the USA, Sweden, and, particularly important to the British debate, the proposed laws in Canada and Australia – this chapter outlines the different ways in which public access can be put into practice.

A number of countries around the world, with a wide range of democratic political systems, have introduced freedom of information legislation and found it to be workable in practice. The best known examples – the USA and Sweden – are presented below, as are the proposed laws in Canada and Australia. Other countries which have made some progress towards greater public access include the Netherlands (1978), France (1978), Norway and Denmark (both 1970), and Finland (1951).

Still more countries have laws giving individuals the right to inspect, and to make corrections to, information about themselves held by government: the USA (1974), Canada (1977), Sweden (1973), France, Norway, Denmark, Austria and West Germany (all 1978). A number of other countries, including Belgium and Luxembourg, are actively considering this step.[1]

The exact formula of public access, either actual or proposed, varies considerably from country to country: the chart on pages 40–41 offers a rough comparison of several important aspects in four leading systems. The implications of the differences will become clearer in the detailed accounts which follow. They can be attributed largely to differences between the societies and histories of the nations concerned: in the Scandinavian countries, for example, populations are small and government traditionally open and informal – which has a double-edged implication for public access, however, in that a good deal of government business may be conducted orally and therefore untraceably.

Differences in the structure and form of public access depend a great deal on the kind and extent of public pressure. In the Netherlands, for instance, it is difficult to detect any sustained opposition to a very generally worded law that lacks both a right of appeal to an independent body, and the absolute right to see the actual documentation. The USA has experienced the most intensive demand for freedom of information, and has a correspondingly tough system. In Sweden, public access has been a pronounced characteristic of social and political life since 1766 – but within a context which differs considerably from that found in America, where pressure groups abound and there is a greater tendency to resort to the courts.

Most countries agree on the general areas of exemption from public access – defence and security, law enforcement, sensitive financial data, confidential information, both commercial and personal (though in the USA this is not necessarily protected), and some kinds of internal working documents. The discussion which follows only stresses alterations to this pattern. The USA is treated as a model and other systems are described in terms of their differences from the American example.

The proposed legislation in Canada and Australia, however, is especially relevant to Britain because both countries apply the doctrine of ministerial responsibility, which is often cited in the United Kingdom as a major obstacle to public access legislation. In the 'Westminster model', the *executive* is formally part of the *legislature*: ministers are directly responsible to Parliament, and thus indirectly to the electorate, for the conduct of their departments. This is said to raise two constitutional difficulties for freedom of information. Firstly, appeal to the courts or even to an ombudsman against refusal to disclose would bypass the relationship of minister to Parliament; and secondly, publication of civil servants' advice and administrative decisions would interfere with the minister's formal responsibility for everything done in his or her name, as well as infringing against the principle of Civil Service anonymity.

The real relevance of this doctrine has increasingly come into question. Douglas Jay MP has remarked that 'if Ministers are going to resign when anyone makes a mistake in a department, there will very soon be no Ministers left. If, on the other hand, everything is referred to Ministers, departments will rapidly grind to a halt.' It is significant to the debate that neither the Canadian government nor the Canadian opposition parties see ministerial responsibility as putting insuperable obstacles in the way of public access legislation – though there are undeniably some differences between the Canadian version of the 'Westminster model' and that of Westminster itself.

United States of America

In the mid-1970s, in the aftermath of Watergate and the Pentagon Papers, the United States embarked on a legislative orgy of public access. The 1966 Freedom of Information Act had led to widespread complaints of delay and obstruction; in 1974 and 1976 it was considerably sharpened and major administrative efforts made to encourage its full application. The 1974 Privacy Act both opened up individuals' files to inspection and correction by themselves, and blocked access by anyone else; and the delightfully named Government in the Sunshine Act (1976) laid certain meetings of departmental heads open to the public.[2]

The Freedom of Information Act establishes the basic principle that public information belongs to the public. 'Any person' may request information held by 'any executive department, military department, government corporation, government controlled corporation, or other establishment in the executive branch of the government (including the Executive Office of the President) or any independent regulatory agency'. This list includes, for example, the Central Intelligence Agency and the Federal Bureau of Investigation; the Treasury Department; the Food and Drugs Administration; the Inland Revenue; and the Consumer Product Safety Commission. (It does *not* include the legislature or judiciary, or the White House advisory staff.)

No reason need be given for requesting information, unless it affects someone else's personal privacy, in which case a 'balance of interest' principle comes into effect. A response must be made within ten days; if it is wholly or partly negative, it must give grounds for refusal, and identify a different and more senior official to whom an appeal can be made. Appeals must be answered within twenty days; if rejected, the applicant can then take the matter to court – where it is given priority over all other business – and the agency must generally respond within thirty days.

If a case comes to court, the burden is on the agency to justify its denial of access (after all, only the agency knows what the information is). The court must take a new and independent look at the facts; it can examine the documents *in camera*. It can also award legal costs against the agency when the requester has 'substantially prevailed'. Considerable amounts of money are involved, and it is widely felt that the courts do not use this power enough.

Before making a final negative decision, officials are supposed to consult the Freedom of Information Committee, a section of the Justice Department established to 'encourage compliance' with the Act and 'invite the attention of the agency to . . . the central policy of fullest responsible disclosure'. The Justice Department has responsibility for defending freedom of information cases in court; but the Attorney General made it clear in 1977 that the encouragement of disclosure was the Department's major function. 'The government should not withhold documents unless it is important to the public interest to do so . . . [the] Justice Department will defend Freedom of Information Act suits only when disclosure is demonstrably harmful, even if the documents technically fell within the exemptions of the Act.'[3]

This raises an important feature of the legislation: disclosure of exempt material is not necessarily forbidden. Officials may, and sometimes do, choose to release material which they are entitled to withhold. There is also provision for 'segregation' – releasing documents from which exempt material has been culled, sometimes sentence by sentence. The exempt categories are basically those listed on page 29, with the addition of internal personnel rules and practices; material protected under other statutes; certain kinds of commercial and financial information (a controversial area); and geological and geophysical information regarding oil wells. Advice contained in internal working papers, described as inter and intra-agency memoranda, is also exempt.

The whole tenor of the Act, and of its interpretation, has until recently been towards maximum access. Applicants are required to give only a 'reasonable description' of the information required – defined by the House of Representatives as one which would enable 'a professional employee of the agency . . . familiar with the subject area of the request to locate the record with a reasonable amount of effort.'[4] Descriptions are frequently the subject of discussions between civil servants and applicants in order to define exactly what is needed. To help applicants, the Act requires each agency to 'maintain and make available for public inspection and copying current indexes providing identifying information for the public as to any matter issued, adopted or promulgated'. This must include a description of the organisation, functions and procedures of the agency, and staff manuals that may affect the public: any rules used by an agency against an individual must have been indexed and made available. Indexes are revised quarterly; and are said to be valuable to the staff as well as the public!

This provision is of great importance: it is clearly little use having the right to information if one doesn't know that it exists, or where to find it. It is also clear that an *attitude* of openness is crucial in making the spirit of the Act work in practice. As well as discretion to release exempt material, officials also have discretion to waive or reduce fees for search and copying if the information is considered to be in the public interest. This has often been an area of contention, since the amounts involved can be prohibitive: the Union of Concerned Scientists was asked for $30,000 for three Nuclear Regulatory Commission documents! Many agencies have also made life easier for all concerned by setting up public records offices, where people can inspect and copy at their leisure. It seems that some individual civil servants are still resistant to the notion of maximum access, either through inertia or considered opposition; but the overall atmosphere has been strongly pro-disclosure.

The Freedom of Information Act has been used by individuals, public interest pressure groups, business corporations, journalists and scholars. For pressure groups, it has been of crucial importance, liberating huge amounts of valuable information. For example: the Union of Concerned Scientists, through intensive use of the Act, established gross negligence and concealment by the authorities over the fire at Browns Ferry nuclear power plant; the Consumers' Union, after a two year battle, gained access to Veterans' Administration comparative test data on hearing aids; and the same body obtained information on violation of minimal nutrition standards in New York City schools.[5] In 1972, Ralph Nader set up the Freedom of Information Clearinghouse to coordinate legal action under the Act and build up a body of case law.

Commercial organisations frequently use the Act for what is best described as jungle warfare against agencies trying to regulate their activities – Exxon Oil responded to a Federal Trade Commission investigation by demanding everything it had on energy! – and against each other, trying to obtain or to block access via the Act to commercial information. The Act has undoubtedly become a weapon of industrial espionage in a manner which was never intended.

The media in general has made rather less use of the Act than one might imagine; apparently because even the quite short delays involved are too long for news purposes, except for issues of historical importance, and also because there is a journalistic *esprit de corps* about getting one's information through contacts rather than over the counter. However, a good deal of material has been obtained through the Act: for example, on the FBI's tapping of Robert Oppenheimer's phone, and the CIA papers on Lee Harvey Oswald, as well as a mass of less sensational documents.

Individuals frequently use the basically similar procedures of the Privacy Act's inspect-and-correct provisions. These are exceedingly important in a society where, according to the 1978 Privacy Act Annual Report, 96 federal agencies then held 3,652.6 *million* records on individuals in 5,881 record systems. The scale of use is less astronomical, but still considerable: in 1977, the Defence Department agreed to amend 14,939 inaccurate records, 99 per cent of those requested (a proportion only slightly higher than other agencies). Perhaps this mass of cases is even more important than the well-known demands by public figures like J. K. Galbraith and Jane Fonda for their own FBI records.

The Freedom of Information Act and the Privacy Act are intended to complement each other, providing for both public access and the proper protection of personal data. A further right of access exists under the Family Educational Rights and Privacy Act (1974): individuals over eighteen can inspect and correct their own children's schooling records, and limit their release outside the school.

The cost of the Freedom of Information Act in 1977, the most recent figure available, was slightly under $26 million. This figure compares very favourably with the $1.5 *billion* for public relations spent by the U.S. government in 1978 – in other words, for telling people what the state wants them to know rather than what they ask about. It also compares very favourably with initial alarmist predictions by official bodies of what such legislation would be likely to cost.[6]

American freedom of information legislation has not been without its critics, though even the sceptics have been forced to acknowledge its value. One critic, the former Attorney-General Mr Civiletti, told the Canadian Bar Association in August 1980:

The Act has, I believe, worked somewhat of a revolution. It has made our federal government far more open and it has exposed government wrong-doing. The consequence has been that many of these wrongs have been righted. The Act tends to make our citizens better informed and provides them with the data needed for intelligent debate. In addition to these benefits, the Act undoubtedly has served to deter wrongful conduct by government officials because of fear of disclosure as a result of the commands of the Act.[7]

However, since the inauguration of the Reagan administration, pressure to amend the Act in the direction of tighter controls on disclosure has intensified. Most of this pressure has come from the law enforcement and intelligence agencies who are seeking to be exempted from the Act's operations completely.

Sweden

The environment in which the Swedish public access system operates is altogether different. To begin with, it has existed for over two centuries as a fact of life and as a constitutional principle: 'the right to an access to official documents is an essential part of the citizen's right to obtain and receive information and thereby one of the conditions for the free democratic moulding of opinion.'[8]

Every ministry or agency – in Sweden many government decisions are executed by semi-autonomous agencies – keeps registers of incoming mail, which are immediately available to enquirers. Documents requested are either brought to the registry, or the applicant is told to which office to go. Applicants may remain anonymous – a truly bizarre picture from the British point of view of unidentified strangers wandering in off the street and going through government mail. The press uses agencies to keep a watch on registers, which are updated daily or twice weekly.

Since 1973, individuals have had the right with a few exceptions to inspect and correct personal files. In fact, it is not very difficult for third parties to obtain access to personal information; a situation ameliorated in some respects by the media's strict self-imposed respect for privacy (not even the names of convicted criminals are usually printed). The press also engages in comparatively little of the hard-hitting investigative journalism which is characteristic of other countries, notably the United States.

Exempt categories are listed in specific detail in separate secrecy legislation – a new Act was passed in 1980 – and officials have little or no discretion to release such material or vary its classification. The types of exemption are basically similar to those of other countries, with the addition of material endangering 'decency and safety'. Working papers are protected until a decision has been reached – at which point, by convention, a good deal of preliminary documentation will be destroyed. As already mentioned, there is also a tendency for the small and informal ministries to talk rather than to write.

There seems to be little dissatisfaction, and few problems, with the Swedish system – however cataclysmic its transplantation to most other countries would be. Applicants may appeal to the courts against refusal of access, but such cases are not common. It is impossible to identify the costs of the system, since they have long been absorbed into general administrative overheads.

Australia

Australia has been moving slowly towards public access legislation since 1972. The first Freedom of Information Bill appeared in 1978, and was widely criticised as being too weak. The Bill's critics successfully fought to have the whole issue referred to the Senate Standing Committee on Constitutional and Legal Affairs.

Under the 1978 Bill, 'every person' has the right to apply to any Commonwealth (that is, federal) ministerial department or authority (but not Parliament or the courts) for 'reasonably identified' information. As in the USA, departments were to publish details of structure and functions – but they were *not* to be obliged to produce registers of documents held. Requests for access were to be answered within sixty days (six times the equivalent US time limit) and, if refused, reasons were to be given.

The categories of exempted information were considerable: as well as broad versions of all the standard exemptions, they included information which would adversely affect the national economy; information which would be in contempt of Parliament, court or tribunal; Cabinet and Executive Council documents; and documents protected from disclosure by ministerial decree. Furthermore, although officials were to have discretion to release exempt material, there was to be no test of damage – no criterion to which an inquirer could appeal which would allow for an independent assessment of the harm that would allegedly be caused by disclosure.

The Senate Standing Committee tabled a lengthy and critical report in November 1979, making 93 recommendations for improvements to the 1978 Bill. The Committee's most fundamental criticism was that the Bill attempted to preserve traditional ministerial responsibility and power in such a way as seriously to undermine the concept of a public *right* of access. The Committee argued that true ministerial responsibility would in practice be strengthened by greater openness since, it claimed, only a well-informed Parliament can genuinely call a minister to account for his actions or those of his department.

Other criticism of the 1978 Bill dealt with the absence of any effective appeal to the courts. Refused applicants were to have recourse to an Ombudsman, and then to an Administrative Appeals Tribunal – which could make angry noises, but which was to have no power to enforce its views. Some categories of information were not to be open to appeal at all: Cabinet or Executive Council papers certified as such by the responsible officer; and defence, security, international and Commonwealth/State papers, together with internal working papers certified by a minister or senior official as against the public interest to disclose.

The Fraser government replied to the Standing Committee's recommendations in September 1980 and has since published a revised Freedom of Information Bill (1981). Implicitly the new Bill rejects the Standing Committee's more serious criticisms. For example, the sixty-day proposed time limit for departmental responses to access applications is preserved. Most important however, the government has retained the proposal that ministers should be entitled to deny access to information by the use of a 'conclusive certificate' with no right of appeal.

It is difficult to anticipate what effects the 1981 Australian Bill might have should it become law. While the government has conceded in theory that 'A Freedom of Information Act should provide a right of access to government information except in those cases where the denial of access can be justified by reference to a positive provision of the law,'[9] in practice it seems to be proposing arrangements which are far more limited. Indeed *The Canberra Times* has described the 1981 Bill as 'an enshrining of the status quo'.[10]

Canada

The turning point in the Canadian debate on freedom of information came in May 1979 with the election of the Progressive Conservatives as a minority government. In October, the new administration redeemed a major campaign pledge by introducing Freedom of Information Bill C-15. This Bill broadly followed the

US model providing a general public right of access to official information subject to exemptions.

Bill C-15 was generally regarded as a strong proposal, but the Clark government had other problems and so the Bill fell early in 1980 with the dissolution of the Canadian Parliament. The Liberal party returned to power in the ensuing federal election and soon committed itself to the re-introduction of access legislation. The new draft duly appeared in July 1980 as Bill C-43. This second attempt at legislation aims to put onto the statute book both an Access to Official Information Act and a new Privacy Act, the provisions on privacy being intended to replace Part IV of the Canadian Human Rights Act. Current proposals are therefore based on a recognition of the close inter-relationship between access and privacy issues.

The Bill begins with an expression of intent given the force of law:

The purpose of this Act is to extend the present laws of Canada to provide a right of access to information in records under the control of a government institution in accordance with the principles that government information should be available to the public, that necessary exceptions to the right of access should be limited and specific and that decisions on the disclosure of government information should be reviewed independently of government.

Citizens, permanent residents and corporations are given the right of access to 'any record under the control of a government institution' (including publicly owned industries like Uranium Canada Ltd). Departments must keep registers and publish descriptions of structure and functions; they must normally respond within thirty days, and must justify non-disclosure.

The exempted areas are the normal ones, along with federal-provincial relations and Cabinet records. But stringent tests of damage are proposed: defence and international material should only be withheld if disclosure would be 'reasonably expected to be injurious', and financial data if disclosure 'could reasonably be expected to be materially injurious to the financial interests of the government of Canada'. There is discretion to release technically exempt documents.

A two-tier appeal system is proposed: first to an Ombudsman-type Information Commissioner, directly responsible to Parliament; then, if the Commissioner recommends disclosure and the agency refuses, appeal to the courts who will have power to order disclosure. The intention is to resolve ninety per cent of cases before they reach court; but the crucial judicial review element is strongly present. John Turner, a former Justice and Finance Minister, has said that 'no forum is better suited or more familiar with balancing private as against public interests, giving meaning to statutory language, or deciding the application of exemptions' than the courts.

Nor does the proposed Canadian system allow for any ministerial veto of the appeal procedure. In this respect – as in its provision for the use of public registers of documents and for the application of tests of damage to refusals to disclose – it is far more radical than the system proposed in Australia. Bill C-43 received its second reading in January 1981 and at the time of writing, though overshadowed by other constitutional business, is proceeding through a clause-by-clause examination at the hands of the Justice and Legal Affairs Committee. It is expected to become law by the summer of 1982.

The significance of the Canadian Bill is that it has attracted all-party support for proposals which go far beyond anything contemplated by Whitehall and which implicitly refute the proposition that access to information legislation is constitutionally incompatible with Westminster-type government. Its relevance to the United Kingdom was unwittingly recognised by the Civil Service Department itself: 'Canadian experience on openness in government is particularly relevant to the UK because of the similarity in British and Canadian constitution and practice and in spite of the obvious differences between the two nations in terms of size, population, density and composition.'[11]

Canada, therefore, is set to become the first British-style democracy to endorse the principle of a public right of access to official information.

REFERENCES

1 *Disclosure of Official Information: A Report on Overseas Practice*, Civil Service Department, HMSO, 1979; *An Official Information Act*, Outer Circle Policy Unit, 1977, pp. 7–18 and pp. 34–64.
2 American legislation is described in detail by Dresner, Stewart, *Open Government: Lessons from America*, Outer Circle Policy Unit, 1980.

3 Quoted *ibid.*, pp. 21–22.
4 Quoted *ibid.*, p. 11.
5 *Ibid.*, pp. 61–9.
6 *Ibid.*, pp. 132–8.
7 Quoted in Riley, T. B. (ed.), *A Review of Freedom of Information around the World*, International Freedom of Information Commission, London 1980, p. B12.
8 A former Swedish Minister of Justice (responsible for the operation of the Act) quoted in *Disclosure of Official Information*, *op. cit.*, p. 11.
9 Statement by the Attorney-General, Senator the Hon. P. D. Durack Q.C., September 11 1980.
10 *The Canberra Times*, 6 April 1981.
11 *Disclosure of Official Information*, *op. cit.*, p. 31.

	USA	Sweden	Canada	Australia
DATE OF INCEPTION	1966, amended 1974 and 1976	1766, variously amended	Proposed (1980 Bill)	Proposed (1981 Bill)
WHO CAN APPLY	'Any person'	'Every Swedish national' (but effectively includes foreigners)	Citizens, permanent residents and corporations	'Every person'
ACCESS PROCEDURES Registers of information held?	Yes	Yes; updated daily or twice weekly	Yes	Qualified yes
Description of departmental workings?	Yes	No	Yes	Yes
Description required from applicant	'Reasonable description' – open to negotiation	Document identified from register	'Reasonable description' – open to negotiation	'Reasonable identification' – open to negotiation
TIME LIMIT FOR RESPONSE	10 days; 20 days for appeal; 30 days for court complaint	Immediate	30 days	60 days
APPEAL AND REVIEW	First to senior department member, then judicial	Ombudsman and judicial (rarely invoked)	Ombudsman then judicial (Ministers will have final say on some kinds of exempted information)	Ombudsman then appeal tribunal (no enforcement power. Ministers would have final say in many areas)

	USA	Sweden	Canada	Australia
EXEMPT MATERIAL Scope	Broad and extensive	Closely specified in separate Secrecy Act	Broad but negotiable	Very comprehensive
Discretion to release	Yes	No	Yes	Yes
Tests of damage?	Yes	Largely inapplicable	Yes	No
RETROSPECTION (ie. right to see material predating Act)	Yes	Inapplicable	No	No
CLASSIFICATION PROCEDURES	Strictly controlled	Closely defined by legislation	No specific control, but subject to review	No safeguards against over-classification
PRIVACY SAFEGUARDS	Yes, both in Act and in Privacy Act 1974	Limits largely set by convention but safeguards introduced in 1980	Yes: separate Privacy Bill	Yes
RIGHT TO INSPECT AND CORRECT FILES ON ONESELF	Yes (1974)	Yes (1973)	Yes (1977) and 1980 proposals	Inspection – qualified yes; correction – not specified

Housing   4
Stuart Weir

On our behalf, government plays a major role in the housing field.
More than a dozen major housing and rent Acts have been passed
since the war. New towns have been created, cities redeveloped, slums
cleared. One family in three now rents from the council in England and
Wales, while private sector housing is governed by rent controls, tax
subsidies, repair grants and the like. How much information do we get
about how policies are decided, the facts and figures on which housing
decisions are based and indeed the way individual housing authorities
manage and allocate their housing stock? Stuart Weir reviews three
case histories – the 1977 *Housing Policy Review*, the 1979 spending
white paper, and the council house sales issue – which illustrate the
limitations of current central government policy on disclosure. At local
level, he argues that a council's behaviour as a public landlord is constrained scarcely at all by the few measures that insist on public
consultation.

In the 1930s, George Orwell asked a miner when the housing
shortage had first become acute in his district. The miner answered, 'When we were told about it.' The anecdote illustrates
the importance of full and intelligible information in creating
public understanding of housing issues, as well as in raising consumer aspirations. Orwell noted that 'until recently people's standards were so low that they took almost any degree of
overcrowding for granted.'[1] The current growing demand for open
government takes us a stage further: it assumes that the public
should be fully informed about decision-making processes in government and the facts and figures on which policies are based, to
allow people to make well informed judgements and to influence
and possibly change policies.

House and home stand at the centre of people's lives. It has
long been established that bad housing is linked to ill health and
mental stress and that inequalities in housing are reflected in
educational, economic and cultural opportunities.[2] The standards,

design, density and location of houses and flats also affect the whole environment – they make a real impact on the look of our cities and countryside, and shape the quality of life of those who live near them as well as in them.

Post-war governments have in practice assumed increasingly comprehensive responsibilities for housing the population, although in the mid-1950s the Conservative government did make an effort – as the present Conservative government is doing – to extricate itself from participation in housing and to let the 'free market' meet normal housing needs. In reality, both Conservative and Labour governments have been pulled into a deeper involvement. Both have assumed official objectives which tacitly acknowledge the inability of the free market to meet normal needs. In 1971, Peter Walker's *Fair Deal for Housing* described one of the Conservative government's basic aims as 'a fairer choice between owning a home and renting one'.[3] In June 1977, the Labour government's long-delayed *Housing Policy Review* declared that 'The traditional aim of a decent home for all families at a price within their means must remain our primary objective.'[4]

It is still true that: about seventy per cent of housing stock in England and Wales is owned by owner-occupiers or private landlords; at least half of new building or improvement work is undertaken as a result of private decisions; in 1979 the building societies loaned £8,856 million for house purchases as against the £5,372 million public spending on all housing activities in 1979/80, of which about fifteen per cent was given in grants and subsidies to the private sector; the construction industry is almost entirely privately run; and that land is bought and sold in the private market, subject only to taxation and planning control.

Nevertheless, government's commitments are so extensive and deeply rooted that to a large extent they shape and dominate the entire housing market. Since the war more than a dozen major housing and rent Acts have been passed. New towns have been created, cities redeveloped, slums cleared – all by public action. Local authorities and new town corporations administer and maintain a public housing stock of well over five million dwellings. One household in three rents from the council in England and Wales. Government gives subsidies for public housing, controls rents in the private sector, allows tax privileges to owner-occupiers, awards rebates on rents and rates to needy householders, makes grants for repair, improvement and insulation to private owners, and advances loans for house purchase. Local authorities have powers to control housing conditions in the private sector, they exercise planning control over development and they can designate whole areas for improvement. Government conducts and promotes research on a vast scale and, at least until 1981, assumed a basic obligation for setting housing standards.

This range of commitments and powers – over areas of life so basic, as we have seen, to people's well-being – demands a high degree of democratic control and public accountability. Now that Britain has a crude surplus of houses over households, and a large majority of the population is comfortably housed, it is widely assumed that the housing problem is over. But though the political and electoral pressure on government for a vigorous performance in housing has waned, major responsibilities persist.

Not everyone has shared in the progress that Britain has made in raising housing standards since the war. Homelessness is widespread and rising: more families are homeless now than in 1966 at the time of *Cathy Come Home*. Some fifteen per cent of Britain's households live in unfit, sub-standard or over-crowded properties, or share their home unwillingly with others. Ethnic minorities remain at a disadvantage in the housing market, both private and public. So, too, do one-parent families. We are short of suitable homes for elderly and disabled people. Obsolescence is creeping through our ageing housing stock faster than our ability – or will – to repair and improve these older houses. A significant minority of council estates are for varied reasons so unpopular that only the most desperate people will move into them. They degenerate into squalid 'dump' estates.

This chapter looks at the contribution which open government proposals for public access to official information could make to greater public understanding of often complex housing issues, and to the democratic control and public accountability which government's responsibilities in housing demand. It concentrates entirely upon central government and local authorities. Although other semi-government agencies are active in housing, even the most directly involved – the Housing Corporation and local housing associations – provide only two per cent of the country's housing stock. Bodies outside the public domain have, of course, a strong influence on the shape of the housing market.*

---

* The building societies, in particular, dominate the owner-occupier market. A National Consumer Council discussion paper[5] has discussed the lack of information for investors and absence of formal means of redress for rejected applicants for loans. The wider

National Housing Policy:
Three Case Studies in Secrecy

Nationally, a huge hoard of information about Britain's housing record, future prospects, the state of the housing stock, households in need, homelessness, and so on, is generally available. The *Housing Policy Review* (HPR) green paper in 1977, with its three technical volumes of data and detailed analysis, represented a major milestone in information-giving.[6]

Even so, it is known that the Department of the Environment collects a great deal of valuable information from local housing authorities which it does not publish. This unpublished information often has important policy implications. For example, in 1977 the DoE analysed local authority returns of their progress in housing action areas (HAAs). Created under the 1974 Housing Act, HAAs are areas of acute housing stress where poor physical and social conditions interact. The intention of the 1974 Act was that local authorities should carry through vigorous five-year programmes to deal with 'unsatisfactory living conditions' in the HAAs.[7]

The analysis showed that barely one-third of 'target dwellings' in HAAs were being dealt with; and that cost limits, and particularly a stop on repair costs, were seriously inhibiting the take-up of improvement grants by private owners. HAAs were then the sharp end of the Labour government's housing strategy; Reg Freeson, the Housing Minister, described them as 'a vital component of the new housing strategies of those authorities with problem areas suffering from acute housing stress'. Plainly, the DoE analysis contained urgent lessons from councils' immediate experience – lessons which should have been debated and then acted on. But this was at a time when the Labour government was beginning the cutback in public spending on housing. Unfortunately the lessons of the analysis – especially on the need to make generous allowance for repairs – would have meant more cash for local authorities, not less. The government sat on the Department's

---

public too has a legitimate interest in the policies and practices of these major institutions. In view of their dominant role in the housing and financial markets, it is arguable that the societies should be made publicly accountable and required to make certain categories of information available. But such proposals lie outside the scope of this book.

findings; and they weren't published until they were leaked to Shelter's *Roof* magazine two years later.[8]

Interestingly enough, in March 1977 Peter Walker, the former Conservative Environment Secretary, asked the government to lodge the HAA returns in the House of Commons library – which would have given limited public access to them. Mr Walker was seeking information on the effects of the rule that highly rated properties should not be eligible for improvement grants. Ernest Armstrong, then a junior front bench spokesman, replied that there was 'no evidence that rateable value limits are causing difficulties generally in HAAs'.[9] It all depended on what he meant by 'generally'. Shelter collected figures that showed that significant numbers of houses in HAAs were above the rateable value limits. But why wasn't the information available so that Walker, Armstrong, Shelter and the rest of us could weigh the evidence and make up our own minds?

But all this largely concerns background information: valuable as a measure of government's performance and plans for housing, but not much use as a guide to the judgements which lie behind a government's policies. How far government is prepared to allow the public to penetrate the blinds which surround the policy-making process can be judged by taking three case studies: first, the Labour government's *Housing Policy Review*; secondly, the Conservative government's 1979 public spending plans; and thirdly, the vexed issue of council house sales.

The Housing Policy Review

Anthony Crosland came to the Department of the Environment better informed on housing than any Secretary of State before or since. He had, in opposition, set up a high-powered informal 'think tank' on housing. Crosland was determined to establish a firm base of statistics and information for housing policies and, in particular, to initiate a 'searching and far-reaching inquiry into housing finance . . . to get back to fundamentals, to get beyond a housing policy of ad-hocery and crisis management'.[10] His primary interest was in the financial issues: about the extent to which subsidies by way of mortgage tax relief to owner-ocupiers and government subsidies for the public rented stock – were growing at the expense of investment in the basic tasks of building and improving houses. No sacred cows were to be spared[11] – a promise which seemed to foreshadow changes in the existing arrangements for mortgage tax relief, which he had condemned three years previously as 'wasteful' and 'inversely related to need'.[12]

The review he set up on taking office was originally to have been in public. But Mr Crosland had to overcome stern resistance to the wide-ranging nature of the review from DoE officialdom (which wanted merely a review of council house subsidies) and the price he paid was an agreement to hold a departmental review *in camera*.[13] He had spared the first sacred cow – the Civil Service's tradition of closed decision-making. Mr Crosland insisted on consulting his outside experts, but they were shunted on to a housing policy review advisory group, and required to sign the Official Secrets Act. They were thus effectively shut up for the two years the review was to take. Instead of stimulating a prolonged and educative public debate about crucial housing issues, the review suffocated it at birth.

Peter Shore succeeded Anthony Crosland at the DoE halfway through the review. He, too, appreciated the significance of the subsidies versus investment issue. In 1976, he said to the Labour Party conference: 'We have, within the total housing budget, to weigh up, and it is difficult indeed, what is the right balance between increased investment in housing, and to go into tax allowances and housing subsidies. We cannot dodge that issue.'[14]

It is, therefore, all the more surprising that the *Housing Policy Review* green paper and three accompanying technical volumes, did not in all their 25 chapters, 26 appendices, 3 annexes, 13 figures, 405 tables and 772 pages give any projections of the likely costs of subsidies – either in mortgate tax relief or for public housing – over the next ten years; even though the mounting costs of subsidies had been one of the major impetuses of the review; and even though the government was able to give projections over the same period for investment in both the private and public sectors.

It was not that the projections weren't made. They were given in one of the many confidential background papers which were prepared for the review. Why then were they not published? The most obvious answer is that they would have embarrassed the government. For Mr Shore had dodged that critical decision about the balance of subsidies to investment about which he had talked at the Labour conference. He wrote in the foreword to the green paper: 'we certainly do not believe that the household budgets of millions of families – which have been planned in good faith in the reasonable expectation that present arrangements would broadly continue – should be overturned, in pursuit of some theoretical or academic dogma.' In other words, he had decided not to touch subsidies: mortgage tax relief was to remain undisturbed and modest savings would be made through limited changes to the council house subsidy scheme. The unpublished projections would have given ammunition to those who were urging the government to begin the politically sensitive task of curbing both sets of subsidies – so that more public funds could be invested in new and improved housing. The projections, which were leaked to the *Guardian* in November 1976, showed that subsidies for public housing would rise by forty-three per cent in the ten years to 1984–85 and the cost to the Exchequer of mortgage tax relief would increase by over two-thirds in the same period. Meanwhile, investment in public housing would fall by nineteen per cent, and only seventeen per cent more would be devoted to homes for owner-occupation.

But at least the figures *were* leaked. Can we then rely on the press to make good the deficiencies in open government? The answer must of course be *no*. Official papers are very often leaked by people with an undeclared interest in the issues to which they are pertinent. Leaking is by definition a politically selective process which is biased towards those few who have access to official data. The leak in August 1976 to the *Sunday Times* of another background paper, prepared for the review by Alex Henney, a London housing official, illustrates this process perfectly.[15]

This background paper achieved brief fame as the 'Henney report': Alex Henney had argued that, with a *notional* (his italics) surplus of housing over households in London possibly by 1981, there was no case on housing grounds for increasing the public stock of housing in London, particularly inner London, and certainly no case for building high-cost homes. This report was somewhat simplistically interpreted by the *Sunday Times*, and it was used thereafter as a platform by those opposed to further council house building in London, and served to discredit existing council programmes. It seems reasonable to assume that this was the purpose of the person who leaked the report. For there was another background paper, by a group of housing professionals at least as 'expert' as Henney, which expressed considerable scepticism about Henney's interpretation of the data and the prospect that outward migration and additions to the housing stock would make 'sufficient inroads into the heavy concentration of sharing and overcrowding in London' to justify the complacency which the leaked report inspired.[16] This second report was not leaked.

Nor were any other of the background papers produced for the review, valuable though some of them were; among them, for example, is a great deal of information about local authority housing finances – their strengths and weaknesses. This information is still under cover. This kind of review should have been conducted publicly; its research work should have been openly published; and any point that seized any interested party's attention should have been allowed to find its own level in the public debate. That chance was lost.

Public Spending Plans: The 1979 White Paper

The most important instrument for planning social policies – housing, health, education, social services and social security alike – is the system of public expenditure planning developed by the Treasury in the 1960s. Each year the government draws up its housing and other social plans on a five-year rolling programme basis, and sets them against its estimates of the likely growth of the economy and revenue. Since 1969, this process has been partly revealed in annual public expenditure white papers. These papers have gradually given additional information, partly as a result of the urgings of the House of Commons Expenditure Committee through its regular hearings and reports.

Even so, every white paper is like a shark's fin: it gives sight of the direction in which the shark is travelling, but no idea what the beast below the surface is thinking or doing before it is too late. Most of the key decisions in social policy-making are taken during the review of public expenditure. This normally takes place in the summer and is approved in the autumn. The review is begun by a Whitehall committee of finance officers from the various government departments and Treasury officials. A Treasury mandarin sits in the chair. Treasury intimations of what can be afforded are communicated to the departments which then seek to have their estimates agreed by the committee. The committee's report is then put to Cabinet for broad approval, and may differ considerably from the subsequent white paper. The review is, of course, part of the larger process which leads up to the Budget. Needless to say, none of the papers or discussions belonging to these crucial stages of the process which culminates in the white paper is ever published; and when it comes out, all the decisions have effectively been taken. The white paper is merely a formal curtsey towards open government.

Consider how well the 1979 white paper illuminated the government's intentions in housing policy. It came in two instalments: in November 1979, the government's plans for retrenchment in 1980–81 were set out; in March 1980, the plans for the current year were augmented, as usual, by projections for the following three financial years (1981–82 to 1983–84) and, for comparison's sake, the figures for the previous six years.

First, it must be said, the white paper is now far more informative about the government's plans for housing than it used to be. As recently as 1976, the white paper's main source of information on housing expenditure was contained in a table which covered ten items only. Capital and revenue spending could not be distinguished. The white paper made no mention at all of tax relief on mortgages (nor, indeed, of any tax relief), though this was as much a public subsidy and cost to the Exchequer as any item in the official public spending programme. The explanation of the government's plans was scanty, crude and uninformative.

Thanks to pressure from the Commons Expenditure Committee, the presentation has been greatly improved. The Committee demanded an adequate breakdown of the items in the main housing table, better presentation and a fuller explanation. The 1979/80 white paper broke the housing table down into thirty-one items, split between seven sub-groups, and the explanation was much fuller.[17] But the housing chapter still left us largely in the dark about what can only be described as drastically bold plans for future housing expenditure. The white paper showed huge and continuing cuts in housing expenditure – from £5,372 million in 1979–80 to:

£4,700 in 1980–81
£3,840 in 1981–82
£3,250 in 1982–83
£2,790 in 1983–84

In 1974–75, the beginning of the period under review in the white paper, the total allocation was £7,154 million. (All figures are at 1979 survey prices.)

What was being cut by half in this four-year plan was not simply housing subsidies: these allocations were for all capital spending on housing by councils and other public bodies, subsidies and rate fund contributions for council housing, rent rebates and allowances, improvement grants, mortgage loans from local councils, and grants to housing associations.

What, then, were the government's intentions? And how did they square with the government's assessment of future housing needs? Here, the white paper is less informative. It makes no bones about its intention to 'reduce further the level of housing subsidies' which means further increases in council rents. But what else? This is all the housing chapter has to say by way of explanation:

The provision for the years from 1981–82 to 1983–84 reflects the Government's judgment of the amount of public expenditure which the nation can afford to devote to housing. In forming this judgment the Government have had regard to the present size and condition of the housing stock, trends in household formation and the capacity of the private sector to meet housing needs both through owner-occupation and private renting. The size of the investment programme which can be accommodated will be affected by the level of housing subsidies and of receipts from council house sales. The relative shares of the capital and current expenditure and the further breakdown of the programme for these years have yet to be determined.[18]

Henry Aughton, a former chief executive and adviser to the Commons Expenditure Committee's housing sub-committee commented:

For the first time, there is very little breakdown of the total for the coming year (1980–81), and none whatsoever for the following three years. Yet relatively precise global totals are given . . . No rounding up to the nearest £100. The figures must, presumably, be based on something. Perhaps the final paragraph of the housing chapter says it all, two sentences that strain one's credulity, a third that states the obvious, and a fourth that says there is no policy.[19]

The publication of the white paper didn't mark the end of the formal procedures for public accountability. The Commons Select Committee on the Environment decided that it wanted more information. How well did it fare? Perhaps the best illustration of its power to get at the facts (and figures) lies in its examination of Michael Heseltine, the Environment Secretary. Mr Aughton's view that the housing figures must be based on 'something' was corroborated by the Chancellor of the Exchequer, Sir Geoffrey Howe, and Adam Butler MP in their evidence to the Commons

Treasury and Civil Service Committee. They said that itemised estimates had been made of the ways in which the very substantial reductions in public expenditure were to be achieved in the various departments of state.

What were these 'itemised estimates' in housing's case? After being pressed, Heseltine told the Environment Committee:

. . . obviously one does do a range of illustrative calculations to see what possibilities there are; but we do not commit ourselves in advance to those and they are purely illustrative. There would be no point in publishing them. We do not ourselves regard them as policy imperatives or decisions. The individual elements [i.e. decisions about the rate of public house-building and slum clearance, the level of mortgage lending, the budget for improvements grants, rent increases, etc.] will each be decided upon much more through local authorities' own decisions than was the aggregate. They may propose to spend it in various specific ways.[20]

He further declined to produce figures for a whole variety of significant issues – the rate of council house building, sub-standard housing, the contribution of the private sector in producing new houses for sale and homes for rent, the balance between public investment in new council housing and council rents, and – perhaps most important of all – the DoE's assessment of housing need over the period under review and how many newly built or improved homes would be required to meet it. In fact, he said, the government had not updated the 'highly speculative' figures which had been calculated for the *Housing Policy Review*. He threw one sop to the Committee: they could have figures which threw light on the government's estimate that thirty per cent of the funds for council house sales would come from the building societies and other private sources. Nicholas Scott, a Conservative MP, pithily summed up his performance: 'Secretary of State, you have been robust in refusing to give us assessments of various things or declining to admit their usefulness. . . .'

Were the reductions based simply upon what the Treasury wanted the government to do, or upon a calculation of housing need year by year?

Heseltine: They are based on a range of discussions which took place between myself and the Treasury as to, broadly, what the country can afford, broadly what money is available for housing in the context of the public expenditure constraint which the government has to introduce, and in order to be sure that it is met – you are not actually going to bring the whole housing programme to an end – you have to do a range of calculations to see what types of packages could be possible. You have to be sure that there are possible packages. But the question then arises: Are those the packages that are going to emerge? And how can you say yes to that, because you do not know?. . .

Chairman: To enable the Committee to form an opinion as to the options open to local authorities, would it be possible for the range of assessments to which you have referred to be made available to the Committee?. . .

Heseltine: . . . The Committee itself, with its officers, is as perfectly able to work out as I am what you can get with this money. The Committee's conclusions would be just as valuable as mine. I do not know what is going to happen; I only know what the total sum is.[21]

As a result of Heseltine's obduracy, the Committee failed to discover on what information the decision to cut public spending by half on housing was based; what the impact on council-house building was likely to be; and how many people in housing need would be affected. Heseltine made much of the independence of local authorities; it was they who would be taking the final decisions. But the freedom they will have to exercise this independence is like the freedom to move for someone in a straitjacket. The overall allocation of public cash is being reduced, and it is not least the local authorities who would benefit from knowing the government's own assessments of how they might cope. But that knowledge was adamantly withheld. Why? Some of the explanation is to be found in the Environment Secretary's reply to Frank Dobson MP; if the Labour backbencher were to draw the conclusions that he might from this information, he said, 'they would not be accurate conclusions and therefore there would be no purpose in providing what are in essence Government discussions but not Government decisions.'[22]

Heseltine's scepticism about the value of gathering information and making assessments about, for example, future housing needs requires comment. If we are to have informed public discussion about the complex issues which housing and other social policies raise, then people must be given the facts and figures with which to weigh up the various alternatives. Open government does not simply depend upon giving the public access to the information which government decides to collect; informed debate demands that there is also some definition of the kind of information which every government will provide.

Council House Sales

As well as 'set pieces' like the housing policy and spending reviews, governments naturally have reports on policy issues as they arise. Take council house sales. During the last years of the Labour government 1974–9, the Conservative party proposed ambitious sales programmes at local authority level and the promise of a 'right to buy' nationally should they regain power. Proposals of this kind raise issues which perhaps only a metaphysician could resolve: on the one hand, the Conservatives argue that it is right to sell council houses to meet the widespread demand for owner-occupation; on the other hand, the Labour party warns that sales would strip the public housing stock of its best properties and leave a stigmatised rump of sub-standard welfare housing for the poor and disadvantaged.

In the late 1970s, however, the Conservatives pressed another argument hard: council house sales produced profits which could be ploughed back into housing. The Tory group in Leeds, for example, won national publicity for their claims that both sides gained: tenants bought a 'cashable asset', while the council saved at least £200 annually on every house sold. They hoped to save £1 million annually by selling off five thousand houses over a three-year period.[23]

In July 1978, the government received a confidential report from the DoE which turned these kinds of calculations on their head: over time, lost rent revenue and tax reliefs turned immediate profits from sales into long-term losses. By the end of the century, these losses could vary from £2,735 to £8,535 on each council or new town property sold. These long-term projections are perilously difficult; they depend on assumptions made about the rate of inflation, rent increases, house prices, management and maintenance costs, and so on, over a long period of time. Even so, at a critical point in the political debate, public understanding of the issue would have been increased by publication of this report. It was finally leaked to the *Guardian* in November 1979 – by which time the Conservative government was in power, and committed to a vigorous sales policy. (Curiously enough, the report had been withheld from the Tories under the convention that documents prepared for one government are not shown to its successor.) The government thereupon produced yet another appraisal of the financial implications of council house sales which showed that council house sales would make long-term profits.

To sum up: central government's influence on the housing market, and its direction of public housing activity, are of decisive significance. But while much background information is made available, the government's decision-making processes are concealed both from the public and Parliament. It would seem that this secretiveness is taken for granted; and even where it might be to a government's political advantage to release information (such as the Labour government's review of the costs of council house sales), this information is almost automatically kept back. In the past few years, two major opportunities to inform and involve the public have been spurned: the first, at the insistence of DoE officials; the second, by the Secretary of State, perhaps to protect himself from critical analysis of his policies for public spending. It is to be hoped that the Environment Select Committee's dignified protest about Heseltine's attitude to its inquiries will have a long-term influence on ministerial behaviour. But there is plainly no immediate prospect of more open policy-making in housing at national level.

Housing at Local Level

The divorce between the public processes of democracy and actual national decision-making is reflected at local level. Formally, local people can take advantage of a wide range of rights and opportunities to enquire, to be informed, and to participate in the actual decision-making itself. These rights are part and parcel of the processes of local government and are not confined to policy-making in housing alone. National statistics on housing contain basic information about the local housing stock, and a variable amount of information about a local authority's finances, policies, own surveys, and so on, is available in council minutes and reports. But, in practice, the public is kept at a remove from the real decision-making process. Though the meetings of committees and the full council, at which decisions are formally taken, are open to the public and some policy papers are available, the actual decisions are often taken at private 'caucus' meetings of the political party in power, or by less formal meetings of leading officials and elected members, and simply ratified in open committee or council. Papers and information are circulated here which do not reach the public, and might even be withheld from a majority of elected councillors. It would be misleading to suggest that local authorities are generally more secretive than Whitehall.* It would also be unfair not to record that many authorities try hard to make a reality of public participation and are increasingly more prepared to open up how they behave to public scrutiny.

The Greater London Council, London boroughs, metropolitan and district councils act as housing authorities. So far as issues of open government are concerned, their general housing activities can be separated into two fronts: preparing and carrying through strategies to meet local housing needs and to maintain the area's housing stock; and administering, managing and allocating the council's own stock. But both areas of activity spill over into another dimension which most distinguishes local from central government: a council's exercise of its housing powers and duties directly affects people as individuals. The council might decide to buy a family's house by use of compulsory powers, to give or refuse an improvement grant to an owner-occupier, or to transfer a household from one council flat to another.[24] The people involved have a right to know how fairly the council is behaving in their own case, and to be informed about the council's general policy in such cases. Thus, while the public at large has a legitimate interest in a council's exercise of its powers and duties in both areas, and in the quality of administration locally, individuals too should have access to personal files and other information with a bearing on their cases.

The public has no coherent overall right to be informed about, or to participate in, a council's exercise of its housing responsibilities. Access for the public depends on a confusing mixture of local authority duties and powers and official exhortations. Strategic housing decisions – to redevelop or improve an area of existing housing, or to build a new estate – raise planning issues and bring into force statutory rights of consultation; and the traditional respect for property has long been enshrined in legislation which requires a council which wants to clear single houses or an area to advertise its plans and give owners individual notice. If local residents object to the plans, they have the power to take the issue to a public inquiry at which the council must explain its decision. Under the huge political pressure from central government to adopt large-scale new house-building programmes in the 1950s and 1960s, many local authorities – particularly in inner-city

---

* But see Peter Stringer's contrary view in Chapter Seven, Local Government and Planning.

areas – ran roughshod over local people's wishes. The formal procedures proved to be no defence against the juggernaut of redevelopment since they reflected government policies: the final arbiter in the inquiry process is the Minister! So began the pressures for real public participation in local authority planning, which since have had the seal of approval from the same central government which encouraged the excess of redevelopment in the first place.

Additionally, when a council decides to designate an area as a housing action area or general improvement area, it must again consult, inform and involve local residents. The government's motive here is rather different: it is recognised that there is enormous scope for voluntary and private action in the rehabilitation of rundown houses in these areas, and consultation and involvement is believed to encourage this action.

The degree of public participation in strategic housing decisions of this kind is therefore limited. First, it is largely confined to residents of the area in which the council plans to act. Secondly, apart from the statutory right of notice, a council's duties to inform and involve residents are vaguely defined, and cannot easily be enforced by people who feel they have been neglected. Much depends on a council's own enthusiasm for public participation. Thirdly, it is the *planning*, not the *housing*, aspects of the council's policy which are really opened up.*

Housing Investment Programme

The introduction since the late 1970s of housing investment programmes (HIPs) at local level has created a framework for more open exercise of a council's strategic housing planning. HIPs are drawn up as part of a local authority's housing strategy. They set out the authority's proposals for investment in its housing activities for four years ahead, against a double background: first, a strategy statement which assesses local needs, special issues and the council's general plan; and secondly, a statistical summary of population levels, the number of households, the extent and state of the housing stock, and so on, with projections over the four-year period. The *Housing Policy Review* anticipated that, in the process of preparing their HIP submissions, authorities would develop 'their existing working relationships' with tenants' and community

---

* For a full discussion of the lessons for a right to information from the experience of participation in planning, see Chapter Seven, Local Government and Planning.

associations and other bodies concerned with housing in their areas.[25] Though it was recognised that the authority's own investment programme would often lie at the heart of the local housing strategy, it was envisaged that the strategy would cast its net wider and consider the contribution that the private sector was likely to make. HIPs – which involve an annual 'bid' for the allocation of funds by central government – are revised every year on a rolling-programme basis.

The HIP system effectively began in 1977–78, but at first the government refused to make the submissions from the authorities public. The DoE argued that they had been sent to Whitehall in confidence, and that their release would be a breach of that confidence. Under pressure from Shelter, the government finally gave in, and local authority HIP submissions are now lodged in the House of Commons library. This makes them open to the public in a typically limited way: anyone who can persuade an MP to give them the status of a research assistant, if only for a day, can get access to them. At a local level, authorities are asked by the government to make the HIP submissions available to the public. Indeed, in August 1979, the government informed authorities that 'providing the public with opportunities to express views on authorities' policies, and taking account of their views, should become an integral part of the HIP process throughout the year.'[26]

How readily available are copies or details of councils' HIP programmes? Leicester Shelter Group asked the nine district authorities in Leicestershire for their HIP plans two years running. In the first year, all nine supplied them with the plans; in the second year, only seven handed them over. Paul Herrington, research officer with the Leicester group says,

The trouble is that there's no obligation on authorities to make this information public. You can usually get the background information, if you're prepared to dig for it in the national statistics, council minutes and reports, etc. But of course it is much more convenient to have a single mine of information, and the way it is presented is important. The crucial information in the HIPs is the strategy statement, but there is resistance to releasing that if it's going to be criticised.

A random sample of eight authorities (two London boroughs, two metropolitan authorities, four smaller districts) found that none published the papers for the general public, and none gave full details of the 'bid' to the Department of the Environment in the council minutes; the DoE's response was more fully reported. None consulted the public in the process of drawing up the programme. But what would they do for the interested citizen? The answer seems to be that, for all their muddled goodwill, precious little. Only two out of eight local residents managed to get a look at their council's programme for the year. In Hackney, an east London borough, a town hall spokesman said that the papers were available at the housing department. At the housing department they said: 'Try the town hall. The chief executive's deputy has the papers.' Back to the town hall. Alas, he was on holiday. 'We think there are a couple of copies, but we wouldn't know where to look.' 'I'll leave my name and address. Can you please send a copy when he gets back? And here's my telephone number in case of difficulty.' That was in May 1980. Nothing more has been heard from Hackney.[27]

Take Leeds, too. Here a persistent citizen telephoned the city's library information unit. 'It will be in the reference library,' they said. So he went to the reference library, which didn't have the HIP papers at all. On a librarian's advice, he went to the council's housing advice centre. 'Oh no, we don't have anything like that here. Try the reference library.' Back home, he telephoned the 'town hall' inquiries desk. After consultation, they said confidently: 'It's at the housing department.' Off to the housing department. But he was out of luck again. 'If you try the housing advice centre,' they said, 'they will give you details.'[28]

At a time of continuing reductions in public expenditure, central government uses HIPs as dressed-up schemes of 'cash limits' and escapes from its responsibility to fund local housing activities adequately by shifting the onus for adjusting activities to straitened circumstances onto local authorities in the name of local freedom. Nevertheless, HIPs offer a realistic framework both for creating a flexible national policy for housing and for fully involving local people in its preparation. Plainly, the first requirement is that HIPs should not be used nationally as a rationing instrument, but rather as a measure of housing's need for investment. Secondly, central government should lay down criteria for the kind of information which the strategy statement should contain, as it does for the back-up evidence. Some authorities put in detailed documents; others could write their strategy on the back of an envelope. Thirdly, the government should make public participation in the preparation of HIPs mandatory, and the HIP submission should contain evidence of the local authority's efforts to inform and involve the public and interested bodies, like tenants' associations, locally. Fourthly, the government should reintroduce 'housing default' powers to make a reality of the public's participation: if a substantial number of local residents were dissatisfied with a council's plans, they should have the power to demand a public inquiry under the aegis of the Secretary of State. If they satisfied the Minister that the authority's plans were inadequate, he would have power to authorise additional investment in housing locally.

How Council Housing is Managed

The HIP process, of course, incorporates a local authority's investment plans for its own housing stock, and information about its state of repair, the provision of amenities, environmental schemes and the like. To this extent, there is an opening for public participation in the strategic investment decisions in public housing. Generally, however, a council's behaviour as a public landlord is scarcely constrained at all by any requirement to be open.

The management and allocation of public housing is the last major area of discretion which central government has left almost entirely untouched to local authorities. It is also an area of central, continuing and occasionally urgent importance to some five million households in council housing, to at least another million families on local authority waiting lists, and (most critically of all) to around two million people who find themselves homeless each year. It is an area in which councils may adopt discriminatory practices, knowingly or unknowingly; neglect the interests of sections of the population; fail to plan or budget adequately for the proper maintenance and repair of people's homes; take an arrogantly unresponsive attitude towards tenants and applicants for housing; and deliberately keep major policies confidential. Racial minorities and one-parent families have suffered most from discrimination, but it is often more general: estates may be reserved for those whom officers consider to be 'the better sort of tenant' or turned into ghettoes of those whom officers regard as unsuitable tenants.

Up until the Housing Act 1980, local authorities were not obliged even to allow their tenants to participate in the management of their estates. Such participation was, perhaps inevitably, poorly developed. 1980 figures showed that only just over four per cent of councils allowed tenant representatives to sit on the council's housing committee – and so get full access to council papers – and only 2.5 per cent allowed them to vote (and so share in the actual decision-making). A further twelve per cent had a tenants' liaison or advisory panel, and fourteen per cent additionally held regular discussions with tenants. Well over a third had no participation of any kind.[29]

A series of official reports – most notably the Cullingworth report, *Council Housing: Purposes, Procedures and Priorities* in 1969[30] – have argued the need for a more open and responsive exercise of the far-reaching responsibilities of local authorities involved in managing and allocating the public housing stock. Academic and community-based reports have drawn attention to shortcomings in the exercise of these responsibilities,[31] and anec-dotal evidence abounds. However, the DoE has always resisted the most modest changes – not simply changes which would make local authorities more open and responsive, but also any which would enforce national standards and remove the opportunity to practise unfair and discriminatory policies. The argument for this resistance has been, at its best, that local authorities are better placed than Whitehall to respond to local needs and pressures; and, at its worst, that interference in this last major area of its discretion would make local government less attractive to officers and council members. But its real base has always been that the local authorities have maintained a persistent pressure against any tampering with their powers. Both the Department and the two major parties have been vulnerable to this pressure. The interests of local bureaucracy and politicians have, therefore, been put before those of the large number of people who depend on pub-licly rented housing. The strong case for reform has been ignored.

By the 1970s, however, the enormous divide between owner-occupation and council housing was increasingly obvious. Both the Labour and the Conservative parties are committed to the expansion of owner-occupation and, for a varying mix of ideo-logical and electoral motives, are unwilling to contemplate any curbing of the financial advantages of buying over renting – ad-vantages which inexorably drive public housing into a residual role. To make some show of redressing the considerable imbal-ance, a bipartisan 'tenants charter' emerged. This has been en-acted in the Housing Act 1980. Its main foundation is the granting of a form of legal security of tenure to council tenants. But it also contains reforms which are relevant to demands for more open government. Local authorities must now publish summaries of their schemes for allocating tenancies to applicants for council

housing, for organising transfers of existing tenants, and for allowing exchanges between tenants. They must inform their tenants
of their rights and obligations under the law and their tenancy
agreements. They must introduce consultation schemes for their
tenants and formally consider any representations made by their
tenants.

The proposals for making public a council's allocation, transfer
and exchange schemes represent a real advance – especially as it
is in allocating tenancies that a council's discretionary powers are
most critical. But whole areas of discretionary power will be left
in the dark, which the half-hearted commitment to consultation,
not participation, of tenants is hardly likely to redress. It is also
important at this juncture to point out that even the opening up
of allocation policies to public scrutiny will not necessarily reveal
discriminatory practices which aren't the result of formal rules.
Inquiries into discrimination against racial minorities in allocation
procedures have all depended on access to confidential files on
applicants. The public could not be given that access. Open government is sometimes put forward as a panacea for all the ills of
government; it is, however, important that further pressure for
open government should be accompanied by a realistic appraisal
of other reforms which are needed. One of these is mandatory
monitoring of procedures, such as allocation schemes, where discrimination is alleged to take place.

The Rights to Information of the People Affected

This discussion leads naturally to the 'extra dimension' of local
activity which has already been noted: a council's exercise of its
powers directly affects people as individuals. What right of access
to information which affects them personally do they have? As
property owners and residents, people do have rights to be informed of council plans which might affect their homes or environment, and a limited right to consultation. They can, as we have
seen, even insist on a public inquiry at which they can question
council officers. But they are not entitled to access to relevant
official information and reports, and the inquiry process does not
extend to any kind of disclosure of official documents.

Respect for property owners' rights again secures for private
landlords right of notice when a council has resolved to use any
of the confused jumble of powers and duties it has to enforce and
maintain standards in privately-rented housing, and to require

repair or improvement works. The council must serve notice in advance of practically every action, and the landlord can normally turn to the courts for protection if he feels aggrieved. Tenants are not so favoured, even though it is they who actually live in the properties. They are not always entitled to notice of a council's intentions. It is even known for councils to refuse to tell tenants, who have complained, say, about damp and a leaking roof, what action they are taking on the grounds that it is *sub judice*.

Most encouragingly, at first sight, government has increasingly attached rights to information to a council's exercise of its range of discretionary powers in housing. An individual who is refused a rent rebate, or an improvement grant, or shelter for their family when they are homeless, can demand an explanation in writing from the council. In some cases, they are entitled to make representations. But these rights do not represent a move towards more open government. No real access to the local decision-making process is granted. The rights disguise a compromise. The government is reluctant to give people in such circumstances what they really need – recourse to an independent tribunal or the courts. This would certainly offend local authorities and would cost money. Thus, in place of a proper right of appeal, aggrieved individuals are given limited rights to information and a hearing by the very body which has made the original decision. (Fortunately, in the case of homeless families, the Housing [Homeless Persons] Act 1977 makes it a duty for the local authority to rehouse certain categories of homeless people, who are thus enabled to get access to the courts.)

Lastly, there is the issue of the personal files which housing authorities keep. The most important of these are the files on applicants for council houses, and the individual tenancy files. But housing authorities also keep personal records on applicants for transfers, exchanges, rent rebates and home loss payments, as well as on homeless families. Files on the maintenance and repair of council properties may contain personal information. It is well known that files on applicants for housing often contain prejudicial information and subjective assessments, especially on what is described as the applicants' 'housing standards', by housing officials, known as housing visitors.[32]

Recent research by a team from the Open University in North Bedfordshire uncovered the following subjective remarks by housing visitors:

She is obviously a very clean woman. Her standard would warrant modern accommodation.

Reasonably clean Asian family

She appears to have plenty of visitors who appear to be mainly West Indian men. This is indeed a problem family and I understand Mrs X is something of an alcoholic. The children are usually very unruly and the place never of a high standard.

Flat is very overcrowded. This was self-inflicted as they knew what problems would arise before they moved in. Would make poor tenants.

Below average type of applicant. I would not have thought this family was suitable for new accommodation.

Good/very good cleanliness. Miss C's room seemed generally well looked after and was full of the usual technicolour bric-a-brac favoured by West Indians.

If Buckingham Palace became available she might accept.[33]

These reports have a marked influence on the type of council home which is offered to a family. Once in council housing, confidential reports are kept on tenants which may contain newspaper cuttings and other personal information not directly relevant to the tenancy. The Housing Act 1980 merely insists that councils should allow applicants for housing to check that 'the relevant information they have supplied' has been correctly entered in the council's files. This is a useful step forward, and with the right to information about a council's allocations policy, should provide applicants with the means to check that they are being fairly dealt with. But it by no means gives the full access even to the files of applicants for housing which is necessary to guard against the entry of prejudicial information, and does not extend to the tenancy or any other files which a housing department may hold.

The arguments against going further are not convincing. It is said that officials will be inhibited from recording full information on files if the people affected have a right to see them. Additional staff would have to be appointed. Extra costs would be incurred. As it happens, Haringey Borough Council, in north London, adopted a scheme to give local residents access to any file or record kept on them by the Housing Department in 1979. The council also abandoned the dubious practice of making records of 'housing standards'. In all, over 64,000 files are now accessible to the people concerned. A tenant or housing client who wishes to see a file first approaches the council's own 'Ombudsman', who works from the chief executive's office, and produces proof of identity. The 'Ombudsman' obtains the file and removes from it only documents which would transgress professional etiquette or privilege (for example, comments by a GP or social worker) or which could cause damage or distress to another person (like a libellous remark.) The intention, however, is to make the files as 'open' as possible, and clearance is usually sought to keep items in the file. The tenant or client can then inspect the file, and enter on it comment on any of the information the file contains. In the first year of operation, the council had 150 requests to inspect files. No extra staff were taken on and no great cost was involved. But a huge step towards more open and accountable government locally was taken. It is not apparent why the government was not ready to take such a step nationally; but it is to be hoped that other authorities will use their discretionary powers to follow the example of the handful of authorities which, like Haringey, have taken the initiative in opening up their files, and that, in the next Housing Act, a government will be prepared to build on their experience.

The processes of decision-making in housing at local level are no more open, then, than at national level. In recognition of the fact that a council's decisions often have a direct impact on the lives of local residents, government has legislated for a somewhat confused range of rights to be informed and consulted, but without considering people's needs in a coherent and overall fashion – and certainly not with any ideal of open government in mind. If any immediate advance is to be made, it probably lies in opening up the files held by local housing departments on individual applicants for council housing and council tenants. Local authorities can take the initiative here themselves, and if enough do so, then government will more easily be able to legislate for such a change nationally with a body of experience behind it.

REFERENCES

1 Orwell, George, *The Road to Wigan Pier*, Penguin Books, 1962 edition.
2 For a review of the literature in this field, see for example, Lansley, Stewart, *Housing and Public Policy*, Croom Helm, 1979; Schorr, A.

L., 'Housing Policy and Poverty', in Townsend, P., *The Concept of Poverty*, Heinemann, 1970; and see also Davie, Ronald, Butler, Neville, and Goldstein, Harvey, *From Birth to Seven, A Report of the National Child Development Study*, Longman, 1972, p. 57.

3 *Fair Deal for Housing*, HMSO, Cmnd 4728, 1971, p. 1, para. 5.

4 Department of the Environment, *Housing Policy: A Consultative Document*, Cmnd 6851, HMSO, 1977, p. 7, para. 2.16. This document is referred to in the text as the *Housing Policy Review* (HPR) green paper.

5 National Consumer Council, *Problems of House Purchase and Mortgage Lending – A Consumer View*, NCC, 1978.

6 *Housing Policy: A Consultative Document, op. cit.*

7 'Housing in Action Areas', *Roof*, September 1979.

8 *Ibid.*

9 *Hansard*, 10 March 1977.

10 *Hansard*, 18 November 1974.

11 Speech to Housing Centre Trust (see *Housing Review*, September-October 1975), quoted in Kilroy, Bernard, *Housing Finance – Organic Reform?*, Labour Economic Finance and Taxation Association pamphlet, September 1978, p. 5.

12 Quoted in Weir, S., 'How Labour Failed to Reform Mortgage Relief', *New Society*, vol. 46, no. 835, 3 October 1978, p. 14.

13 Kilroy, Bernard, *op. cit.*, p. 9.

14 The Labour Party 1976 Conference Report.

15 *Sunday Times*, 22 August 1976.

16 'London Has Still Got to Rehouse Worst Off', *Roof*, November 1976, p. 176.

17 *The Government's Expenditure Plans 1980–1 to 1983–4*, Cmnd 7841, HMSO, March 1980.

18 *Ibid.*, p. 72.

19 Aughton, H., 'Demolition Job Planned on Housing Expenditure', *Roof*, May/June 1980, p. 76.

20 First Report from the Environment Committee Session 1979–80, *Enquiry into the Implications of Government's Expenditure Plans 1980–81 to 1983–84 for the Housing Policies of the Department of the Environment*, July 1980, HC 714 HC 578 – i, p. 2.

21 *ibid.*, p. 4.

22 *ibid.*, p. 18.

23 See Kilroy, B., 'No Jackpot from Council House Sales', *Roof*, May 1977.

24 For a general guide to the statutory powers and responsibilities referred to in this section, see Smith, Mary E. H., *A Guide to Housing*, Housing Centre Trust, 1977. A brief guide to the 1980 Housing Act is given in National Consumer Council, *New Rights for Tenants*, NCC, 1980.

25 *Housing Policy: A Consultative Document, op. cit.*, p. 43, para. 6.08.
26 Department of the Environment, circular letter to housing authorities.
27 Personal research by the author.
28 Personal research by Lewis Minkin.
29 Institute of Housing, *Annual Review 1980*, p. 7.
30 *Council Housing Purposes, Procedures and Priorities*, Ninth Report of the Housing Management Sub-Committee of the Central Housing Advisory Committee, HMSO, 1969.
31 See, for example, Murie, Alan, Niner, Pat, and Watson, Christopher, *Housing Policy and the Housing System*, Allen and Unwin, 1976.
32 Examples are cited by Ward, Colin, *Tenants Take Over*, Architectural Press, 1974, p. 17.
33 Examples taken from 'How Blacks Lose Out in Council Housing', by Richard Skellington, *New Society*, 29 January 1981.

Education

Peter Newell

The one public service that might perhaps be expected to foster a spirit of lively enquiry and the full and frank exchange of information is education. Public debate about schools and schooling is often intense. Nearly everyone has some first-hand experience of the service and almost one in three households has a child in full-time education. About two-thirds of local authority revenue expenditure goes on educational services. So is there a more liberal approach to the release of official information about this crucial public service? Not at all, argues Peter Newell. The Department of Education and Science and local education authorities are as loathe to share background details about plans and policy formation as other departments of government, while at local level the schools even keep secret from parents – although not always from other outsiders – the information, whether accurate or not, that they record about the children themselves.

At every level of the education service, traditions of bureaucratic or professional secrecy rule. Whether your interest is in finding out the basis for some dramatic and unexplained change in central government policy, discovering who does what in your local education office or simply seeing what is in your own child's school record, you will find obstructions – many of them insurmountable within existing legislation – all along the way.

A service that consumes billions of pounds of our money and involves all of us as students in compulsory institutions should not be able to decide for itself how little or how much information it makes available. As national and local electors, we may play our token democratic part in choosing who administers the service nationally and locally, but accountability should begin, not end there.

This chapter cannot hope to document in detail the huge gaps in information available to the public at central government, local authority and individual institution level. Nor can it prescribe in detail the sort of legislation required to give the users of the service adequate access. General right of access legislation would solve some of the problems, though much would depend on how widely its provisions were drawn; and at school level, recently published regulations on information for parents arising from the 1980 Education Act show a welcome move towards openness, although they ignore the vital issue of parent and student access to school records.[1] This last issue, generally regarded with some impatience by both administrators and teachers, provides an excellent introduction to all the principles of freedom of information and privacy: it demonstrates a classic example of political and professional paternalism, and is therefore covered at some length in this chapter. It may be strategically important for historians to have access to Department of Education and Science policy planning documents, but in human rights and consumer terms it is far more important that teachers should not be able to write down things about children and their families, keep them in secret files, and pass these files on to others without the knowledge or consent of the subjects.

The education system and its institutions should be a practical training ground for an open, fair democracy. Currently, they look and act like an effective conditioning process for a secretive and discriminatory society.

'A National Service . . .'

'A national service locally administered' is the traditional historic view of the English education system; the balance of power between Department of Education (DES), local authorities and individual heads and governing bodies is set out in the 1944 Education Act and succeeding legislation. During the period of broad consensus and the expansion of the service, in the 60s and early 70s, the Department's position and the closed nature of most of its decision-making was seldom questioned.

Maurice Kogan, in *The Politics of Educational Change*, suggests that although the DES is exceedingly powerful within the education service, within the Civil Service it is regarded as a little separate: 'It has the appearance of a Vice-Royalty, something akin to the style of the British Raj in India, a prestigious part of the main system but somewhat remote from it.'[2] In 1975, a report prepared by examiners from the Organisation for Economic Co-operation and Development (OECD) criticised the DES for undue general secrecy, and for effectively preventing alternative strategies from being discussed before policies were decided.[3] When Sir William Pile, the then Permanent Secretary at the DES, went to Paris to defend the Department against OECD criticisms, he accepted 'that the British system of decision-making was private, but argued that planning the allocation of resources did not lend itself to full and open consultation.'[4]

A journalist, who in the 70s achieved some distinction for his record of leaking sensitive DES planning documents, later wrote a detailed account of the handling, or mishandling, of the reorganisation of the colleges of education.[5] David Hencke sees secrecy as endemic to the political and administrative system:

The world of government is dominated by a plethora of confidential committees where ministers and civil servants meet to discuss issues. It is supported by that peculiarly British tradition, the gentlemen's club, where confidentiality is the rule and where many Government matters are discussed in advance among the *cognoscenti* before they are made more public. The Department of Education is no exception to the secret traditions of our society.[6]

When, following the OECD criticisms, a committee of MPs looked at policy making in the DES, they repeated the charges of undue secrecy and lack of proper consultation procedures. The report, by the Education, Arts and Home Office sub-committee of the House of Commons Expenditure Committee, was published in 1976.[7] Its chairperson, Miss Janet Fookes MP, said that the Departmental Planning Organisation planned behind closed doors; nobody was taken into its confidence; and when the Committee tried to get some of the major planning papers, it was rebuffed. The Committee's report 'reluctantly' defended the constitutional tradition of the confidentiality of advice from individual civil servants to individual ministers, but argued that many planning papers could and should be published. (The Committee itself was refused access to Programme Analysis Review (PAR) material.) There was, for instance, a wide range of empirical evidence behind the 1972 Education white paper, which could have been published to encourage debate:

In the UK it is normal for an 'official' paper to be restricted and so it becomes the habit for an official to withhold. We believe that the habit of secretiveness – the instinct to withhold rather than voluntarily to share information – lies at the root of most of the criticisms of DES' consultative processes.[8]

The report also suggested that the Department 'does not encourage interest groups, or indeed the wider public, to participate in discussion of long range planning and of the overall purposes and shape of the educational services.' The MPs found it 'ironic' that in defending its record of consulting interest groups, the DES made no mention of Parliament, 'the group with the widest range of interests of all. The elected representatives of the people may ask questions of the DES or speak in debates on education but they are never consulted.'[9] The irony was underlined when this Parliamentary study was briefly dismissed in a departmental reply (of a mere eight pages),[10] and no significant action on its recommendations taken.

Education policy is inevitably susceptible to rapid reversals with a change of government. The successive about-turns in legislation on comprehensive reorganisation illustrate this, as most recently do the radical changes brought about by the 1980 Act. Parliamentary procedure allows MPs publicly to debate such policy reversals, on the floor of both Houses and at committee stage, but really it is the size of the majority of the ruling party which determines the speed and confidence of change.

The unwillingness of the present administration to collect information on the local results of central policies and centrally-imposed cutbacks in public expenditure is understandable, in that for the first time for several decades the Secretary of State for Education and his Department find themselves presiding over a severe pruning job rather than planned growth. The Cabinet's search for economies within all branches of government has not ignored the DES, and a particular section that is going to be drastically hit is statistics: while serious researchers already criticise the DES' six volumes of annual statistics for making long-term comparisons and predictions difficult and for lengthy delays in publishing them, they are going to be less than happy with the announcement in the white paper on *Government's Statistical Services* (published in April 1981) that the publication of annual volumes of statistics will cease altogether. The white paper suggests that the Department of Education will be looking at 'more effective ways' of meeting the demand for essential and historical data.[11]

Writing to the *Times Educational Supplement* in July 1980, the Education Secretary of the National Association of Teachers in Further and Higher Education said:

Education is a major and inevitably costly service, and it is nonsensical that the relatively small sums spent in collating and publishing information on its performance should not continue to be made available. The statistical information which is now under threat is essential to effective administration and democratic policy making.[12]

To a large extent, the public rely on the press, and in particular the education correspondents, for any revelations about the internal workings and decisions of the DES. But the education correspondents, like their colleagues the political correspondents, the industrial writers and so on have their own 'lobby club' – the education correspondents' group – which arranges off-the-record meetings and lunches with ministers and representatives of interest groups. It is debatable whether this collusion between journalists and government information officers acts in the best interests of the public, enabling as it does politicians and officials to inhibit what is written and published about their actions.

During the Committee stage proceedings of the 1979 Education Bill, one (Labour) MP said:

I see no harm in publishing, within an authority, the names of schools that are available to the parents living in a particular area . . . Certainly the names of the schools should be published . . . There is certain minimum information to which parents are entitled. What I am afraid is that, if we take this too far, we are on the slippery slope of giving information that the parents – I say this advisedly – may not understand fully.[13]

Try phoning up a local education authority office, and asking for basic information about the schools in the area; after transfer from one unhelpful department to another, you are lucky if you end up with a duplicated list of names and addresses.

Central encouragement of better information for parents on education became politically fashionable a few years ago, and while Shirley Williams was Secretary of State, the then government issued a circular entitled *Information for Parents* setting out the 'nature and extent of the information she [Mrs Williams] considers should normally be made available to parents in written form as and when appropriate in relation to their children's school careers'.[14] It listed such uncontentious items as names of head and senior staff, name and address of the chairperson of governors and any parent governors, times of visiting, special facilities, arrangements for religious education, outlines of teaching and pastoral care organisation, and so on.

The Conservative administration which came to power in 1979 had before the election made a great deal of its commitment to 'opening up' the education system. Norman St John-Stevas' parents' charter was echoed by rather less enthusiastic commitments in the Party manifesto and then in the Queen's Speech; the manifesto said: 'Schools will be required to publish prospectuses giving details of their examination and other results' and, contributing to the debate following the Queen's Speech, Mark Carlisle, then Secretary of State for Education, said: 'If parents are to be able to make a choice they need the information on which such a choice can be based, and we will make it a requirement for LEAs to provide the widest possible information about their schools.'[15]

The 1980 Education Act does give local education authorities, and governors of aided schools, a duty to publish their rules governing admission to schools, the arrangements for parents to express a preference, and the appeals procedure. They must also publish details of the number of places available at schools. The Act also gives the Secretary of State the power to issue further regulations outlining what other information about schools LEAs and governors should be required to make available.[16]

The first moves towards implementing this section of the Act were a minor but classic example of the kind of partial consultation for which the Department of Education and Science should be famous. In April 1980, a preliminary consultation document on information for parents was sent privately to local authority and voluntary school associations.[17] The document was inevitably leaked fairly widely, and at the same time the local authority associations and others let their opposition to it, and in particular to the suggested timetable of implementation by September 1981 (finally agreed for implementation for school admissions in September 1982), be known. A government that directly or indirectly had taken away much of the authorities' educational spending power, and had expressed its commitment to reducing central direction, leaving more to local decision, was now intent on imposing a centrally dictated and expensive administrative exercise. It was typical of the Department of Education to organise this initial consultation so that the providers of the information, rather than those who need it, were the first to be consulted; there is simply no tradition within the DES of consulting non-professional bodies at the stage of policy formation.

The particular aspect of information-providing which most appeals to Conservative education ministers is the publication of individual schools' examination results. So it is no surprise to find that the consultation document devoted considerable space to discussing this aspect; the 'Government's aims', summarised on the first page, seemed laudable:

(a) to enable parents, now that they are to have a statutory right to express their preference as to the school they wish their child to attend, to make an informal decision;
(b) to contribute generally to openness and the avoidance of reputation by rumour;
(c) to make generalised and exaggerated claims impossible and to ensure that present provision and achievements are clearly distinguished from future plans; and
(d) to contribute towards the establishment of an informal and mutually supportive relationship between parents and the schools that their children attend.[18]

When the regulations were finally published in May 1981 (as the Education [School Information] Regulations 1981), they generally followed the lines of the original Shirley Williams' Circular. But despite representations from parent groups and others, the government had not taken the opportunity to include a requirement, for instance, that governors' names and addresses should be published, nor that schools should make a clear statement on equal opportunities.

The section on the publication of individual schools' examination results – which in prospect had greatly upset the teacher unions and others who put paternalism before freedom of information – turned out to be less rigorous than expected. Schools are required to give the numbers taking each public examination in the most recent school year, and the numbers attaining each grade in each examination.

But of course these regulations do represent a major step forward towards an open and accountable service – schools and authorities will have to get into the habit of providing a great deal more information, and hopefully this will lead them to question some of their largely concealed policies on, for example, how pupils are to dress, and where applicable to give the approximate cost of each item of school uniform; and also their arrangements for discipline, including, in particular, the practice of the school as respects corporal punishment and the arrangements for bringing school rules to the attention of pupils and parents.

'. . . Locally Administered'

Local education authorities have certain obligations to conduct their business openly. For instance, the Public Bodies (Admission to Meetings) Act 1960 directs that all meetings of education committees must be open to public and press (although they retain some discretion over defining as 'confidential' certain items of business and so excluding both public and press).[19] And part of Schedule 1 to the 1944 Education Act says that 'The minutes of proceedings of an education committee of the local education authority shall be open to the inspection of any local government elector for the area on payment of a fee not exceeding one shilling, and any such local government elector may make a copy thereof or an extract therefrom.'[20]

The public meetings of education committees are seldom quite the open forums for democratic debate that they may appear from the gallery. In most areas, local elections follow normal party lines, and the majority and minority on the local authority normally represent political parties. These groups usually hold 'shadow' private meetings before the public meetings, go right through the agenda and decide how to vote as a block (with penalties imposed by the local whips for any party dissidents). Politicians find it very hard to understand why, to others, this system may appear to give less than adequate attention to real local issues. It certainly reduces to a meaningless charade the open face of most local education committees. The committee is also given power under the 1944 Act to appoint sub-committees, to which the same obligations to operate 'openly' do not apply.[21]

While the 1944 Act does place a duty on the Secretary of State for Education to make an annual report to Parliament,[22] no such duty is placed on LEAs, and very few of them voluntarily produce either annual reports or regular statistics.

In April 1980, the Inner London Education Authority (ILEA) started consultations on a series of proposals designed to give parents and school governors more information about schools. The Authority proposes that each school should produce an annual report; that there should be an annual review prepared by the head and staff for governors; and in secondary schools a more detailed five-year report, based on an examination of the school by head and staff in cooperation with ILEA inspectors. The first of these reports, covering the school year 1980–81, will be published in 1982.[23]

Given the huge areas of discretion allowed to them in performing their vague duties under the 1944 Act (providing 'sufficient' schools, 'efficient' instruction, 'adequate' facilities for further education and so on), it is vital that consumers should be able to check how their own LEA compares in generosity or meanness with others. The 1980 Education Act increased the areas of discretion, and while the Secretary of State may *require* LEAs to provide him with information on the services they provide, they are not otherwise under any general obligation to do so voluntarily.[24]

The only comprehensive source of comparative statistics, published annually, is the statistical information service of the Chartered Institute of Public Finance and Accountancy (CIPFA). The education volume contains both non-financial statistics – pupil and teacher numbers, ratios, etc. – and financial data. These include total costs, analysed in some detail, and also unit costs per pupil for different aspects of the service at different levels. Local authorities regard these statistics with some scepticism, presumably linked to their attitude to filling in the returns on which they are based. Two volumes are published each year, one based on estimates and the other on final accounts, and – accurate or not – they do document remarkably large variations in spending on such items as books and administration and in primary and secondary unit costs from one LEA to another.

A standardised system of accounting analysis, allowing fair and accurate comparisons to be made, is vital to the consumer, who also needs to know on what basis LEAs exercise their discretion; the whole field of non-mandatory grants for further education is a good example. There is no central direction and little central advice in this area. In some parts of the country, Leeds and Ealing for example, an enthusiastic response to demands to cut local spending has resulted, for a period, in no more 'discretionary' grants being awarded. So the chances of receiving non-degree-level further education now depend even more on place of residence (or of course the ability to 'buy' a course without a grant). There is no obligation on an LEA to publish its policy on discretionary grants, if indeed it has one. On school closures – the issue which has probably caused more active community attempts to participate in LEA policy-making than any other – there are obligations to publish notices and invite comments, and a DES circular encourages 'full consultations'.[25] But political paternalism tends to protect schools and the public from any long drawn-out debate on falling rolls' policies. The justification is that any school threatened with closure is likely to lose public confidence and support. In practice, the opposite appears to be the case: there is no better way to mobilise active parental involvement than to introduce a closure threat.

When things go wrong with a particular school, and local education authorities ask for officers' reports, or send in their own inspectors/advisers, those most directly affected – the students and their parents – might expect to know what the inspection reveals. But they generally expect in vain. Such reports are seldom circulated outside the education committee, governing board and perhaps the head teacher (unless of course some dissident councillor or governor leaks them to the local press).

Confidentiality at local level reflects the similarly restricted circulation of Her Majesty's Inspectorate (HMI) reports. HMI, an officially independent 'watchdog', has a duty to report to the Secretary of State on the efficiency of the system. Individual HMIs can visit and comment on all publicly maintained and grant-aided institutions, independent schools and certain independent further education colleges. Their advice goes to the Department, to local authorities, and to teachers and governors; but reports are not to be made available outside the school (the official reason often given is that schools might use them to 'advertise' themselves).

According to the Department of Education, 'only two or three HMI reports on schools have been published in the last 20 years'. In Autumn 1980, the Inspectorate broke with their traditional secrecy by agreeing to publish – at the request of the Inner London Education Authority – their full-scale report on London's schools.[26] In the case of an authority-wide report like this, which would have been made available at least to the heads and chairpeople of governing bodies of all the capital's schools, it is of course hard to see how secrecy could have been maintained, and the brave political decision to publish was probably no more than a calculated desire to avoid inadequate, leaked reports, concentrating on HMI's many criticisms. Should the decision to allow publication rest solely with HMI and with the providers of the education service?

Looking at the content of the London report, surely it becomes obvious that parents and students using ILEA schools have an absolute right to know, for instance, that HMI believe: 'Too many secondary schools expect too little from their pupils at all levels, and much work lacks pace, variety and interest'; shortages 'frequently contrast with lavish over-provision and waste in other parts of the school'; roughly two-thirds of the fourth and fifth year classes observed contained 'much dull repetition with mindless copying of notes; where children are rude or lethargic, it may well be a consequence in these classes of the work they are being offered'; 'too frequently teachers assume that children from ethnic minorities need an extra year to prepare for public examinations in all subjects'; 'standards in some day schools for the maladjusted are disturbingly low'.

In 1978, HMI surveyed twenty-one community homes (the old approved schools) offering education in England and Wales. Two years later, a report of the survey was published which in deadpan official language documented shocking gaps in the facilities and education provided in many of these institutions.[27] The schools were not identified. The children in them, in the care of local authorities, have no active representatives to insist on proper care and education, and are already in social and educational terms at a considerable disadvantage. The maintenance of such institutions on a basis of administrative secrecy, with the collusion of HMI, does not inspire public confidence.

HMI collectively are in a better position than anyone else to assess the real extent of the damage to educational standards being done by continuing cuts in education budgets. Yet the report containing the collated results of their inspections had until 1981 only been made available to the Expenditure Steering Group for Education, a small secret working group of senior central and local government officials.

After references to the existence of this evidence appeared in the press, the Advisory Centre for Education pressed the senior chief inspector to publish the report. After some delay, it and a similar report by the Welsh Inspectorate, were published in February 1981.[28] But further demands that the local authorities referred to in it as providing an inadequate service should be named were refused. It would not be fair, was the argument, to name names when the information had been collected by HMI in confidence. So much for the 'independent watchdog' role of the Inspectorate.

The Commissioners for Local Administration (local government Ombudsmen) were greeted with some hope by those who believed local government to be a closed and unaccountable service. But their powers of intervention in education are severely limited; they cannot investigate any action taken by a local education authority relating to the instruction, curriculum, internal organisation, management or discipline in any school or college. They can only investigate complaints of maladministration – for example, unjustifiable delay, incompetence, neglect or bias.

The local Ombudsmen themselves are not happy with this limitation; in their 1978 annual report they argued that:

The Commission consider that "internal" school matters should be within jurisdiction. The present exclusions are illogical. A complaint about allocation to a school can be investigated; a complaint about allocation to a form cannot. A complaint about the management of a children's home can be investigated; a complaint about the school attended by the same children cannot.[29]

But the 'representative body' which comments on the Commission's work, including its annual report, and which is made up almost entirely of representatives of local authority bodies, rejected this argument out of hand:

Under the education system, councils, as local education authorities, school managers and governors, all have responsibilities for various aspects of education and it would be both impracticable and undesirable for any outside body such as the Commission to be able to investigate complaints about the internal arrangements of schools. In any event, it would be premature to consider change at the present time because of the recently published consultation document on education and the report of the Taylor Committee on School Government and Management which is under consideration.[30]

The government accepted the representative body's argument, although by implication the argument would seem to question the validity of letting an Ombudsman look at *anything* which other bodies have a responsibility to provide. The teacher unions are known to be opposed to letting the Ombudsman inside schools, but it seems inevitable that pressure will grow from both inside and outside the Commission to break down the barriers which allow schools, and particularly their powerful head teachers, to operate largely unchecked.

If the policy and decision-making functions of central and local government seem largely inaccessible, those of some of the other bodies that exercise influence and power within the education system might as well be on another planet. The various church authorities exercise wide powers both locally and nationally over voluntary schools: there is no right of access to their decision-making bodies, or to information which underlies policies of such crucial public importance as the determination of the criteria on which individual voluntary schools, even in areas where secondary education has been reorganised on non-selective lines, continue to select students.

The examination boards which still dominate the structure of the secondary school curriculum, and themselves remain generally dominated by the universities, keep their pass levels, marking standards and moderation techniques shrouded in secrecy. Those who wish to challenge a mark can usually get a clerical check, to ensure that everything was marked and the results added up correctly, done without charge; but only some of the boards are prepared to go further and arrange for a re-marking, and the fee may be over £20. (None of them, apparently, allow candidates to have their own papers back.)

The universities have not given up their more or less complete autonomy in return for government finance. The period of student unrest in the 60s did lead to some significant changes in the relationship between the individual student and the institution, for example, rights of appeal in disciplinary procedures and of participation in internal government. But universities are still not under any obligation to publish explanations of their (often eccentric) admission criteria or statistics of results, despite the vast amounts of public money they consume.

Then there is a whole range of quangos, with varying degrees of government direction, and varying degrees of influence on the system – the Schools Council, the National Foundation for Educational Research and the Assessment of Performance Unit are just three. The idea that consumers of the service should be represented in the government of such institutions is quite new, and where, as in the Schools Council, some element of parent participation has recently been allowed, it is of course on a purely consultative basis.[31] And while all these bodies produce mountains of publications and reports, access to their policy-making committees, and to the papers that circulate internally prior to policy decisions, is strictly controlled.

There is insufficient space here to consider in detail what safeguards the users of the system should be given in respect of such quasi-public bodies. Instead, it is necessary to turn to those compulsory institutions which almost all of us experience as students, and many of us as parents or teachers – the schools: it is in them that the most universal denial of rights – of access to information by those most concerned and its proper protection *from* others – is consistently defended by both administrators and professionals.

In the Schools: Secret Files

The systematic keeping of secret files, which starts the moment a child enters a state nursery school at three years old or even before, must contribute towards conditioning all of us to accept the oddly secretive habits of those in authority in education, both in institutions and at local and national government level.

The 'secret school files' issue first surfaced in the media during the mid-70s when a Campaign Against Secret Records on School-children was launched. In 1975 the Advisory Centre for Education (ACE) surveyed the record-keeping policies of local education authorities throughout Britain and their policy on confidentiality and access.[32] The survey revealed the usual confusion of control: in most local authorities the whole matter is left to the discretion of the head teacher to keep whatever records he likes and show them to whomever seems appropriate. With very few exceptions, those authorities which did offer any central directives did so to stress the confidentiality of records.

A follow-up survey carried out by ACE in 1978 showed that more than half the LEAs offered no advice to heads whatsoever.[33] For example: Salford – 'The authority recognises the professional responsibility and competence of head teachers in this matter;' Doncaster – 'Schools are given no advice/instructions either to make records available to parents or to withhold them. This is regarded as a matter for the professional judgement of the head, as is also the question of informing parents of the existence of school records. It would, of course, be a naive parent who believed schools kept no records.'

In a few authorities, there is a clear instruction that secrecy must prevail: Wirral – 'record cards are confidential and should not be shown to pupils, parents or unauthorised persons;' Bedfordshire – 'The Education Committee have decided that record cards should be confidential within the Schools and Education Service.' And the outer London Borough of Harrow appears to win all prizes for the most comprehensively secretive policy:

1 Confidential information or reports or references given by other Authorities, employers, agencies or departments should not be given by

schools to a member of the teaching staff, non-teaching staff, pupil, parent or legal guardian concerned.

2 Confidential reports given by the Headteacher (or a member of his staff) for prospective employers or other educational establishments on pupils, teachers, or members of the non-teaching staff should not be shown to the person concerned although the Headteacher may wish to discuss the report in general terms.

3 Headteachers should not be obliged to show their own reports of children's home circumstances, etc. to the pupil, parents or legal guardians concerned.

This particular LEA policy is interesting in that it brackets together school students and their families with teaching and non-teaching staff – all at the mercy of the professional judgement of heads and all those external agencies who are given access to records and references.

In a few authorities now, a two-tier system has been introduced, with some basic educational records made available to parents on demand, but any other records, reports or letters which may be accumulated still kept in closed files – closed, that is, to the students and parents concerned. For example: Clwyd – schools are advised to make the day-to-day educational working record of the pupil available to parents; 'However, there is no access to confidential professional records from the helping agencies such as, educational psychologist, child guidance, etc.;' Leeds – 'Schools are advised to make records and reports [on attainments and developments of pupils] available to parents, but it is left to the discretion of the Head and staff whether or not they keep any records for their own information only.'

Britain's largest LEA, the Inner London Education Authority, has introduced a new type of primary school record card which head teachers are instructed to make available to parents on request. But a question to the Education Officer from ACE revealed that heads are under no obligation whatsoever to make other records and reports available, nor even to tell parents of their existence.

So no local education authority in Britain instructs schools to allow parents, let alone students, access to all records and reports kept about them and their children (although in May 1981, Labour gained control of Derbyshire County Council, and part of their education manifesto was to make secret school records available to parents; consultations with teachers were to proceed during 1981). The amount and type of information kept in files, both at schools and in LEA offices (special education files are frequently kept at the offices) varies enormously. Some authorities issue standard folders, with detailed tables of personal characteristics for teachers to assess. An Essex County Council 'character profile' ('strictly confidential, for information of careers service, Colleges and potential employers') has spaces to tick under these headings:

Intelligent and quick to understand.	Fairly intelligent.	Rather slow to understand.	Dull. Limited understanding.
Original and creative.	Sometimes shows originality.	Rarely shows originality.	Unimaginative.
Always cooperative.	Usually cooperative.	Sometimes uncooperative.	Uncooperative.
A very capable leader.	Good leader.	Usually follows.	Always a follower.
Highly adaptable.	Reasonably adaptable.	Unadaptable.	Inflexible.

A parent was accidentally given access to one of these reports filled in on her son; she regarded the assessment as 'totally irresponsible and thoughtless', as it was based on a period when her son was ill. When she took the matter up with the head, he replied in a letter, 'I am sure you will appreciate that I am not in a position to discuss the content of a report which was issued under strict confidentiality.'

Health authorities in several areas send a form to teachers to fill in on new school entrants – usually after one term.[34] This includes such assessments as:

is friendly towards other children
is friendly towards adults
is unusually quiet or withdrawn
has had tears on arrival at school, or has refused to come into the building
frequently fights with other children
does he appear neglected or unnaturally tidy?
does he generally look unduly tired?
does he dislike getting dirty?

Teachers are also asked whether there are other things about the child which they wish to discuss with the doctor and whether they want the parent to be present.

In Walsall, notes of guidance to teachers completing the primary/secondary transfer card say:

PERSONAL PROFILE   Give brief comments on characteristics so as to construct a 'thumb-nail sketch' of the personality of the child. You may find it necessary to comment on all of the characteristics listed – dependability, honesty, sociability, initiative, powers of concentration, industry, etc. . . . Home background: Information on Parents/Guardians (absence of?). Financial circumstances as they affect school life (school dress, maintenance grant); parental contact and attitude to school. Is the child adopted, being fostered, in care?[35]

During a student's progress through school, from nursery through secondary, folders may expand to contain the most astonishing variety of bits of paper: basic educational reports, test results, transfer reports, psychological and medical assessments, notes from child guidance, education welfare, social services, absence notes from parents, press cuttings about the family, court reports and so on.

I have a number of London secondary school records (many of them containing records going back to students' first years at nursery school); there is no reason to believe the collection to be unrepresentative, and it contains a frightening variety of subjective judgements made by teachers, and retained in files which may be available to all sorts of outside agencies; at no point may the student or parent concerned check or challenge, or even know of the existence of the file:

Written under 'special medical conditions' on cover of secondary school folder: 'Father is in prison unfortunately. X seems very easily distracted and lacks concentration understandably.' Inside the same folder, in a letter from education welfare to the head: 'The following is some information we have on this family. Mr X is in prison and help has been given with clothing.'

Confidential primary report, filled in when a girl was eight, still in her secondary school folder when she was fifteen: 'An emotionally disturbed girl. She is prone to sudden fits of screaming tantrums when annoyed or disturbed, reason or comfort only make her worse. Her temper can be uncontrolled, and her language, rudeness and attitude is distressing . . . A real "Jackal [sic] and Hyde" personality . . .' And under 'special needs' . . . 'Stable home, endless amounts of love and possibly psychiatric help.'

Notification of decision of the Juvenile Court, sent to secondary school on a standard form: 'Charge: stole child's pedal cycle. Decision of court: case dismissed.'

Letter from education welfare to secondary school at transfer age: 'I fully realise that this child comes from a problem family, which has been well-known to the education welfare service since 1962 . . .'

Psychologist's report in secondary school folder: 'Mrs X is at present living on social security in rather poor housing. From time to time she has a co-habitee there, so the home situation is unstable.'

Letter from education welfare to secondary head: '11-plus confidential: Mr X suffers from severe arthritis and has been unable to work for some time now. Mrs X suffers from mental illness from time to time.'

Primary record on eight-year-old, found in secondary folder seven years later: 'Far too much pressure is put on X to look after young brother and sister and she is frequently kept at home for domestic reasons. Mother is unkempt and always telling the children how she longs to return to her home in Germany.'

It is, of course, the families and children in most difficulty with their lives, or at least their school lives, who accumulate the thickest folders. They are also the children most vulnerable to drastic professional action – transferring them to special schools or units, or bringing care proceedings to take them away from home.

In most cases the subjective judgements, the casual assessments, the mistakes and out-of-date information are never seen by those in a real position to challenge their accuracy. One Lancashire family, recently told by the education authority that their son should be transferred to a school for the educationally sub-normal (ESN), tried to obtain copies of the reports that formed the basis for the transfer proposal. They argued, after taking legal advice, that by refusing to allow them to see the reports, the LEA were making it impossible for them as parents to fulfil their duty to see that their son is educated in accordance with his age, ability and aptitude (section 36 of the 1944 Act). They refused to take any further part in the assessment procedure unless the reports were made available. A reply from the specialist in Community Medicine (Child Health) to the Area Health Authority states baldly:

You will not receive a copy of the doctor's report. You will not receive copies of the Observation Class and Educational Psychologist's reports from me – I am not authorised to send them to you. I consider that the Observation Class and Educational Psychologist's reports which were completed by highly qualified professional colleagues to be completely acceptable in every way.

The parents replied asking who did have the authority to forward the reports to them:

Perhaps if you would be kind enough to inform us who is preventing you sending the reports, we would then know against whom to direct our claim that we are being prevented from fulfilling our statutory duty by not having access to these reports. Further, whilst we are forbidden access to our son's assessment reports, we shall not be presenting the child for any further assessment by your department; we also refuse permission for any examination in our absence on the grounds that we are being prevented from pursuing a statutory duty under Section 36 of the 1944 Act by not receiving copies of the reports . . . Finally, your blind faith in the professional performance of your colleagues who are not accountable in any real sense to the parents of the children whom they assess, neither are they accountable to the children, is rather disconcerting to say the least.

Most parents will not risk the possibility of victimisation of their children by protesting in this way, so most such assessments go unchallenged, despite the often irreversible consequences for the children concerned of being labelled as sub-normal or maladjusted.

It appears that, legally, all records and reports made by those employed by the Area Health Authorities remain the property of the Secretary of State for Health and Social Services. But while this glib justification for not allowing parents access is trotted out as a fact of life by professionals, it does not prevent reports and records being made available to an astonishingly wide range of other individuals and agencies. Replying to the ACE survey, LEAs indicated their liberal attitude to such third-party access.[36] Most authorities describe it as being limited to the 'helping agencies' or those 'professionally concerned with the education and welfare of the child'. This can include, for example: Gwynedd – education welfare, careers service, social services, police; Kent – teachers, members and officers of the authority 'in appropriate cases' (why should elected councillors need or want to see confidential school files?); Clwyd – education social workers, education psychologists and police liaison officers. The careers service in Clwyd also receive a 'confidential abstract of pupil's educational progress and achievement'. Others have vague policies, or none at all: Barnsley – 'So far schools have been left to decide for themselves what information should be available to the interested parties;' Doncaster – 'The head controls access to school records by other organisations, such as social services, the police, etc.'

A primary-secondary transfer form in use on the Isle of Wight also indicates that there are other ways of using school records to transfer information from one professional to another without the subject knowing; a box on the form is captioned: 'Please signify by a tick if there is further information which you wish to amplify in discussion.' In Devon, where after two years' study a working group (composed, of course, entirely of professionals) came up with new proposals on school record-keeping, allowing a very limited degree of access for parents, the primary/secondary transition card contains a box saying 'Consultation essential'; teachers are advised that 'a tick must be put in the box if there are any personal particulars, other than those on the cover card or the transition card, which will help the secondary school to respond to the needs of the child.'

The campaign for parents and older students to gain access to their records has not yet (1981) made a great deal of progress, although it has led to some parliamentary discussion of the issue and the introduction of an unsuccessful private member's bill in the House of Commons in November 1979. The School Records Bill, based on a draft prepared for the National Council for Civil Liberties, would have given parents and students over sixteen the right to see all records and reports kept about their children or themselves; to challenge and if necessary correct anything in them, and to control who else, outside the school, is allowed to see them. Similar legislation – the Family Educational Rights and Privacy Act (FERPA) – has existed in the United States since 1974.[37] FERPA gives access to parents and students over eighteen, and schools have to have written permission from the parent or eligible student before releasing any information from a student's record. The Act is administered from a Washington office, and while there have been criticisms that local school boards do not rigorously implement the Act, the fact that parents have to be informed of their rights each school year has certainly led to an extensive change of attitude and practice. In the period immediately before implementation, according to an article in the official US Department of Health Education and Welfare journal, 'many schools across the country conducted massive house cleanings of records. A few school districts even closed for several days to enable the staff to empty the files of undesirable material.'[38] Canada, Sweden and Norway have similar legislation.

But in Britain, there remains a refusal to grasp the significance of the issue, and a willing readiness on the part of politicians to accept traditional professional defences of confidentiality. Usually such defences are made in terms of extreme examples. How could you show a parent a record including details of their incestuous relationship with a member of the family; or suspicions of child-battering? But the real questions are whether a school record is an appropriate place for such information, and whether it is in the least useful to communicate such information from one professional to another, without enabling the subject of it to either check or challenge its accuracy, or indeed to change their behaviour on the basis of some direct communication.

It should not be necessary to argue for a right of access to personal information on the basis of examples of malpractice: the obvious human rights issues involved should be enough, linked to what one would expect to be a natural desire of professionals to encourage trust and communication with their 'clients'. How can a parent, or a student, be expected to trust a teacher who finds it necessary to keep secret their assessments and comments? Of course, to introduce a policy of open records where there has formerly been no access must imply a change of attitude as well as practice. It is perhaps more difficult to have to justify what is written about someone else, to them or their parents; but surely this sort of direct communication must inevitably replace professional paternalism in time.

The Report of the Committee on Data Protection (1978) raised the spectre of cradle-to-grave computer educational records maintained on a large proportion of the population (and no doubt tied into all sorts of other national computer-based record systems).[39] While the terms of reference of the Committee made their primary concern automated or computerised information systems, the report's conclusions clearly apply equally to manually prepared and stored records, and the Committee did provide strong support for parental access to school records, student access to records in further and higher education, and subject access to social work records. The Committee suggested that the time when at least some school records would be computerised 'is not far distant, and we certainly expect this to happen within the lifetime of the proposed data protection legislation.' Early in 1980, the Highland Region Education Authority in Scotland became the first to authorise computerisation of some of their school files, provoking opposition from both teachers and parents, and the Scottish Council for Civil Liberties.

The Data Protection Committee stated that parents should be allowed access to 'almost all' the information kept in school files, 'particularly where it is factual or about the home and family circumstances, if for no other reason than to ensure accuracy'. The Committee were heavily lobbied by the doctors' professional body, fearful of patient access to their files, which may explain their illogical insertion of 'almost all' into their recommendation. There is no immediate sign that the government will act on the recommendations of the Committee.

When the Advisory Centre for Education wrote (in 1980) to the then Secretary of State for Education, Mark Carlisle, urging him to support legislation to provide for parent access to school records, his reply echoed that of previous ministers: 'The question of confidentiality and parental access to school records (both educational and non-educational) is a complex one and it is unlikely that the Government will seek to introduce further regulations on these matters until the issues have been more fully considered.'

Mr Carlisle confirmed that his government

believes that there should be a large degree of openness between schools and parents. Indeed the educational records kept on school children will usually consist almost entirely of the sort of information that is made available to parents in term reports and at parents' evenings and the like. A small number of cases may arise, however, when records may contain observations which it is considered should be dealt with in confidence: these might refer for example to suspicions that the child is being neglected or ill-treated at home or otherwise at risk in some way, and in such cases the need for confidentiality is primarily in the interests of the pupil. There is also the question of respecting the confidentiality of professional medical, psychological or social work reports many of which will not in any cases be the property of the local education authority.

The 1980 white paper on *Special Needs in Education*, while trotting out the usual clichés about parents needing to be given access to information 'in the most effective way possible', came down firmly against disclosure of 'professional' reports: 'The Government agrees with the widely-held view that it would be wrong to require full disclosure to parents of the professional reports . . . Professional reports must remain confidential if they are to give the LEA fully and frankly the information it needs in assessing and meeting special educational needs.'[40] So under the new special education legislation which followed the white paper, the LEAs have access to all the reports, but the parents – who have the primary legal duty to see that the child is suitably educated – only have access to the 'statement' prepared by the LEA on the basis of these reports.

There has been no sign of the policies of confidentiality I have described helping to limit cases of parental violence against children. On the contrary, it is possible that more direct and open communication of 'professional' suspicions rather earlier in the day could actually reduce the number of children at risk. And it is significant that the Department of Health and Social Security have recommended that parents should almost always be informed before their names are included on any register of suspected child abuse. A case of one government department not knowing about another's change of policy?

There is nothing to stop parents and students asking to see their records, and increasing numbers do. But while the largest teachers' union, the National Union of Teachers, has successfully argued that the reports and references written by one teacher about another should be shown to them, they have not yet applied the same principle to their relationship with students and parents (and the Union has turned down a request from ACE and other consumer organisations for a meeting to discuss confidentiality).

The significance of the secret school records issue lies in its universality, and in its obvious and direct connection with other freedom of information and privacy issues – access to medical and social work records, police and security service records, insurance, banking and credit agency records, employment references and record systems.[41]

The defence of confidential files by the teaching profession and local administrators, so far backed up by politicians of both parties, also reflects a much more general defensiveness on the part of many professional groups, a defence of a kind of professional authority over 'ordinary' people which is no longer appropriate (if it ever was) and which must in time give way to a healthier, open and accountable relationship with clients or consumers.

REFERENCES

1 Section 27(d) of the 1980 Education Act does allow the Secretary of State for Education to make separate regulations about educational records. However, there is no immediate prospect of such regulations being introduced.

2 Kogan, Maurice, *The Politics of Educational Change*, Fontana, 1978, p. 150.

3 Organisation for Economic Cooperation and Development, *Educational Development Strategy in England and Wales*, OECD, Paris, 1975.

4 *Times Educational Supplement*, 13 June 1975.

5 Hencke, David, *Colleges in Crisis*, Penguin, 1978.

6 *Ibid.*, p. 126.

7 *Policy Making in the Department of Education and Science*, Tenth Report from the Expenditure Committee, session 1975–6, HMSO, 1976.

8 *Ibid.*, paras. 86–7.

9 *Ibid.*, paras. 80 and 98.

10 *The Government's Reply to the Tenth Report from the Expenditure Committee Session 1975–6 HC 621, Policy Making in the Department of Education and Science*, Cmnd 6678, HMSO, November, 1976.

11 *Review of Government's Statistical Services*, Cmnd 8236, HMSO, 1981.

12 Letter in the *Times Educational Supplement*, 11 July 1980, from Janey Rees, Education Secretary, NATFHE.

13 Caerwyn Roderick MP, *Hansard*, 8 March 1979, col. 786 (13th sitting of the Committee).

14 Department of Education and Science circular 15/77, p. 1.

15 *Hansard*, 16 May 1979, col. 222. See also Norman St John-Stevas, *Standards and Freedom*, Conservative Political Centre, 1974, pp. 10–11; and Conservative Party Manifesto, 1979, p. 25.

16 Education Act 1980, section 8.

17 Department of Education and Science preliminary consultation document, *Education Act 1980: Regulations on Information for Parents*, April 1980.

18 *Ibid.*, p. 1.

19 Public Bodies (Admission to Meetings) Act 1960 Schedule 1(d). See also pp. 15–19.

20 Education Act 1944, Schedule 1, Pt. II. para. 9.

21 *Ibid.*, para. 10.

22 *Ibid.*, Pt. I, Section 5.

23 The ILEA Schools Sub-committee agreed these proposals, after pilot studies, in April 1981.

24 Education Act 1944, section 92 (Reports and returns) gives the

Secretary of State wide powers to oblige LEAs to supply him with information. Only he or she can exercise this power.

25 Department of Education and Science circular 5/77, para. 6.

26 *Report by HM Inspectorate on Educational Provision by the Inner London Education Authority*, Summer 1980.

27 *Community Homes with Education*, HMSO, 1980.

28 *Report by HM Inspectorate on the Effects on the Education Service in England on Local Authority Expenditure Policies: 1980–81*, DES, February 1981.

29 Commission for Local Administration in England, *Your Local Ombudsman*, Report for the year ending 31 March 1978, p. 27, para. 134.

30 *Ibid.*, p. 31, para. 159.

31 See Bullivant, Barbara, 'Parents' Voice on Schools Council', *Where?*, no. 152, October 1979.

32 *Where?*, no. 109, October 1975.

33 Reported in *Where?*, no. 148, May 1979.

34 For this and other examples see *Where?*, no. 155, February 1980.

35 Walsall Local Education Authority, *Notes for Guidance on the Completion of the Transfer Card – Primary/Secondary*.

36 *Where?*, no. 148, May 1979.

37 The Family Educational Rights and Privacy Act, also known as the Buckley Amendment, became law on 19 November 1974. See Hayden, Trudy, 'Lesson from America', *Where?*, no. 155, February 1980.

38 Knight, Lucy, 'Facts about Mr Buckley's Amendment', *American Education*, June 1977, p. 7.

39 *Report of the Committee on Data Protection*, chairman Sir Norman Lindop, HMSO, Cmnd 7341, 1978.

40 *Special Needs in Education*, HMSO, Cmnd 7996, 1980, pp. 18–19, paras. 57 and 61.

41 There is a precedent for statutory subject access in the Consumer Credit Act 1974. This provides for the individual's right to see and challenge any file kept on him or her by a credit reference agency. Consumers can insist that inaccurate information is corrected. The Director General of Fair Trading has the power to deal with complaints from consumers about particular files and can, where necessary, order that files be amended. This part of the Act came into force in May 1977.

The Environment   6
Maurice Frankel

Members of the public, their elected representatives, the press or environmental organizations often seek information about environmental protection in order to make individual decisions or to evaluate policies
. that affect the wider community. Maurice Frankel argues that information in this field is deliberately withheld by some agencies whose job it is to monitor pollution; that much research done on some pesticides is inadequate because it is not allowed to be scrutinised by independent scientific organizations; and that the now-discredited argument that secrecy must be maintained to protect commercial interests is still used.

In 1977 the Department of the Environment published a report describing the UK's environmental standards. The report emphasised the benefits of an open approach to information, declaring that: 'the flow of adequate information between public and Government is an essential part of the process of standard setting . . . Better availability of information should help the public to understand the ways in which watchfulness is being maintained.'[1] Despite these sentiments, the report demonstrated just how deeply seated the secrecy instinct is in British government.

The report was described in its title as the product of an unspecified 'inter-departmental working party'. *Social Audit*, which had been asked to review the publication, contacted the Department of the Environment (DoE) to ask which government departments were involved. It was told that, as the report had been prepared for the Cabinet Office, the DoE was 'not free to release' any information on its authorship. 'It is policy that they (the Cabinet Office) don't release the names of the participants or any other information on cabinet committees', a DoE spokesman apologised. 'All I can tell you is that the relevant departments were represented.'

The Need for Information

There are numerous individual circumstances in which members of the public, their elected representatives, the press or environmental organisations may seek information about environmental protection. The issue may be one of national importance, such as the development of a nuclear energy programme, or the introduction of new pesticides into the environment where they may affect not only wildlife but everyone who eats treated food. Or the subject may be primarily of local interest: an objectionable nuisance may have occurred or a possibly polluting factory may be planned.

Normally, such issues will concern a whole community – but at times individuals may have a special need for information. They may (as, farmers, anglers or beekeepers, for example) make special use of their property or the surroundings; or they may be unusually vulnerable to pollution – as are sufferers from respiratory illnesses that may be aggravated by air pollution. Thus individuals, or the community as a whole, may need information in order to decide whether to accept or formally object to a proposed new development, press for stricter controls for an existing one, prepare a legal dossier in anticipation of suing for damages, or – ultimately – abandon their homes and move to a less polluted area.

In all these situations, three kinds of questions may have to be asked. These concern:

The quality of the environment and the size of any possible risk. How toxic is a particular contaminant; how much of it is, or may be, in the air, water or food?

The adequacy of the discharger's precautions. What measures are used to prevent contamination of the environment; how effective and reliable are they?

The competence of the control authority. For instance: Does the authority know enough to do an effective job? Does it have information about individual discharges, environmental quality, the toxicity of pollutants, the extent of any damage? Are its standards adequate? All safety standards involve a margin of risk. Decisions about how much risk to allow are political rather than scientific. How willing or able is the authority to act effectively – either when standards are broken or when new evidence of a hazard comes to light?

Information about environmental quality – if it is collected at all

– tends to be publicly available. For example, there are national monitoring programmes for certain air and water pollutants, and full results – showing both national trends and local details – are freely available. The Department of the Environment periodically issues a *Digest of Environmental Pollution Statistics*[2] and this describes, among other things, the level of radioactive emissions from individual nuclear power stations, the volume of sewage sludge dumped at sea, the concentration of toxic metals in the air, and the levels of pesticides in shell-fish taken from British waters. The information allows gross trends in pollution to be monitored and in some cases shows how much progress has been made towards specific goals, such as the introduction of smoke control areas or the cleaning of polluted rivers.

It is usually much more difficult to obtain information about the contribution to pollution made by individual dischargers, and the way in which authorities take enforcement decisions. There are several obstacles to such disclosure. One of the most important is the protection of actual – or alleged – trade secrets, whose disclosure would harm the commercial interests of the discharger.

There are two main kinds of environmental information which industry claims must be kept confidential in order to protect its commercial interests. The first concerns details of tests carried out on new chemicals – this is dealt with later in the chapter. The other relates to the nature and volume of industry's wastes.

Industry maintains that there are several ways in which the study of a factory's wastes could reveal valuable information to its competitors. The presence of new or unusual chemicals in a factory's effluent may identify a new and secret product or process. Changes in the factory's output may be reflected in the volume of waste discharged. Even the fact that an authority has given a firm special exemption from meeting a legal limit can supposedly convey something of value to competitors. It may suggest that the authority has been privately informed of some so-far unannounced plans. The factory may be due for closure shortly, or the authority may be waiting for better controls as part of a so-far secret investment programme. On occasions there may be some truth to some of these claims. However, in the past these arguments were accepted unquestioningly and embodied in such wide secrecy clauses that *all* information about a firm's pollution was protected from public disclosure by an authority.

In the field of air pollution control, both the 1936 Public Health Act[3] and the 1956 Clean Air Act[4] made it an offence for an official to disclose information about '*any manufacturing process* or trade secret' at a factory. Not only trade secrets – but any other information – was protected. Even when the chemicals released by a particular manufacturing process were common knowledge within the industry (as is generally the case) a pollution authority could not divulge their names to the public.

The approach was taken even further by the Rivers (Prevention of Pollution) Act 1961[5] which included a secrecy clause that makes no reference at all to trade secrets. The Act imposed an outright ban on the release of *any* information obtained by an official in connection with an application to discharge an effluent into the river. It forbade the release both of the legal limits applied to such a discharge and of the results of samples analysed to check whether these limits were observed. The rather curious thinking behind these restrictions was that information about a factory's wastes is the property of the factory owners, and should not be passed on to anyone, regardless of whether trade secrets are in fact involved.

The same philosophy is expressed even where there is no legal duty to maintain secrecy. It can be found in the administration of the non-statutory Pesticides Safety Precautionary Scheme, described later, but is most clearly found in the work of the Alkali Inspectorate in controlling air pollution. Until 1974 the Alkali Inspectorate administered the provisions of a succession of Alkali Acts which were remarkably liberal in their attitudes towards secrecy. While inspectors could not reveal process plans, they were free to do what they liked with information about pollution.

Nevertheless, the policy that was to be followed for over a hundred years, and continues until the present day, was laid down by the original Chief Alkali Inspector. In his first report, for the year 1804, he notes:

the opinion of the alkali makers, of at least one district, has been very distinctly expressed regarding the propriety of silence on certain points, whilst some have desired that as little as possible should be said on all points. Of course *every information regarding any work must be considered private*, unless the publication is demanded by the Act or permitted by the owner.[6] (emphasis added)

The importance attached to the protection of 'private' information is underlined by the penalties laid down for unauthorised disclosure. A polluter who wiped out all the life in a river with a chemical discharge faced the possibility of a (fairly small) fine. But a pollution inspector who, out of court, revealed details of the lethal discharge faced the possibility not only of a fine but also of three months in gaol.

When a pollution inspector was forced to protect himself by prefacing a scientific paper with the remarks 'All that can be said is that the events occurred somewhere in England over the last 25 years',[7] the secrecy had clearly got out of hand. The idea that this secrecy actually protected real trade secrets was also regarded with scepticism in environmental circles. *New Scientist* correspondent Jon Tinker commented in 1972:

the notion of industrial secrets leaking away down the plughole is regarded as ludicrous by most chemists. Plants usually have only one outfall, which drains dozens of separate processes, and a firm anxious to protect itself could so treat or mix its effluent that it became unrecognisable. In any case, a competitor wanting details of a rival's waste is more likely to row stealthily upriver on a dark night, and take a sample for himself, than to rely on the meagre information recorded in a local authority's books.[8]

The final collapse of the notion that as a rule secrecy protected trade secrets was brought about by the newly formed Royal Commission on Environmental Pollution. In its second report, published in 1972, the Royal Commission reported that the widespread confidentiality about industrial wastes deprived responsible people of information they needed, and also led to risks of misunderstandings by the public. Processes were not often so well described in the technical literature that competitors had nothing to gain by studying each other's wastes. They concluded that:

As a rule, therefore, the legislation which protects secrecy over industrial effluents and wastes no longer safeguards genuine trade secrets. . . . Its only value is to protect industry against the risk of common law actions or against misconceived or ill-informed allegations that the environment is being dangerously polluted. We fully agree that those industrialists who are concerned to abate pollution are justified in wanting some safeguard against risks of this sort. We believe that more accurate information about the wastes they are putting into the environment, issued and explained by themselves, would provide this protection more effectively than the secrecy they observe at present.[9]

The Royal Commission called on the government to devise

measures to increase the flow of information on industrial wastes to the public, and the response was embodied in the 1974 Control of Pollution Act.

Although the Act covered information about noise and waste disposal on land, the most influential disclosure provisions concerned air and water pollution: the Act either required or allowed the responsible pollution authorities to publish information about discharges in a public register. Special protection – by appeal to the Secretary of State – was allowed for trade secrets, but on the whole, the bulk of the information previously concealed could now be disclosed.

This outstanding attempt to open up pollution control was accompanied by a remarkable exception. The openness prescribed for local authorities and water authorities was not to apply to the Alkali Inspectorate. Under the 1974 Health and Safety at Work Act, the Inspectorate came, for the first time in its long history, under a new, and all-embracing secrecy clause.

So, depending on the authority and the form of pollution, a complete range of different duties or restrictions have now been introduced: Water Authorities are to be *obliged* to provide information about river pollution discharges to the public.[10] (At the time of writing, these provisions had not been enacted, and the traditional secrecy clauses of previous legislation still applied.) Local Authorities are *permitted* to publish information about air pollution emissions in their areas.[11] The Alkali Inspectorate is *prohibited* from disclosing any information about air pollution from works it controls.[12]

The new arrangements prompt several questions about the role of public information in pollution control. Why should two statutes, introduced by the same government more or less simultaneously, require one authority to provide information to the public while forbidding the disclosure of similar information by another? What part does secrecy still play in the control of pollution – and what effect does this have on the public, and on the quality of decision-making?

To some authorities, an informed and involved public is a valuable asset. They show industry that pollution control policies have public support: not only the authority, but the press and the public can be seen to be expecting improvements. Such involvement also helps the authority demand the political backing and financial resources it needs for its work. Alternatively, public involvement may be seen as an obstacle and an embarrassment. This is likely to happen if the standard of pollution control fails to meet public expectations. The authority can respond either by trying to raise the level of control – or by lowering the level of public expectation.

The latter course has now been adopted as official policy at the highest level. A leaked confidential cabinet document, reported in the *Sunday Times* in November 1979, revealed that the Department of the Environment had been instructed, as a matter of priority, to aim to 'reduce over-sensitivity to environmental concerns'.[13] This may, of course, be an invitation to more secrecy. It is easier to suppress reports about hazards than to explain why nothing is to be done in response to them.

The failure to reduce pollution to acceptable levels may have various causes. On the one hand, public awareness about the dangers of chemicals in the environment is increasing. Although conditions may not have changed, public expectations may now be higher. At the same time, pollution authorities may not have the financial resources, or the legal powers, to do an adequate job.

Many inspectorates are so understaffed or overworked that they simply cannot hope to keep all the premises under their control under adequate surveillance. The most extreme example of this is the Factory Inspectorate which in 1979 employed 900 inspectors. These officials were responsible for health and safety in more than half a million workplaces, employing some 18 million workers.[14] On average, they can inspect a workplace once in five years: most premises receive a visit only after someone has been killed or seriously injured in an accident.

The difficulty may be exacerbated when the courts impose trivial fines on those convicted of pollution offences. In the early 1970s, air pollution offences under the Clean Air and Public Health Acts were punished by average fines of around £30. Alkali Act offences led to penalties of around £50 with some as low as £5.[15] Under these circumstances, the threat of prosecution is no real deterrent, and inspectors may avoid the time-consuming, and possibly humiliating, procedure of taking offenders to court.

If the authority cannot impose standards, then it must rely on the good-will and co-operation of industry for improvements. A study of the work of pollution officers in two water authorities during 1970 and 1977 reported that: 'it was generally accepted wisdom that control could not be achieved in the face of widespread non-cooperation from industry. . . . Accordingly, where control so permitted, there was a marked tendency to favour *consent* conditions which were acceptable to industry, on the basis that such conditions were more likely to attract compliance.'[16]

But if the industry has, or convincingly pleads, financial difficulties, then due – or undue – allowance may be made for these problems. The above study of water authority officers reported that for large and influential industries 'the industry's bargaining position would be sufficiently strong to enable it to insist that account be taken of its financial problems.' Similarly, annual reports of the Alkali Inspectorate repeatedly acknowledge that the standards the inspectorate wants to bring in have been delayed because the industries concerned are, or appear, unable to afford them.[17]

In such a combination of circumstances, an authority may find itself unable to adequately respond to severe pollution problems and justified public complaint. Equally, it may not be prepared either to acknowledge its inability to enforce standards or to publicly criticise the industry on whose goodwill it is now heavily dependent. As the Council for Science and Society has pointed out, the danger is that not only power, but also powerlessness, will corrupt. 'An inspectorate that cannot enforce its requirements must either confess its impotence or conceal it from view.' If it chooses the latter path, it maintains that the pollution is under control – but refuses to release the details. In the Council's words, the inspectorate 'denies all cases of abuse except for the most flagrant: and in so doing becomes implicated in their continuation. Thus, a weak inspectorate is pushed towards identification with those who create the risks, to the detriment of those who experience them.'[18]

Both industry and the control authority may therefore feel severely threatened by pressure for disclosure of information that would either reveal the nature of the partnership between them or provide opportunities for the public to influence the way in which control decisions are taken. Faced with this possibility, it is noticeable that both parties repeatedly stress that the public is 'over-emotional' and unfit to participate in the careful technical deliberations of government and industry specialists.

So, although the Confederation of British Industry responded positively to the Royal Commission's 1972 call for the publication of information about river pollution discharges, it drew the line at disclosing applications to make *new* discharges. This might enable the local public to influence decisions:

If applications for consent have to be advertised there is inevitably a risk of public outcry based more on emotion than on the merits of the application. This could well influence the controlling authority (particularly one on which the local authority representation is strong and vocal) into giving a wrong decision. This could be serious.[19]

In a similar vein, a local authority officer in 1977 described the (very weak) disclosure provisions of the Control of Pollution Act as 'the most damaging piece of legislation ever to appear on the statute books in relation to atmospheric pollution'. He referred to the use that would be made of it by 'action groups . . . composed of mischievous and destructive people', identified as 'university research workers, lecturers, people who had failed to gain election to the local authority through the ballot box and including many cranks'. In this unsettled climate: 'the release of even the most simple details of emissions to the atmosphere may well be misinterpreted by the general public assisted by action groups – and eventually frighten away prospective industrial developers.'[20]

It is noticeable here that 'university research workers' – who might well be in a position to make careful but penetrating use of technical information, feature high on the list of people regarded with suspicion. It is hard to avoid the conclusion that it may be precisely because such people *are* qualified to give an independent interpretation that their involvement is resented. A similar worry has been expressed by the former chief Alkali inspector: 'I am a great believer in informing the public, but not in giving them figures they can't interpret. You would get amateur environment experts and *university scientists* playing around with them. People can become scared of figures, they can get the wind up.'[21] (emphasis added)

The Royal Commission on Environmental Pollution has itself experienced the way in which information may be withheld from independent experts. In its 1979 report on *Agriculture and Pollution* it describes:

the response received by a scientist who sought information from a manufacturer in following up a point that was put to him by one of our members about the possible risks posed by a particular chemical. The information was refused with the comment that toxicological data, quoted out of context, could easily be used to mislead the public and create unnecessary concern.[22]

The Alkali Inspectorate

Pollution control in Britain is traditionally characterised by a lack of fixed standards, leaving the various agencies free to set their own limits. This is typically done through private negotiation with industry without the participation of those affected by pollution. In fact, there is some reason to believe that this exclusion may be in some cases quite deliberate, relying on official secrecy as an essential element.

It is worth looking in some detail at the agency which most strongly personifies this approach: the Alkali Inspectorate. Under the Alkali Act, and the Health and Safety at Work Act which superseded it, any works operating one of a number of 'scheduled' industrial processes must register with the Alkali Inspectorate, and subsequently use the 'best practicable means' for controlling air pollution.

After consulting with industry – but no one else – general guidelines on the 'best practicable means' for a particular industry are issued by the Chief Alkali Inspector. On the whole, these require that modern controls be installed at the time industry can best afford them – when new plant is being built, or old equipment being overhauled or replaced. Although complaints of nuisance or damage may arise *before* such a time, these do not normally lead to improved controls. According to the former Chief Alkali Inspector: 'any plant installed to our requirements is allowed to operate for its economic life before further demands may be made on that works to meet more stringent standards.'[23]

Hence, the Inspectorate resists calls for immediate action to deal with pollution problems (other than those caused by accidents or poor maintenance) even when there is considerable local dissatisfaction and pressure for improvements.[24] A former Chief Inspector has explicitly acknowledged this, pointing out that the benefits to a works that meets the Inspectorate's initial requirements are that '*in cases of public complaint etc. compliance will normally ensure the support of the inspector.*'[25]

The Inspectorate's commitment to resisting inconveniently timed local pressures for improvements is confirmed by a confidential minute of a meeting of the Clean Air Council (a statutory advisory body) held in 1977. It notes that one of the advantages of Alkali Inspectorate control is its 'invulnerability to local pressure'. The result is, as even the Inspectorate acknowledges, that 'when inspectors visit complainants, they are often regarded as representing industry.'[26]

Given the Inspectorate's commitment to withstand local pressure, secrecy becomes essential. People living near a polluting factory are unable to learn whether or not the works is complying with its legal requirements. Although broad guidelines of 'best practicable means' for the industry may have been published, specific details are negotiated separately for each works – and never published. The Inspectorate checks compliance by taking samples of emissions, but the results of its samples are never released. Firms may be required to monitor the quality of the air around the factory, but the Inspectorate does not disclose the results of such sampling.

Works that are judged by the Inspectorate to have fallen short of its requirements are informed by private letter – but no acknowledgement is made to the suffering community. Occasionally, when a prosecution takes place details may be reported in the local press, but when in 1972 *Social Audit* asked the Chief Inspector for a list of offenders prosecuted, this was refused on the grounds that further publicity for these companies would be 'unfair punishment'.

Nevertheless, the Alkali Inspectorate acknowledges that the public has a legitimate right to be informed about air pollution problems that affect it. This view, however, is doubly qualified. First, the Inspectorate believes that it is for industry – not the Inspectorate – to do the informing. And secondly, it maintains that disclosure should be voluntary and not obligatory. To this end it has encouraged local authorities to establish local liaison committees in areas of pollution complaint. The industry involved meets with the local authority – sometimes with local people also in attendance – to explain how it is dealing with the problem. The Inspectorate maintains that this exercise satisfies the local demand for information: 'at these meetings, managements have learnt to be frank about their emissions and to give information freely.'[27] However, at least one example suggests that this is not necessarily so.

A liaison committee, representing the Alkali Inspectorate, several local authorities and the London Brick Company has been set up in the area of the Bedfordshire brickworks. The area has suffered damage to crops and livestock from fluoride and sulphur dioxide emitted by the brickworks and the unpleasant smell from the factory chimneys is a perpetual source of nuisance. Periodically, the committee publishes brief statements on the situation which are released to the press. These summaries have in themselves led to accusations of considerable bias. In November 1978 the committee issued a press release entitled 'Evidence indicates fluoride emissions is not a hazard to humans' which concluded that 'if levels in any location or medium give an indication of a possible health hazard, the appropriate government department would investigate and report.'[28]

On close reading, this reassuring statement proved to be highly misleading. It suggested that fluoride levels in every 'location and medium' were being monitored. However, the only reliable fluoride monitoring in the vicinity of two brickworks in the Marston Vale region is done at just two sites, one of which is known to miss the main effects of the emissions.[29] The Deputy Chief Alkali Inspector has acknowledged that this monitoring is inadequate: 'there is no organised monitoring (of fluorides) taking place . . . the measurements that are being carried out by the Company are entirely different, the results having no direct relationship to the atmospheric concentrations of fluorine and because of the limitations of the method that is used neither is there any meaningful interpretation of the figures in terms of chimney emissions.'[30]

Peter Goode, the secretary of a local amenity group, points out that if existing monitoring is so poor, the liaison committee could have no reasonable idea of the actual levels of fluorine pollution: it therefore has no evidence to support the statement that the level of fluorides present 'is not a hazard to humans'. Equally, it had no justification for the assurance that high levels of pollution found in 'any location or medium' would be investigated – since no one had the ability to detect such levels.

The episode casts some doubt on the impartiality of the Alkali Inspectorate. The Inspectorate clearly acknowledges the monitoring to be inadequate, yet it was represented on the liaison committee and endorsed the press release with its inflated claims. Moreover, the Inspectorate has itself given credence to the results of (even less adequate) monitoring carried out in the past. Successive annual reports of the Chief Inspector during the late 1960s and early 1970s reported that: 'The industry continued to monitor the area and submitted to the inspectorate the results of their tests. Ground level concentrations of sulphur and fluorine compounds *continue to be satisfactorily low*.'[31] (emphasis added)

Peter Goode has himself tried to obtain details of the monitoring results, but with no success. The Inspectorate has told him that 'The results of these tests are sent to the Alkali Inspectorate on an "in confidence" basis as a matter of interest and . . . I am not at liberty to send you copies of these reports.'[32] The liaison committee, established to 'keep the public informed of work being done on the control of air pollution' has been no more helpful. The secretary of the committee has told Goode that the committee 'meets in private and considers papers which I have no authority to publish . . . I cannot properly supply Committee papers to a member of the public.'[33]

The Alkali Inspectorate's secrecy has managed to survive the new disclosure laws because the Inspectorate has fought strongly to maintain it, and done so quite publicly. At various times it has argued that: it was prevented from disclosure by the Alkali Act[34] (although in fact the Act was the one piece of legislation with no secrecy clause); that there was no reason for it to provide information as no such duty was laid on it by Act of Parliament; that any information it let out would be seized on and distorted by 'extremists in the environmental movement'; and that information would confuse the public. 'If we were to announce that dust from a certain cement works was equivalent to six or seven tons of dust fallout per square mile per month . . . people would think of tons of dust falling off the back of a lorry. They'd get very worked up about it.'[35]

Of course, it would be easy to avoid using such gross units if the Inspectorate wanted to release information without confusion. The Royal Commission has commented that the Inspectorate's concern that the release of such information might cause public anxiety 'is often overstated'.[36]

Ultimately, the Inspectorate has always fallen back on the terms on which it accepted information initially: since it accepted data in confidence from industry, it could not subsequently publish it. 'The Inspectorate is not free to release information without the permission of owners.'[37]

During enquiries that *Social Audit* was making into the social impact of a major rubber manufacturing company, the managing director of the company wrote to a number of pollution authorities authorising them to release to the researchers any information about the company on their files.[38] The files of one water authority, who granted full access, were found to contain the following intriguing memorandum: 'I believe that we should accede to their [the company's] request allowing involvement only of the [*Social Audit*] staff and in the hope that not too much attention will be paid to the . . . authority by [*Social Audit*]. . . . I think we would find ourselves in this and similar situations in a most unenviable political situation if we refused them access to our files, except so far as these relate to public security.'

In complete contrast, the Alkali Inspectorate revealed no such political sensitivity. The fact that the company concerned may have requested – or in this case waived – confidentiality was clearly not the crucial factor: 'These files and reports are confidential to the Chief Alkali Inspector and it is not our policy to show their contents or to give information about them to anyone outside the Department. We cannot make an exception in this instance.'

It may be argued – as the Royal Commission has done – that in its secrecy the Inspectorate is one-sided. It may be that the Inspectorate actually does give undue attention to industry's needs at the cost of an inflexibly unresponsive attitude towards the public. This latter view was held by Richard Crossman who, as Minister for Housing in the late 1960s, was responsible for overseeing the Inspectorate's work. In his diary he records that 'nearly all my technical advisers were passionately in favour of the producer and against the amenity lobby. This was particularly true of the Alkali Inspectorate.'[39] If this is the case, then secrecy plays a central role in concealing – and thereby preserving – this one-sided approach.

The Alkali Inspectorate's approach to information has been examined in some detail, not only because the Inspectorate has been outstandingly secretive in a field where secrecy has been the norm, but also because of its influence on other pollution authorities. The Inspectorate's flexible, informal approach based on the 'best practicable means' has been widely admired and highly influential. Its example helped to shape the Health and Safety at Work Act; has been held up as the British alternative to uniform emission limits proposed by the EEC; and has been promoted by the Royal Commission as the basis for a new unified pollution inspectorate, based on an expanded Alkali Inspectorate with increased responsibilities. It has also affected information disclosure by a second category of responsible bodies whose legal duties were changed by the 1974 Legislation: the local authorities.

Local Authorities

Air pollution from any process not controlled by the Alkali Inspectorate is the responsibility of local authorities. They administer the Clean Air Acts, which cover boiler emissions, and the Public Health Acts which relate to any emission that causes a health hazard or nuisance. Both sets of legislation contain wide-ranging secrecy clauses.

Following the Royal Commission's call for greater openness, the statutory Clean Air Council set up a working party to investigate possible mechanisms for disclosure.[40] The committee, on which the Chief Alkali Inspector sat and reportedly played an influential role, issued a report that bore the strong imprint of Alkali Inspectorate thinking. Accepting that the public should 'have a right to full and reliable information' the report nevertheless shared the Alkali Inspectorate's objection to the release of raw emissions data on its own which, 'can sound alarming to the uninstructed'. Instead, it recommended that information 'carefully considered and presented to the general public in proper perspective' should be released through local committees similar to those already established at the Alkali Inspectorate's instigation.

The recommendations were embodied in the Control of Pollution Act. The feature that distinguishes these provisions from, say, those on water pollution is that they are entirely discretionary. Local authorities need take no steps to publish information unless they choose to. Before taking any initiative they must set up a cumbersome tripartite committee on which the authority, local industry, and amenity interests or specialist advisors are represented. They can then require any discharger – whether controlled by the local authority or by the Alkali Inspectorate – to supply emissions data, which must then be published on an open register.

Dischargers may be protected from disclosure if, on appeal to the Secretary of State, they demonstrate that trade secrets or military secrets would be jeopardised, or if the information could only be provided at unreasonable cost.[41] A further protection exists for Alkali Inspectorate works: these need not provide any information that is not already being supplied to the Inspectorate.[42]

Brought into force in February 1977, these provisions have had little practical effect on the amount of information available to the public. In the first three years of their operation, only a handful of authorities have established the necessary committees – and few more seem likely to do so in the near future. Those that have set up the necessary committees have not done so primarily to inform the public. A committee was established by the City of Coventry on the mistaken assumption that without one it could not take pollution samples for use in court actions. By the time it had learnt that this view was incorrect, the committee had been formed and was committed to meeting twice a year. It has published useful reports on pollution levels in the city but at the time of writing has opened no public register. It has issued no formal requests for emissions data, but has accepted such information in confidence from industry.

A committee has also been established at Walsall where the object has been to allow the authority to extend its own investigations, especially into pollution from Alkali Inspectorate works to which it would otherwise have no direct access. Surveys commissioned by the Council revealed extremely high levels of toxic metals in the area, at times as much as 100 times above those in unpolluted regions. By using its power to obtain information, the authority hoped to locate the main sources of this pollution.

The committee's first meeting revealed industry's strong concern that information it supplied should be 'treated with the strictest confidence'. The result was that the committee – one of whose aims is to provide information to the public – has resolved to hold parts of its meetings in private.[43] This did not prevent it from sending a questionnaire to local industries asking, informally, for emissions data for publication. The response confirmed that without confidentiality informal requests will generally be fruitless. Only 20 out of some 70 firms approached returned the questionnaire; among those failing to reply was one of the companies represented on the committee itself. At the time of writing the committee was about to decide whether to use its formal powers to demand information for publication.

In the main, however, authorities that already receive the information they need for their own use are under no incentive to seek public disclosure. For example, a long established liaison committee in Bristol gives the City Council all the information it needs – in confidence.

We get possibly more from the things we've built up in Bristol than from a section 79 (ie. disclosure) scheme. If we did this, people would know that the information they gave would be made public and they would probably restrict themselves to what the law requires. We feel we get more from them knowing its not in the public arena . . . (section 79) has strengthened our arm. It might strengthen the case for having a section 79 arrangement if they don't supply information and so they co-operate bearing this in mind.[44]

So provided an authority already receives the information it needs from industry, it has no incentive to use its formal powers, and there will be no disclosure to the public. Indeed, the threat of public disclosure may be used to put pressure on industry to provide more information to the authority in confidence. Despite its good intentions, the Act seems unlikely to open up the private relationship between local authorities and dischargers. In fact, by strengthening local authorities in their private dealings with industry, the effect may be precisely the opposite.

River Pollution

The provisions for the disclosure of river pollution information seem more likely to achieve their purpose. This can be seen both from the way the law has been framed, and from the very positive response of a number of water authorities. Unlike the air pollution provisions of the Control of Pollution Act, disclosure data about river discharges is compulsory, not discretionary. Furthermore, 'raw' discharge data will be made available directly to the public without filtering through intermediary consultative committees.

When the Act is fully implemented, each of the ten regional water authorities in England and Wales will be required to keep a register, open to the public, showing details of all applications for consent to discharge effluent, conditions attached to existing consents, the results of effluent analyses, and enforcement action taken on the basis of such analyses.[45]

These provisions are nevertheless not as strong as they might be. Apart from the standard exemptions for trade and military secrets, two major loopholes have been left open. As a result the public will have only partial access to information about discharges: when water authorities grant consent for a discharge, they may require the discharger to monitor the effluent himself, passing the results on to the authority. Such samples may in practice provide the only full picture of the quality of a discharge, but they will be exempt from publicity. Also, many industrial effluents are not discharged directly into a river but into the sewers where they are treated at a sewage works before being discharged with the sewage effluent. Although information about the sewage works effluent will appear on the public register, details of individual industrial discharge to sewers will remain secret.[46]

By mid-1980, six years after the passing of the Control of Pollution Act, these measures have still not been brought into force and the secrecy provisions of the previous legislation – with gaol penalties for unauthorised disclosure – still operate. Yet in one of the most remarkable developments in recent pollution practice, many water authorities have circumvented the legal restrictions and published the hitherto secret information.

The move was led by Severn Trent Water Authority, which sought and obtained the permission of dischargers in its area to release details of their consents and effluent quality.[47] While the majority of firms agreed to the publicity, some forty either refused or failed to reply to the request. Memorably dubbed 'the furtive forty' by the *New Scientist*, these companies received considerable adverse publicity for their reticence.[48]

Severn Trent's water quality reports have been published each year since then, allowing those who avoided publicity initially to reconsider subsequently. A number of other authorities have either followed this example or undertaken to seek discharger's permission to release data if particular requests for this information are made. Other authorities, however, have made no moves to release information in advance of the legal requirement.

There is, then, a considerably more positive attitude towards the disclosure of information about river discharges than about emissions to the air. This is reflected not only in the attitudes of the control authorities but also in the legal provisions – even though a single Act governs disclosure in the two areas. How can these differences be explained?

It is certainly not because of any stricter enforcement of river pollution standards. The data that has now appeared shows that existing river pollution standards have been widely ignored. However, this poor enforcement of standards was the responsibility of the old river authorities, whose functions were taken over by the water authorities in 1974. By publishing full details, the new authorities underlined the fact that their problems had been inherited from their predecessors, and were not self-made.

Parliament, however, had a very specific reason for requiring disclosure about river discharges. Under the old system, the operation and control of sewage works had been divided. Local authorities ran the sewage works; river authorities set and enforced the standards. Under the new arrangements, a single water authority did both. This presented a serious problem of accountability. How could a water authority be expected to license its own sewage works, set its own standards, enforce them – and take itself to court in case of violations? Moreover, under the existing confidentiality provisions, it would do all this in complete secrecy. This was unacceptable, not only to the public, but also to industry which suspected that industrial dischargers might be unfairly subjected to much stricter enforcement than the authorities' own, possibly more polluting, sewage works. The dilemma was solved by introducing two safeguards. The public was given the right to prosecute any discharger – water authority or other – that exceeded a legal limit;[49] and it was given full rights of access to information about discharges.

Though the openness was welcomed in environmental circles, the right of public prosecution had unfortunate repercussions. Fearing widespread and costly action against the many sewage works that exceed their legal limits, the water authorities have carried out a general revision of all consent standards, including those for industry. The object is partly to set standards that are directly related to the use made of the water. More urgently, the purpose is to lower the legal standards so that the many presently illegal discharges are legitimised, and so protected from private prosecution.[50] As the CBI has commented: 'increased risk of private prosecution provides a substantial incentive to get more relaxed consent levels and to take samples (on which revised consents are to be based) only when effluent quality is good. Such practices would tend to defeat the whole object of the exercise.'[51]

At the beginning of this chapter it was suggested that an authority which could not satisfy public expectations could try either to improve its own performance, or reduce public expectations. The latter course often involves the use, or rather the abuse, of secrecy. The importance of the river pollution saga is that it demonstrates that an authority that cannot solve its problems need not inevitably respond secretively. This can be illustrated by the following report, taken from the publicised minutes of the Yorkshire Water Authority in 1978:

Out of a total of 640 sewage treatment works, 461 (just over two-thirds) failed to comply with the consent standard currently imposed . . . out of a total of 372 industrial premises with direct discharges to stream, 130 (approx. one third) were not sampled and 176 (approximately half) failed to comply with the present consent standard . . . at least half of the consent conditions relating to final effluents from the Authority's own sewage treatment plants, and a similar proportion of industrial discharge consents, will need to be changed.[52]

The level of control described here is depressing, but is probably typical not only of water authorities but possibly of other pollution authorities also. However, the fact that it is openly *described* is important and reassuring, for this is information that most pollution authorities would instinctively suppress.

Similarly, Severn Trent's exercise, although it revealed a large proportion of offenders, and its own non-enforcement of standards, has shown that information about discharges can be released without the dire consequences so often predicted. This impression is confirmed by industry's response to the publication. In the early days of the exercise, seven out of 250 companies contacted refused their permission for disclosure, and a further twenty-five failed to respond. By 1978/79 the number of companies refusing to allow publication had fallen to only two while only fourteen failed to respond to the survey.

Clearly, the release of this data has not caused the public to 'become scared of figures . . . get the wind up' as the Chief Alkali Inspector warned, nor presumably did public use of the figures 'frighten away prospective industrial developers' as a local authority officer suggested. As an officer of the Severn Trent Water Authority suggests, the response may have been just the opposite, with companies finding positive benefits to the disclosure:

I have noticed that companies generally seem happy to point to their record of openness and it is always nice for a company, if they have been accused of secrecy, to say 'Well, look, we've allowed this to be published here' . . . They are not as suspicious of the process as they used to be. There used to be a great thing about keeping everything secret at all costs without thinking why it was necessary.[53]

Pesticides

Not only does secrecy deprive the public of information it may need – it also rules out the possibility of independent evaluation of regulatory decisions. An authority that operates in complete secrecy must inevitably have less chance of detecting oversights or miscalculations than one which exposes its data to review. The benefits of such review – and the dangers of excessive commercial secrecy – can be seen by looking at the control of pesticides in the UK.

Pesticide regulation is based on a non-statutory agreement between pesticide manufacturers and a number of government departments, known as the Pesticides Safety Precautions Scheme (PSPS). Under this scheme, pesticide manufacturers undertake not to introduce a new product onto the market, or promote an existing one for a new purpose, without official clearance. If this is given, they agree to print agreed safety precautions and hazard warnings on pesticide containers. Similarly, they undertake to withdraw a product from sale if officially asked to do so.

The stated object of the scheme is not only to safeguard domestic animals and wildlife, but also to protect those handling pesticides or consuming treated products. It is therefore notable that neither worker nor consumer organisations are represented on the scheme. Wildlife interests, however, are represented by the Nature Conservancy Council – a statutory body established to promote, and advise the government on, wildlife conservation.

The Council has itself complained of the harmful secrecy that characterises the PSPS. For example, it has pointed out that more information from the PSPS or manufacturers would help ensure that pesticides approved under the scheme were not used in excessive amounts. Once a pesticide has been cleared, manufacturers and retailers presumably do whatever they can to promote maximum – rather than minimum – use of the product:

Excessive use of certain pesticides has been suspected but never established, through lack of evidence. Indeed, the whole history of pesticide/ wildlife studies is one of hindrance and gaps in knowledge caused by the refusal of manufacturers and suppliers to give figures for the amounts of pesticides made and/or sold in this country. And even the MAFF (Ministry of Agriculture, Fisheries and Food) and the DAFS (Department of Agriculture and Fisheries for Scotland) surveys do not necessarily give an accurate picture of the range and scale of applications . . . the difficulty and extra work required have militated against the provision of such data, but there has also been *a real resistance from certain quarters with an interest in preserving a state of public ignorance on these matters.*[54] (emphasis added)

The Council's criticisms were endorsed by the Royal Commission on Environmental Pollution which concluded that it could 'see no good reason why data on the quantities of active ingredients manufactured and sold should not be made freely available'.[55]

Equally harmful is the secrecy that applies to toxicity studies on pesticides. Such studies must be submitted to the Advisory Committee on Pesticides (which administers the PSPS) before clearance for a new product can be given. Yet, between 1957 and 1977, the Committee published only five reports. A review of pesticide control in the UK published in 1977 concluded that, while these reports contained much new and valuable information:

At crucial points there is insufficient information to determine why a particular decision has been reached. The references (published and unpublished) have not been disclosed and the assessment criteria which are employed are not stated with any precision and often not at all. . . . Given the largely closed operation of the PSPS together with the type of representation which it allows, the suspicion may remain that the assessments made are inadequate and/or biased in favour of those interests which are predominantly represented in the Scheme.[56]

Independent reviews of manufacturers' data in the United States has revealed that official clearance for pesticides has sometimes been given on the basis of quite inadequate data. Data on twenty-four pesticides cleared by the Environmental Protection Agency were, under pressure from a Congressional Committee of Investigation, submitted for independent review which, in 1976, reported that with one possible exception these data were so inadequate that it was not possible to conclude whether any of the pesticides were safe or whether there would be any hazard in eating common foods with now legal residues.[57]

To what extent similar practices occur in the UK is not known, but there is certainly no reason to believe that they do not take place. A survey published in the *New Scientist* in 1976 was based on over 180 reports from scientists with direct or indirect knowledge of intentionally biased research. Nearly three-quarters of these reported 'unequivocal instances' of scientific cheating of which they had direct knowledge: 'the most frequent kind of IB (intentional bias) detected is data "massage" (74 percent of the total) and experiment rigging (17 percent); complete fabrication of experiment and data, sometimes involving plagiarism (7 per cent) and deliberate misinterpretation (2 per cent), are alternatives.'[58]

Although most of the instances described occurred in university laboratories, seventeen per cent of the reports concerned industrial establishments. In most cases, those found to have cheated suffered no penalty on detection, and indeed the author of the survey noted that 'a qualification frequently included was the response "promoted" '.

There are two conditions which can almost be guaranteed to favour the production of inadequate or biased research; both are characteristic of schemes such as the Pesticides Safety Precautions Scheme.

The first is some strong commercial or other advantage to those producing the research if its conclusions point in one way rather than another. Studies showing that a new pesticide is of relatively low toxicity will obviously be of great value in securing official clearance and encouraging sales. The second is freedom from independent evaluation of data by the scientific community. Academic research is scrutinised by the scientific journals before results are accepted for publication; afterwards, the findings are open to review by other researchers in the field, who will often attempt to duplicate unexpected results. If researchers know that their data will never be published, a fundamental, vital check on the quality and integrity of the work is lost.

Under the present PSPS it is impossible for independent scientists to evaluate the data on which a new pesticide has been cleared, or to know precisely what degree of hazard has been demonstrated. To take one example: a number of pesticides cleared for use in the UK are now known to have been approved on the basis of data produced in an American laboratory suspected of falsification. At the time of writing, these substances were being re-evaluated under PSPS, but it is not possible to discover which substances are under suspicion or known to have been cleared on the basis of false data.

The non-publication of data can have other serious consequences for research. For example, it may be important to identify products turned down by the PSPS in case they are being exported for use in developing countries where the machinery for regulating pesticides may be absent. Export of banned pesticides has been well documented in the US. In 1971, 95,000 tons of wheat and barley grain treated with methyl mercury – a fungicide whose use is forbidden in many developed countries – was exported from the US to Iraq. The poisoned seeds were distributed throughout the Iraqi countryside where they were used not for planting but for baking. Some 6,000 people died as a result, and another 100,000 suffered serious injury.[59] In addition to such effects, the uncontrolled export of banned pesticides may even prove dangerous to the *exporting* country, as agricultural products grown abroad by countries using the banned substances may subsequently be imported, presenting home consumers with dangerously contaminated foodstuffs.

Between 1973 and 1977, forty-eight applications for new products or new uses were turned down under the PSPS in the UK.[60] However, the PSPS secrecy arrangements frustrate any attempt to trace the fate of such banned products: the Ministry of Agriculture refuses to disclose the names of pesticides failing to obtain clearance. When the possibility of dangerous exports was raised, *Social Audit* was told: 'We really don't care what happens to a product once it goes abroad.'

Secrecy 'carried to unnecessary lengths' has concerned the Royal Commission on Environmental Pollution which has suggested that the refusal to provide information about pesticides 'tends to become a reflex action, without specific reference to the question of whether commercial interests are truly at risk.'[61]

New Chemicals

Many of the weaknesses of the PSPS are likely to be replicated in new regulations concerning the pre-testing of all new chemicals. These requirements are due to be introduced in response to an EEC directive.[62] While it is proposed that the manufacturer will have to publish safety precautions and a summary of the chemical's hazardous properties, the actual name of the chemical and the details of the toxicity testing findings will remain secret. Once again, the position of the control authority has become so closely identified with that of industry, that on crucial issues such as public disclosure the two appear indistinguishable.

The Confederation of British Industry (CBI) has argued that even to reveal *which* toxicity tests have been completed might give away 'considerable research and development effort in their own right'.[63] On the other hand, members of the public can hardly be confident of the adequacy of testing under such secretive arrangements. The CBI suggests that secrecy needs to be still more extensive than this because: 'in some cases mere knowledge that a product has been notified to a control authority can of itself constitute valuable commercial information. It may imply to a competitor not only that the notifier considers the product commercially viable but also that the product is acceptable from a safety, health or environmental point of view.'

It is precisely these arguments which have been taken up by the Health and Safety Commission (HSC). In its evidence to the House of Lords Select Committee on the European Communities, the HSC concentrated not on the considerable public benefits that would follow from disclosure, but on the *possible* commercial harm. It testified that: 'There is considerable concern over the possible commercial disadvantages which could occur from disclosures' adding that the proposed directive 'could inhibit innovation and it could introduce an *unacceptable form of control over conditions of marketing*'.[64] (emphasis added)

Given that industry has ample opportunity to give evidence on its own behalf, it is surprising that an authority concerned primarily with safety should give commercial considerations such a high priority, ignoring the possible advantages of disclosure. The HSC's views should be contrasted with those of a panel appointed by the US Department of Health, Education and Welfare to investigate trade secrecy restrictions in the work of the Food and Drug Administration (FDA). Their report recognised that, by keeping toxicity data secret, the original manufacturer of a drug can deprive competitors of valuable information needed for launching similar drugs. Nevertheless there are persuasive arguments for finding a way to release this information. The report argues that if this is not done:

most day-to-day decision making remains closed to public participation and outside review. Present policy thus places FDA in the untenable position of having to justify its decisions without being able to refer publicly to the data on which the decisions are based. FDA's trade secrets policy also deprives the agency of valuable opinions and criticisms from sources outside the agency by preventing scientists and other members of the public from examining and commenting on the facts which underlie agency decisions.[65]

The report suggests a mechanism for releasing this data without harming innovating companies. This would prevent the subsequent manufacturers of a new drug from using the originator's data when seeking approval for the 'me-too' products. They would either have to purchase the rights to the data, or produce their own independent evaluation. By the latter course, they would be not only double-checking and extending the original research but also provide a valuable safeguard against possible inadequacies.

The fact that such measures are feasible is demonstrated by the US Toxic Substances Control Act of 1976. Under this Act, manufacturers of specified new chemicals must submit details of toxicity studies to the Environmental Protection Agency. Provided this information does not reveal manufacturing details or the exact proportions of ingredients in a mixture, the full toxicity studies must be made publicly available. The Act allows for the sharing of test costs between the various manufacturers or importers of such a substance.

Toxicity data is therefore not in any absolute sense a trade secret. Provided the control authorities allow only the originator to make commercial use of his data, there is no need at all to restrict its publication. Given the political will to support such disclosure by safeguarding the position of innovators, this information could safely – and advantageously – be released.

Nuclear Energy

Some of the now familiar themes of this chapter take on a new and more urgent importance in the context of nuclear energy. As the government commits itself to an expanded nuclear energy programme, the reliability of the safety assessments – on which official clearance for the programme depends – has become a critical political issue. The importance of independent scrutiny of official safety assessments is now well appreciated in the United States. A reactor safety study completed in 1975 was so widely criticised for its inadequacies that in 1977 the Nuclear Regulatory Commission (NRC) ordered an independent review of the report. The review panel reported that the Executive Summary of the study:

does not adequately indicate the full extent of the consequences of reactor accidents and does not sufficiently emphasise the uncertainties involved in the calculations of their probability. As a result, the reader may be left with a misplaced confidence in the validity of the risk estimates and a more favourable impression of reactor risks in comparison with other risks than warranted by the study.[66]

Many of these failings had been identified by independent commentators during the consultation process that followed the appearance of a draft of this report. Yet these criticisms 'either were not acknowledged or were evaded'. The NRC accepted the findings of its review panel, withdrew any previous endorsement of the discredited Executive Summary to the report, and re-affirmed its belief that 'proper peer review is fundamental to making sound technical decisions.'

There is ample opportunity for similar faults to find their way into safety studies carried out in the UK – but if they are present, the chances of detecting them are remote. According to Friends of the Earth:

The assessment of designs, and the licensing and construction of commercial nuclear power stations, is carried out behind closed doors by a small group of technically qualified experts. Details of the consultation and review procedure are kept secret as indeed are the records of operating experience at nuclear plants. The public, and sometimes Parliamentary watchdogs like the Select Committee on Science and Technology, have difficulty obtaining information. Even lists of *titles* of reports prepared or commissioned by the industry or the Nuclear Installations Inspectorate are withheld.[67]

Apart from this, there is evidence that successive governments have been prepared to go to considerable lengths to suppress information that might lead to criticism – however justified – of the nuclear programme.

In 1950, Chapman Pincher of the *Daily Express* learnt that a mistake had occurred during the building of the Windscale nuclear reactor, with the possibility of major releases of radioactive material during operation. The story was quashed following a warning from a senior Ministry of Defence official that disclosure would certainly be punished by a prosecution under Section 1 of the Official Secrets Act. Some time later, after the fault had been repaired, the same official acknowledged to Pincher that no security question had been at issue, and that the government would not have been able to prosecute had the original story been printed. The threat had apparently been made only to shield the government from the embarrassment that would have followed from revelations of incompetence.[68]

More than twenty years later, the Official Secrets Act was still serving the nuclear industry well. In March 1973, a *Sunday Times* journalist investigating claims that Windscale workers had suffered from radiation poisoning, reported that: 'There is also the fear among Windscale workers that any public discussion of injuries or compensation might infringe the Official Secrets Act. One man refused to show me a scar on his arm which he said had been caused by plutonium because he thought it might be an official secret.'[69]

Not only press comment, but even Parliamentary scrutiny has been avoided by deliberately withholding information. In 1972, the Select Committee on Science and Technology was denied access to a Departmental working party report on thermal nuclear reactors, allegedly because of 'considerations of commercial confidentiality'.[70]

Former Secretary of State for Energy, Tony Benn, has suggested that even ministers are denied access to official information, if it is felt that by drawing their attention to certain issues a departmental policy might be threatened. Benn has stated that although he was responsible for nuclear energy as Minister of Technology from 1966 to 1970 and as Energy Secretary from 1975 to 1979, during neither period was he informed about a serious explosion at a Soviet nuclear plant in the 1960s. As a result of the explosion a large population was exposed to severe radioactive contamination with heavy human casualties and widespread deaths. The UK Atomic Energy Authority is thought to have learnt of this incident from information supplied by the CIA in America, but no details were publicly revealed nor was the British Cabinet or the responsible minister informed. Instead, according to Mr Benn, it was decided 'to keep it quiet for fear that an accident in the Soviet Union might throw doubt upon the safety of nuclear operations worldwide'.[71]

Any other information that might allow independent scrutiny of technical decisions is, similarly, closely guarded from public disclosure. In 1978, Friends of the Earth asked the South of Scotland Electricity Board for a copy of the preliminary safety study it had submitted to the Nuclear Installations Inspectorate in support of the proposed nuclear reactor at Torness. The Board replied: 'Our submissions to the Nuclear Installations Inspectorate are part of an extensive on-going process of discussion and evaluation. They are necessarily complex and voluminous and publication would not assist the public, whose interests are fully safeguarded by the Inspectorate.'[72] When the group then approached the Inspectorate itself, it was refused access to the document on the grounds that the report was 'proprietary and may not be disclosed to a third party without the express permission of the supplier'.[73] The effect of such non-disclosure is to limit the scope of public discussion on the risks of nuclear energy. It is now clear that this is precisely what the secrecy is intended to do.

An internal Central Electricity Generating Board minute, leaked to the press in 1979, showed that the Board's Director of Health and Safety had, as a deliberate matter of policy, decided to withhold safety studies from publication. Issued after the near catastrophe at the Three Mile Island reactor in the United States, the minute warned that the 'nuclear opposition' was as a result likely to step up its activities and suggested that secrecy would be the best defence:

I think their main line of attack will be to obtain public discussion and debate about the safety of our Magnox reactors and the AGRs (advanced gas-cooled reactors), as well as providing opposition to the PWRs (pressurised water reactors). The Friends of the Earth have already requested that the full AGR Safety Reports are made public and *this has been refused*.

Their current policy is to approach or telephone staff with the objective of obtaining information about existing safety problems . . . I propose to you that any telephone calls of this nature received from the nuclear opposition or unknown callers should be dealt with by *refusing to provide such information*.[74] (emphasis added)

To conclude, some of the secrecy that is found in pollution control may have no particular function: it may exist simply because it is the tradition, and authorities feel that to start publishing new data would give them extra bureaucratic work with no obvious benefits. On the other hand secrecy may have a very definite, and undesirable, purpose. It may be a device for deliberately suppressing public discussion on vital decisions. More generally, it may protect the control authority, the industry it regulates, or a national policy from having to face and respond to criticism, however justified that criticism may be. Naturally, the purpose of such secrecy must be disguised, and the pretext of protecting trade secrets has often provided a convenient camouflage. Trade secrecy continues to be used to justify the non-disclosure of toxicity studies on new pesticides and chemicals. US experience suggests that this data can be published provided the control authorities are prepared to take other steps to safeguard the competitive advantage of innovating firms.

For many years, the argument of trade secrecy deprived the public of all information about industrial discharges. That argument has now been overturned, and the laws protecting trade secrets relaxed. The fact that most authorities still do not disclose details of the discharges they regulate confirms that the secrecy has deeper roots.

Another common objection to disclosure is the suggestion that technical information will be deliberately distorted by alleged extremists, or misinterpreted even by the well-intentioned. In practice, anyone who believes that the public should be warned – or frightened – about the hazards of pollution can raise the alarm quite effectively without the help of specific data. No hard facts are needed to warn that the release of (unnamed) chemicals in (unspecified) quantities undoubtedly presents an (unmentionably awful) risk which the authorities are determined to conceal by secrecy. In fact, those who would really make use of the detailed factual information at present so often withheld are the increasing numbers of individuals and organisations who have the ability to understand the technical issues involved and can assess for themselves the adequacy of the decisions taken in their name.

The consequences of this unnecessary secrecy affect both the public and the control authorities themselves and it denies individuals and communities the information they need to participate in and influence decisions that affect them. It frustrates and angers those who are exposed to actual hazards which they suspect may not have been adequately controlled.

Nor does secrecy necessarily help the control authorities. If lack of resources prevents an authority from doing as effective a job as it would like, secrecy may protect it from criticism. But by concealing rather than acknowledging its failures, the authority commits itself to accepting them.

Secrecy removes from the control authority the vital discipline of knowing that its work will be publicly scrutinised; it may also deprive it of valuable informed comment that may genuinely help it in its decision making. Ultimately, secrecy can only be expected to sap public confidence in the work of an authority, feeding the suspicion that it conceals unjustifiable concessions to industry and a lack of concern for public health and the environment.

REFERENCES

1 Department of the Environment, *Environmental Standards, A Description of United Kingdom Practice*, Pollution Paper No. 11, HMSO, 1977.
2 Department of the Environment, *Digest of Environment Pollution Statistics*, No. 2, HMSO, 1979.
3 *Public Health Act 1936*, Section 287(5).
4 *Clean Air Act 1956*, Section 26.
5 *Rivers (Prevention of Pollution) Act 1961*, Section 12. While some environmental legislation covers the whole of the United Kingdom, there are separate statutes for Scotland as follows: *Public Health (Scotland) Act 1897; Water (Scotland) Act 1946; Sewage (Scotland) Act 1968;* and *Rivers (Prevention of Pollution) (Scotland) Acts 1961–65.*

THE ENVIRONMENT 123

6 Quoted in Ireland, F. E., 'Reflections of an Alkali Inspector', *Clean Air*, Summer 1977, pp. 4–9.

7 Fish, R., 'Some Cases of Quality Affecting Water Use', *Effluent and Water Treatment Journal*, October 1973, pp. 629–636.

8 Tinker, Jon, 'Britain's Environment – Nanny Knows Best', *New Scientist*, 9 March 1972. pp. 530–33.

9 Royal Commission on Environmental Pollution, Second Report, 'Three Issues in Industrial Pollution', HMSO, 1972.

10 *Control of Pollution Act 1974*, Section 41.

11 *Ibid., Section 82(2) (d)*. And: *The Control of Atmospheric Pollution (Research and Publicity) Regulations 1977*.

12 *Health and Safety at Work Etc. Act 1974*, Section 23(7).

13 *Sunday Times*, 18 November 1979.

14 Letter from Chief Inspector of Factories, *Guardian*, 20 December 1979.

15 Royal Commission on Environmental Pollution, Fifth Report, *Air Pollution Control: An Integrated Approach*, HMSO, 1976, p. 65.

16 Richardson, G. M., and Ogus, A.I., 'The Regulatory Approach to Environmental Control', *Urban Law and Policy*, 2 (1979) pp. 337–357.

17 See for example: Health and Safety Executive, *Industrial Air Pollution 1975*, HMSO, 1977 p. 6; and *Industrial Air Pollution 1977*, HMSO, 1979, p. 1.

18 Council for Science and Society, *The Acceptability of Risks*, Barry Rose (Publishers) Ltd., 1977, pp. 43–44.

19 Confederation of British Industry, *Water Pollution Control*, Paper No. 5, 'Publication of Information About Discharges to Inland Water Courses', CBI Comments, August 1972.

20 Holmes, I., 'Why Clean Air?' Remarks made during discussion of papers at 44th Annual Conference of the National Society for Clean Air, 19–22 September 1977, Harrogate.

21 Quoted from Ireland, F. E., *op. cit.*

22 Royal Commission on Environmental Pollution, Seventh Report, *Agriculture and Pollution*, HMSO, 1979, p. 79.

23 Ministry of Housing and Local Government, *105th Annual Report on Alkali Etc. Work 1968*, HMSO, 1969, p. 26.

24 Frankel, M., 'The Alkali Inspectorate. The Control of Industrial Air Pollution', *Social Audit*, 1974, p. 22.

25 Carter, J. F., 'The Alkali etc. Works Regulations Act 1906 and Alkali Etc. Works Orders 1928 to 1958', in: *Chemical Engineering Practice*, Vol. 11, ed. Cremer, H. W., 1959.

26 Quoted from Ireland, F. E., *op. cit.*

27 *Ibid.*

28 Fletton Brickworks Liaison Committee, Press Release, 28 November 1978.

29 *The Environmental Assessment of the Existing and Proposed*

124   CONSUMING SECRETS

Brickworks in the Marston Vales Bedfordshire, prepared for
Bedfordshire County Council by Cremer and Warner, Consulting
Engineers and Scientists, 22 October 1979.
30 Letter from Dr W. E. Grant, Deputy Chief Alkali Inspector, to P.
M. Goode, 19 October 1978.
31 Department of the Environment, *107th Annual Report on Alkali etc.
Works, 1970*, HMSO, 1971, p. 48.
32 Grant to Goode, *op. cit.*
33 Letter from Secretary of Fletton Brickworks Liaison Committee to
P. M. Goode, 4 December 1978.
34 Department of the Environment, *108th Annual Report on Alkali etc.
Works, 1971*, HMSO, 1972, p. 11.
35 Quoted in Frankel, M., *op. cit.*, p. 25.
36 Royal Commission on Environmental Pollution, Fifth Report, *op.
cit*, p. 35.
37 Department of the Environment, *107th Annual Report on Alkali
Etc. Works, 1970, op. cit.*, p. 5.
38 *Social Audit on the Avon Rubber Company. An Independent
Assessment of a Company's Activities as They Affect Employees,
Consumers and the Local Community*, Social Audit, 1976.
39 Crossman, Richard, *The Diaries of a Cabinet Minister. Vol. 1.*
Minister of Housing 1964–65, Hamilton & Cape, 1975, p. 311.
40 Clean Air Council, *Information About Industrial Emissions to the
Atmosphere*, HMSO, 1973.
41 *Control of Pollution Act 1974*, Section 81(1).
42 *Ibid.*, Section 80(3).
43 Meeting of the Walsall Atmospheric Pollution Consultative
Committee, 29 March 1979.
44 Cooper, P. C., Senior Environmental Health Officer, City of
Bristol, telephone conversation, 29 April 1980.
45 *Control of Pollution Act 1974*, Section 47 (1).
46 Department of the Environment, *Control of Pollution Act 1974:
Part II*, Consultation Letter No. 2, 26 July 1978.
47 Severn Trent Water Authority, *Water Quality 1973*.
48 Tinker, Jon, 'River Pollution: The Midlands Dirty Dozen', *New
Scientist*, 6 March 1975, pp. 551–554.
49 When the Control of Pollution Act is fully implemented it will
repeal Section 11 of the *Rivers (Prevention of Pollution) Act 1961*
which allows prosecution only with the consent of the Water
Authority or Attorney-General.
50 National Water Council, *Review of Discharge Consent Conditions –
Consultation Paper*, February 1977.
51 Martindale, R. R., 'The Industrialists' Viewpoint'. Paper given at a
conference on 'Water Quality – the Implications of the Control of
Pollution Act 1974, Part II'. Oyez International Business
Communications Ltd., 12–13 December 1978.

52 Yorkshire Water Authority, 'Review of Discharge Consent Conditions, Progress Report', Water Quality Advisory Panel, 9 November 1978.
53 Breach, Dr. R. A., Scientific Officer, Severn Trent Water Authority, telephone conversation, 9 June, 1980.
54 Nature Conservancy Council, evidence to the Royal Commission on Environmental Pollution, *Study of Pollution in Relation to Agriculture*.
55 Royal Commission on Environmental Pollution, Seventh Report, *op. cit.*
56 Gillespie, Brendan F., *British Control of Pesticide Technology – with Reference to the Occupational, Environmental and Consumer Hazards Associated with the Use of Aldrin and Dieldrin*, Ph.D. Thesis, University of Manchester, August 1977.
57 Epstein, Samuel S., *The Politics of Cancer*, Sierra Club Books (San Francisco), 1978, p. 383.
58 St James-Roberts, I., 'Cheating in Essence'. *New Scientist*, 25 November 1976.
59 Scherr, Jacob S., Paper presented at the Seminar on the Implementation of Toxic Substances Legislation, organised by the European Environmental Bureau, Bonn, 11–14 June 1980.
60 *Hansard*, (HC). Col. 333, 10 July 1978.
61 Royal Commission on Environmental Pollution, Seventh Report, *op. cit.*
62 *Directive 79/831/EEC*, 18 September 1979, O.J.L 259, Vol. 22, 15 October 1979.
63 Confederation of British Industry, 'Release of Environmental and Technical Information, CBI Statement', October 1979.
64 House of Lords Select Committee on the European Communities, Session 1976–77, 29th Report, *Dangerous Substances*, 26 April 1977, HMSO, 1977.
65 US Department of Health Education and Welfare, Final Report of the Review Panel on New Drug Regulation, May 1977.
66 US Nuclear Regulatory Commission, Office of Public Affairs, News Releases, Vol. 5, No. 4, week ending January 23 1979.
67 Flood, Michael, *Torness: Keep it Green*. Friends of the Earth, Energy Paper No. 1, 1979.
68 *Departmental Committee on Section 2 of the Official Secrets Act 1911* Chairman Lord Franks, Cmnd 5104, HMSO, 1972, Vol. 4, evidence of Mr Chapman Pincher.
69 *Sunday Times*, 18 March 1973.
70 Flood, Michael and Grove-White, Robin, *Nuclear Prospects*, Friends of the Earth, 1976, p. 39.
71 Granada Television, *World in Action*, 'Mr Benn's Secret Service', broadcast on 7 January 1980.

72 Letter from D. A. S. MacLaren to Michael Flood, 24 November 1978.
73 Letter from K. M. Paley, to Michael Flood, 8 December 1978.
74 Note sent by R. R. Matthews, Director, Health and Safety, CEGB, to all nuclear power station managers, 6 April 1979.

Local Government and Planning   7

Peter Stringer

Battles between a planning authority and parts of the community it
serves are an everyday feature of local newspaper columns. One of the
issues over which fighting sometimes breaks out is the failure of local
authority officers, and occasionally councillors, to release information
to the public – a failure that is invariably attributed to a conspiracy of
silence at town hall. But poor communication between council departments, the ambiguous role of elected councillors, a muddled commitment to commercial confidentiality and simple misunderstanding can all
frustrate public access to planning information, as Peter Stringer shows
through a selection of case histories in this chapter. A legal duty to
arrange for public participation in planning decisions was imposed on
local authorities in 1968: the way the planning profession has responded
to this duty is examined in the second part of the chapter. The story of
public participation has lessons for any programme of reform for public
access to official information.

The Times of 12 May 1980 reported the end of the 69-year-old
fiction which had denied to the public the very existence of MI6.
On the same day the same paper contained the headline 'Council
planners say government department is hiding behind Secrets Act
over nerve gas move.'

Equipment used for the development of lethal nerve gases and psycho-
tropic chemical weapons is being transferred from Nancekuke, Cornwall
to the Chemical Defence Establishment at Porton Down, Wiltshire.
    The planning committee of Salisbury District Council was advised as
a matter of routine by the Property Services Agency of the move of
processing plant and effluent treatment tanks. Civil engineering construction at the Chemical Defence Establishment has started, and work on
underground lead-lined storage vaults began more than a year ago.
    However the matter has not been examined by the local authority
because some members of the planning committee object to an instruction
from the Property Services Agency that the press and public must be
excluded from any discussion.

Mr Austin Underwood, a councillor, said yesterday that the instruction was an example of the government department trying to hide behind the Official Secrets Act, which he says is the last refuge of the scoundrel.

He believes that development on Crown lands are pursued without much reference to local authorities.

In the case of the transfer from Nancekuke to Porton Down, he says, it was outrageous to attempt to suppress a proper examination after giving out certain details. There could be no question of discussing a formal planning application in secret.

This is a rather melodramatic example of the secrecy with which authorities sometimes cloak their planning proposals. It is not the purpose of this chapter, nor of this book, to argue about the special status given to the development of Crown lands. But the incident is an ironical case of the biter bitten. Several other cases of the relative ignorance or powerlessness of the authorities themselves show that it is not only the public from whom information is kept.

The case studies below recount various episodes in which access to information about planning matters was difficult or impossible. They are not intended simply as evidence that it is often hard for people to find out what is going on. They also suggest some reasons *why* the blockage could have occurred. Unless these are understood, a blunt legal requirement to give access to information would be unlikely to remedy the situation. Secretiveness is not a deeply rooted trait of government; it is a symptom, very often, of structural and organisational ills. The most important conclusion to be drawn from the case studies is that an effective improvement in the public's access to information will only be achieved if the organisational procedures and professional values of local government are changed as well.

The second part of this chapter discusses some of the experiences which followed the introduction of statutory public participation in planning in 1968. Again, many of the successes and failures have depended on the extent to which participation has become an integrated and essential component of the planning process, rather than being an appendage loosely tacked on. Some local authority planners have recognised that anything more than token participation entails a shift in their conventional ways of working. Another important lesson is that the legislation basically only 'enables' an authority, whereas the full implementation of the spirit behind the statute book demands a positive and outgoing approach. For a legal right of access to make a difference we need to do more than agree the principle of information disclosure: we need a positive and practical commitment to open government.

Missing Information in Barnsbury

An early and unusually well-documented example of the difficulties people can have in finding out what the planners are doing has been given in a paper by John Ferris,[1] who is concerned with events in Barnsbury, London, in the period 1964–71. It is an apposite example, because it was subsequently referred to by the government-appointed Skeffington Committee in their report on public participation in planning.[2] In 1964 the Barnsbury Association was set up in the London Borough of Islington. The Association objected to the redevelopment of a local site for housing. The area had been a working-class neighbourhood greatly lacking in social amenities: more recently, in one of the best known examples of inner city 'gentrification', many new middle-class owner-occupiers had moved into the area. They did not altogether sympathise with the need for redevelopment.

One of the points made by the Barnsbury Association at the Bewdley Street Public Inquiry [in 1965] was that there was no detailed plan for Barnsbury as a district and that the proposed re-development represented piecemeal planning. This was a rhetorical point rather than a statement of fact. Planning policy for the area was contained in the 1963 Islington Town Map and the Greater London Development Plan. These plans had laid down very precisely future land use patterns, housing densities and so forth. What the Barnsbury Association were really saying was that it was not possible for ordinary citizens to find out what the local authority departmental plans were, particularly with regard to housing and roads.[3]

To fight 'piecemeal planning' the Association had intensively lobbied elected members of the councils involved to discover departmental plans; but to no avail.

Coun. Bayliss, a former chairman of the Islington Borough Council Housing Committee said in a private interview that the [London County Council's] Architects Department in conjunction with [Islington Borough Council] had during the early 1950's drawn up a long term housing programme and listed future redevelopment areas. He also said that these departmental plans were only known to senior housing and administrative staff and a few members; junior staff, other departments and the public could have no knowledge of these re-development plans. It would seem in view of this that the Barnsbury Association were quite correct in accusing the authorities of official secrecy although it is of course debatable as to whether this secrecy was in the wider public interest.[4]

In fact, as regards traffic, what was concealed was the lack of any plan at all.

The arrangement described by Councillor Bayliss is based on a dangerous principle. It implies that information can pertain to individual officers or members rather than to an authority or department. Organisationally this may be the case. It may be strictly permissible, but it gives an escape route to the authority which wants to avoid disclosing information. The Royal Town Planning Institute seems, at least in part, to accept this principle. In its 1979 draft policy statement on open government it said that information exempted from disclosure should include: 'Procedural confidences – such as the advice given by officials to Ministers and committee chairmen, or the exchanges between officials and their colleagues, including early drafts of official documents.'[5]

At a later point in his interview Councillor Bayliss possibly tried to offset his revelations about the secrecy of the councils with an interesting attack on the Barnsbury Association itself. His views were attributed by Ferris as typical of those of a number of councillors and officers. Councillor Bayliss alleged that the young professional people who were moving into Islington at that time had an overriding and excessive concern to see the value of their property rise; the Association was motivated by considerations of personal financial gain rather than by social and environmental goals:

One aspect of the Barnsbury Association that particularly annoyed Coun. Bayliss and officers of the Council was that some of the more prominent Association spokesmen were planners and architects who had been employed either by the L.C.C. or the London boroughs. The feeling was that they had been given the opportunity to 'cut their professional teeth' with these authorities and now showed their gratitude by spending their time attacking them. The hostility was further aggravated by the suspicion that much of the Barnsbury Association case at the Bewdley Street Public Inquiry was based on information that was available to them as local authority employees and also that they had informal contacts with Ministry planners prior to the Inquiry.[6]

But, as Ferris points out, this suspicion is somewhat belied by

Bayliss' own statement that the relevant information was very severely restricted even among officials. There was certainly no evidence of the disclosure of confidential information. What is true, however, is that information that is withheld from the general public may be accessible to middle-class professionals working in their own personal interests – an élitist form of participation that is fostered by secrecy.

As the Barnsbury Association pursued its course it continued to have difficulty over the availability of information. In 1968 it was publicly complaining of an exhibition of planning proposals being mounted in such a way as to prevent many people from attending it; and of the withholding of a planning report with the effect of minimising the time available to the Association to study the proposals in depth and make constructive criticisms.

The Barnsbury example highlights several important issues about the operation of secrecy in local government. The failure to disclose information may be due to the fact that it does not exist, either deliberately or by neglect. The refusal to formulate a detailed plan may be a way of keeping options open. It may be due to lethargy. Or it may be intended effectively to prevent the public from getting an overall picture of what is planned. Piecemeal information disclosure can be as effective as total secrecy.

Sometimes information is 'hidden' in the structure of local government. Only certain officers or members may be aware of it. It may be tacit information, a matter of informal understanding between a few officials. If they are in different departments, these are very difficult sources to uncover.

Finding the Way in Sheffield Town Hall

The difficulties faced by the layman in finding out about planning proposals have been documented in another case, by John Peaden, a Methodist minister who became involved in an action group in Sharrow, an inner-city area of Sheffield beset by familiar housing and traffic problems.

Initially the main difficulty for the group was in obtaining information on the clearance programme and the major by-pass proposal. When as Minister of a local church I asked about the latter I was shown a plan which was covered by sheets of foolscap paper revealing only the church site and a small section of the road about thirty feet from the rear door. Rumours were stimulated by the local authority's secretive manner. Uncertainty was producing rapid deterioration of property and a great deal of social stress. The origins of resident activity lay in the increasing anger caused by uncertainty.

A few months after the formation of the action group the chairman and I discovered once again how difficult it was to find out about policy at the Town Hall. We had to deal with different receptionists and several departments before getting the beginnings of a picture. Information is still the most pressing issue in redevelopment areas like Sharrow. When the local councillor was chairman of the group, information came through her internal contacts. After she resigned it was less easy.[7]

In the face of these difficulties the action group set up their own information and action centre. The officials in Sheffield, according to Peaden, gave little or no help with the venture, perhaps because they saw it as a threat to their own information service. But in the end local authority officers were actually using the centre, even though it was still not recognised by the authority, to help them in their work.

John Peaden describes some of the nitty gritty of secrecy and the attempt to combat it. An official was careful, for instance, to show Peaden only the effects of the new road on the property in which Peaden had shown an obvious interest and to conceal the rest with blank paper – an absurdity that created more uncertainty and resentment than it allayed.

Cases like Sharrow highlight the problem of where to go to find information that may not even exist. This is a matter of local government management. There need to be clear, quick, reliable paths to information. To facilitate access, people need intelligible and comprehensive guides to the structure of their local authority, with the names of individuals who can help them find their way in.

It is regrettable that local councillors either cannot, or sometimes choose not, do more. Why should Sharrow's elected member have had to chair the action group in order to be helpful? Was her time only available if she had that status? Did she find a conflict of interest when she had resigned? The form of representative democracy which we have in this country surely places responsibilities on elected members to keep their electorate informed. To ask officers to take on this role is to bypass the councillor. But councillors may wish not to disclose information, perhaps for political reasons. Alternatively, some information may only have been made available to them 'in confidence'. More generally, councillors at present have neither the time nor the expertise to digest and pass on to each other, let alone their constituents, even quite salient background information on policy formulation. It is an issue that councillors themselves ought to be asked to face.

Deliberate Misunderstandings

In Sharrow the residents faced the all-too-common and familiar problems of getting access to the local authority. The 'sheets of foolscap paper' concealing the supposedly irrelevant parts of a plan may appear petty. But the events described by Norman Dennis in his two books on people and planning in Sunderland are an even more outstanding instance of the pettiness and ambiguity into which people get sucked in their legitimate search for information.[8] (Indeed, the victims become tainted with the same shortcomings. Dennis is forced into a peculiarly contorted narrative in parts of his *Public Participation and Planners' Blight*[9].)

The motif of *Public Participation and Planners' Blight* is control of the content and flow of information by a planning authority. Sometimes issues were clouded by apparently deliberate misunderstandings by the planners. The following sequence is an example. On 31 March 1969 Sunderland Borough Council held a public meeting at which a map of redevelopment proposals for Millfield was introduced. The format of the map – for example, its small scale – made it difficult for the audience to read. The Millfield Residents' Association wrote to the planning department asking for a copy of the map which they might show to a meeting of their group on 14 April. No response was made to their request. After further requests by telephone the Association eventually received a letter at the end of July promising that the map would be made available. After further prompting the map was finally handed over on 14 August.

This is a very small incident. But it was one of many which served over a long period to keep the residents of Millfield in considerable uncertainty as to what was to happen to their homes – when they might be demolished and for what purpose. Its significance is not just that the map was not handed over when it was first requested, but that the planning department claimed in their letter of 28 July that the map had not been completed until the middle of June. According to Dennis the map handed over in August was identical to that referred to at the public meeting in March. The planners appear to have allowed themselves to misunderstand just which map the Association was asking for. The planners ought reasonably to have assumed that the Association only knew about the map shown in March, and was unlikely to have been asking for one that was apparently still being drawn and to which it could scarcely have had access. However trivial and stupid this incident may appear, it is typical of very many anecdotes about people's experience when they try to find out what planners are devising.

When novel events are threatened – and the redevelopment of one's neighbourhood is novel enough – people are in a hurry to learn the facts. It is important to recognise just how irritating delays can be to the public in their contacts with government, and how destructive of a workable relationship between the two. The Royal Town Planning Institute, however, apparently supports the principle of deferment: 'The Institute is aware that the publication of carefully selected information, out of context or before a full picture is available, can prejudice decisions in a harmful way. . . . The authority should therefore have the right to withhold information until a reasonably comprehensive picture is available, provided that it is released well before any decision is taken.'[10]

It is assumed here, without justification, that planners but not lay people can think and act rationally in the absence of comprehensive information – whatever that may be. It is also implied that there is only one terminal decision of any significance. Of course a council takes that final decision. But there are many technically more significant decisions beforehand. The Millfield map episode is ambiguous as well as petty. One feels for Dennis and the residents. But of course the motivation of the officers in a case like this may not have been to obstruct legitimate public involvement and comment. There may have been a genuine, if unfortunate, misunderstanding about a map; a lack of sympathy for the residents' urgency; or a failure to communicate between officers themselves. The explanation may again lie in local government management, as well as perhaps in the calibre of its staff.

My own impression has been that local government is more secretive than central government in its routine operations, and that this is partly due to personnel factors, particularly at the junior levels. In local government, junior officials have more contact with the public, but with inadequate briefing and with an imperfect understanding of much of the work of government. The committee system makes of elected representatives a burden on officers which is not paralleled in central government, and there is an insecurity among local government officers on matters such as accountability and local politics which is apt to make them much more cautious about disclosing information.*

Commercial Confidentiality
Property Developers in London

Two other well-documented cases revolve around issues of commercial confidentiality of a kind which planners are frequently drawn into and which raise legitimate problems for freedom of information reform. The first again involved a neighbourhood threatened with redevelopment – the area around Tolmers Square in central London. The second concerned projected pit closures in Nottinghamshire.

The Tolmers Square neighbourhood was a twelve-acre site just off the Euston Road, in the central London Borough of Camden. Its story is a typical one, of central city redevelopment and of events which closely affect the lives of the people who live and work in such areas. Originally Tolmers Square was a residential area of Georgian and Victorian terraced houses, but by the 1960s its buildings and uses had become much more diverse. It offered both housing and a wide variety of employment to working-class native English people and a changing population of many other nationalities. As one resident described it, 'It was a place with atmosphere, always alive – everyone knew each other'.[11]

For eighteen years, from 1957 to 1976, a battle was fought between property developers, who wanted to redevelop the area for offices, and the community which stood to suffer considerable disruption and loss if the development occurred. The community was represented by the Tolmers Square Tenants' Association and subsequently by the Tolmers Village Association. The story of their efforts is told by Nick Wates in *The Battle for Tolmers Square*. He concludes that as a pressure group the Village Association was effective enough; but because it was not allowed to become involved in the decision-making process its long-term impact was small. Underlying this was a lack of information which greatly limited the potential for community action.

The crucial areas of ignorance concerned land ownership and the substance of the negotiations between the developers, Stock

* But see, for example, Chapter Four, Housing, for a different view of town hall *versus* Whitehall secrecy.

Conversion, and the London Borough of Camden. Negotiations were under way for five years before Camden publicly acknowledged them. By this time Stock Conversion had been acquiring property in the area for nine years and had become the major landowner. Negotiations between the two parties were confidential. Not all matters of potential interest to third parties were recorded; and many of the records which did exist were only available in a file in the town clerk's office. Even if one knew of their existence, neither a member of the public nor a councillor would have had a right of access to them. The appeal to commercial confidentiality in such cases effectively keeps a very tight control on the disclosure of information.

Even if there had been a right of access, an applicant might have been 'caught between' the planning and the town clerk's departments, particularly if the crucial information was split between them or existed only as an interdepartmental 'understanding'. Any scheme of reform as applied to local government should stipulate that responsibility for the release of information rests with the council as a whole and not with constituent departments. Otherwise the transfer of applications for access from one council department to another could be used to create delays in meeting requests from the public.

For the Tolmers Village Association the dearth of information went further. They were denied access to any statistical details about the area and had to conduct their own time-consuming surveys. In 1975 Camden Borough published an extensive planning survey containing information on population, housing, employment and traffic. Its function was 'to provide information which can be used by everyone to discuss problems and needs and to evaluate the worth of the various policies which the Plan might contain'.[12] But, as Wates pointed out, the plan revealed nothing about land ownership, land values, office rents or the activities of development companies. Without details of these a discussion would necessarily be ill informed. Yet not only were details not revealed to the public, adequate information was not available to Camden Council itself. If the information had existed, it might well have been difficult to locate or collate. Workable right of access proposals must contain safeguards against hard-pressed or inefficient authorities for whom any complex application would cause some disruption. Because of the possibility of hiding behind 'missing information', we need to consider too whether freedom of information legislation might not require authorities in certain circumstances both to collect information and to make it available. Many urban and county councils have intelligence units to whom the task could be given; more could be established.

I have already pointed to the local councillor as a weak instrument in the exercise of more open government. His or her own lack of the right of access to certain information, as in Camden and the Barnsbury case discussed earlier, underlies the threat to representative democracy which secrecy can entail. But if any solution to secrecy bypasses or discounts the elected representative, the threat will not disappear. Another instance both of this factor and of commercial confidentiality is found in the case of the Nottinghamshire coal fields related below.

Commercial confidences are held by local government as they are by central government, the nationalised industries and other bodies. Most legislative proposals for freedom of information have incorporated an exemption clause for the purpose of protecting confidentiality. The difficulty is to devise a means of counterbalancing the competing claims of *genuine* confidentiality with those of public interest. One solution would be to allow for the disclosure of parts of documents, but in practice this might well awaken considerable scepticism – shadows of the pieces of foolscap paper in Sharrow. Partial information, I have already suggested, can be more disruptive than total secrecy.

The Coal Board in Nottinghamshire

In the autumn of 1976 Ken Coates, an adult education lecturer, was told by a former student that he had heard of a plan for the phased closing of all the collieries in the Ashfield area of Nottinghamshire, together with others to the west of the county.[13] The plan was apparently contained in information supplied by the National Coal Board to the Nottinghamshire County Council, as part of the process of preparing a structure plan for the county. (Structure plans are written statements of a local authority's general policy for large-scale structural change over twenty-year periods. They deal with such matters as employment, industry, housing and commerce.) On enquiry it emerged that neither the area executive of the National Union of Mineworkers nor county councillors knew of the plan, despite its consequences for those whom they represented. As Coates puts it:

. . . about one-third of the miners of the large condemned area are young enough to be compelled, within a relatively short time, either to uproot themselves, or to commute for considerable distances, in order to be able to carry on in their chosen jobs. Firstly, they have a right to know what to expect. Secondly, they need to know in time to be able to put up any alternative proposals which seem sensible to them. Thirdly, and crucially important, they have a right to insist that any new mining developments will avoid the dreadful and callous mistakes of the Robens era.[14]

Over the next few months the hornets were very active, with the upshot that by February of the following year:

As far as the newspaper reader of Ashfield would have known up to this time, then, this was the state of affairs: allegations that a secret County Council planning report existed, and that it forecast widespread pit closures in West Nottinghamshire, had first been denied, and then confirmed, by a variety of public officials. Having confirmed them, the chairman of the appropriate Council committee had first called for their publication, and threatened to invoke the assistance of the Secretary of State for Energy [Tony Benn], and then later offered the view that the report in question was unimportant, outdated, and inaccurate, even though, at the time in question, he admitted he had still not seen it. Rightly or wrongly, important union spokesmen had been quoted as dismissing the whole notion that there might possibly be something to worry about in the scheduled report. The Coal Board had denied giving the County Council any information which was not already openly available to the miners.[15]

Quite apart from any doubts about secret consultations between two public bodies, without reference to the electorate, the elected representatives or the trade union concerned, the confused sequence of allegations and denials – not uncommon when concealment is attempted – is in itself highly damaging to people's faith in political and industrial democracy.

Why was secrecy thought necessary? The planning officers had accepted the need for it because the Coal Board would only supply the information in the offending report on condition that it was confidential to them. The extraordinary result was that one of the twelve topic reports prepared for the Nottinghamshire structure plan's 'report of survey' – that dealing with coal mining – was available only in summary form. But not even the severest critics of the Ashfield incident suggested that the planners were acting in any way that was not entirely proper.

The Coal Board's justification after the event was that the information in the report was tentative and could unnecessarily raise fears in the community about events which would not be realised. In a meeting with the miners' union in March 1977 the Board explained that '. . . the mining estimates provided by the Board reflected the situation as it then appeared two years earlier. Similar estimates provided for an earlier planning study had proved to be about 50 per cent wrong as a result of changed circumstances, such as oil price increases and improved mining methods.'[16]

Projections had been requested for up to twenty years in accordance with structure planning procedures at the time. However, this was outside the normal planning time-scale of the Board and made accuracy impossible. The Board said that already, after two years, the predictions for 1986 had been shown to be wrong and that anything beyond that was guesswork.

It is difficult to know what to make of these admissions. Is it not possible to publish tentative projections, and at the same time to underline why they are necessarily tentative? What is the status of the structure plan if parts of it are based on inaccurate information? And, what is the value of the £60,000 public participation exercise which Nottinghamshire mounted for the draft structure plan? As the local newspaper commented in January 1977:

The public, local authorities and other organisations and bodies are being asked to make their comments on the proposals in the plan.
What, it is being asked, is the use of bothering to make these comments if they will be ignored because those who have made the proposals have not revealed the true reason for making them? Anything which is said, possibly after a great deal of research and trouble, would be a waste of time because the planners have unrevealed information to use against them.[17]

Astute research and interpretation by Coates suggests that the Coal Board may not have been bothered so much by the possible inaccuracy of their manpower projections as by their social implications. Firstly, in the material which was published, a decline in mining employment was given separately for the ten-year periods 1976–86 and 1986–96. Despite the implication at several points that the decline would be spread over a twenty-year period, Coates concludes that pit closures would be likely to bunch near the middle of the period, with obvious consequences for communities. Secondly, the impression was given that the decline would be due primarily to the exhaustion of geological reserves. The alternative interpretation, however, is that it would enable manpower redeployment to occur. Faced with an ageing work-force the Coal Board could not hope to recruit sufficient numbers to keep existing short-life pits in operation given their relatively high manpower requirements. The new generation of ultra-modern pits, for example Selby or the Vale of Belvoir, will require many fewer miners. Coates' interpretation is that older collieries would only be kept open so long as necessary to 'store' younger labour until redeployment to the new pits was possible. In other words, what the pit closures are essentially about is the necessity for the younger generation of miners to accept a considerable upheaval in their lives in middle age. The secrecy around the plan deprives them of any chance of making adequate preparations, of whatever sort, for that outcome.

Many of the issues underlying what happened in Ashfield featured in our other case studies – the ignorance of councillors, the uncertainty produced by denials and counter-denials, and the ambiguity of the commercial customer's motives for secrecy. A new element in the Ashfield case is the defence of imperfect information, its tentative nature being used as a reason for not disclosing it. This suggests that there is a distinction to be made between different levels of information. How are these levels to be defined? Is it possible in practice to distinguish between factual matter and expert opinion or technical judgement? Would a defective legislative expression of this distinction enable the National Coal Board, for instance, to cover itself in future on the grounds that the information available consisted of 'guesstimates' and not fact? Should the Ashfield miners be kept in ignorance, in the wider public interest? Depending on the answers to such questions, the possibility may arise of officials learning to hide behind tentative information. In planning matters a great deal is highly tentative.

The Nottinghamshire coal mining example raises a slightly different question about commercial confidentiality. What are the commercial interests of a state monopoly in this context? Could education or health authorities plead the overriding considerations of their competition with the private sector as a justification for refusal to disclose? Might planners apply an excessively broad interpretation of any confidentiality exemption because not to do so would, in their view, impair their ability to obtain such information in the future? What implications would such a policy hold for the involvement of planners in participation exercises? Their stance during public discussions of structure plans could be an awkward one. Inconsistencies in official information and policy revealed at an inquiry do not have to be settled then and there. But where jobs, homes, and communities are at stake they can leave a bad taste in the mouth.

Public Participation in Planning

The availability of information on planning matters is not a new issue. As a result of incidents like those described above there was increasing pressure from the public during the 60s for a more open approach. Government also came to recognise the potential value of telling the public more, largely as a result of the confusion into which the inquiry system had fallen. Public dissatisfaction had led to a volume of planning inquiries which was difficult to handle. The atmosphere of confrontation at many inquiries was obscuring the administrative goal, which was to use them to better inform government on contentious issues. (See Chapter Eight for examples of secrecy engendering confrontation at road planning inquiries.) The planning profession was also moving towards a more participatory mode of operation.

The ground was prepared, in the late 60s, for a form of statutory participation with the 1968 Town and Country Planning Act.[18] Despite the ambitious discussions in those years of what participation should or could be, the Act went no further than to make a general statement to ensure that the public who wanted to be involved in commenting on statutory planning proposals had an opportunity to do so and had sufficient information to enable them to understand and judge the proposals. In other words, there was to be a limited publication of information. No definition was offered of how to judge the adequacy of the information.

'Public participation' is a different concept from 'freedom of information'. But because of its recent history, its statutory concentration on the release of information and the careful monitoring of a number of early cases of participation, it may be worth examining its course to look for lessons for the subject of this book. Certainly, where local authority planning departments are concerned, the question of freedom of information is and will be seen in the light of experience with public participation.

As a profession, planning has in the past been more active in collecting information than in disseminating it. In local government its task is control rather than service provision. It seeks information in order to have a rational basis for the control of applications to develop land. The information is drawn from many fields – architecture, engineering, economics, agriculture, and so on – and is highly technical. Information collection, and particularly the development and use of 'data banks', became a skill on which planners prided themselves. It was assumed that the information was too specialised and complex for anyone but the professional to digest.

In the 60s the public inquiry was the medium which gave the widest scope for effective public involvement in planning. But that, too, was based on the principle of information *collection*. Its primary administrative purpose was to enable the public to inform the Secretary of State on relevant matters which might not otherwise come to his attention and thereby improve the quality of his decision.

More recently, in the era of participation, information collection has been pursued as a high art, in the form of the sample survey of public attitudes, priorities and reactions.[19] Many authorities have now used surveys, and have claimed that they are participatory, even though, since they canvas only a sample of opinions, they actually 'disenfranchise' most of the population. However, not only do they illustrate the penchant of planners to turn an activity, such as participation, into a specialised and quantitative craft, they also promote an aura of secrecy. Surveys are usually conducted in a vacuum. Respondents are rarely told why questions are being asked nor the use to which their answers might be put – except in the most general and uninformative terms. Technical reasons to do with survey interpretation are used to justify keeping respondents in ignorance of what is behind it all. The point to be made is that behind much apparent secrecy is an assumption of self-justifying expertise and a belief that the planners' job is to find out, not to tell. The coyness over sample surveys extends to their results. It is extremely rare for them to be fed back to the respondents who gave their time and thought to providing them.

Many of the participation exercises of the 70s appeared to show a measure of public involvement. Certainly a small percentage of the population responded in most cases. But people are not used to participation nor to a free flow of information from government. When it is offered they may not recognise it nor know what to do with it. At the same time, there is evidence from a number of sources that people do feel under-informed.

For example, my own research, conducted in north-east Lancashire, suggested that a majority of the population feel that they

are given too little information about what was going to happen
in their area, specifying road planning and housing as particular
examples.[20] The concern over lack of information exceeded any
desire for a greater involvement in decision-making. (Presumably
people have a right to information and are free also to disregard
it or not act upon it.) This work also brought out people's ideas
on how they would like to be kept informed: by notices in the
newspaper and by leaflets delivered to their homes. People do
seem to understand that to be informed about events is to gain
control of them, if only by having the opportunity to anticipate
change and adapt their view of the world. To be surprised by
events through ignorance is to be powerless and deprived.

The Benefits of Participation

Some critics say that participation in planning has achieved very
little. But against the situation prior to 1968 it has achieved a
great deal. Much more information is published than before. Public meetings, exhibitions, newspaper supplements and leaflets have
become commonplace in any planning exercise. Efforts are made
to tap public opinion. Public reaction to proposals is noted and in
a number of cases has led to significant changes in a plan. Inno-
vative techniques have been introduced – tape-slide presentations,
planning 'kits' and community forums.

What can be achieved is best seen at local level, and particularly
when the planners have something specific to 'sell'. It may be that
the benefits of a freer access to information generally will appear
in similar circumstances. For example, one of the first housing
action areas (HAAs) to be declared in Wales was in Pennar, an
urban community in south Pembrokeshire. The initiative came
originally from the residents. But the local authority's response
was striking. Participation was, unusually, mounted as an inter-
departmental and cooperative exercise. The aim was to explain
the HAA scheme to the local inhabitants and encourage them to
take up the grants for house improvement which were available.
An action group of street representatives was formed, together
with local councillors and officers, which met every six weeks. A
newsheet was published every two months. Public meetings were
held, which were attended by residents of nearly all the 179 houses
eligible for a grant; a highly imaginative and successful tape-slide
show was given. A show house was opened to exhibit the possibilities of improvement grant work, where residents could talk
informally with councillors and officers. The two Pennar district

councillors also toured houses, talking to people, explaining the scheme and encouraging the take-up of grants. Everyone concerned with the exercise, as well as research workers who monitored it, agreed that it was a success.[21]*

When a local government department has a clear motive for issuing information and does the job itself, it can make a success of it. The difficulty about a lot of planning work, however, is that it is unclear to the planner what might be his objectives in participation, technically or professionally. It has been very difficult to show that development plans covering more than one or two streets or a localised facility, such as a recreation area, are any the better for participation. One could hope that an informed public could use (or boycott) more purposefully the results of a plan when implemented. But again it is difficult to demonstrate this.

One of the main conclusions of research into participation has been that planners neglect to specify their objectives. Their exercises then become formless and their effectiveness cannot be properly evaluated. But as far as freedom of information is concerned, they have learnt by this past mistake. In their draft statement on this issue a committee of the Royal Town Planning Institute took care to spell out the benefits to planning of a greater availability of information:

The constraints within which planning must operate would be better understood, leading to more realistic proposals.

The difficulties which arise where one authority is effectively advocating the policy of another authority or Government department about which it has reservations would be reduced.

An informed public will expect and appreciate a better environment.

In an activity which involves much co-ordination, secrecy is an obstruction to action.

The opportunities for corruption will be reduced as more people know what is going on.

Those affected by planning decisions will better understand the reasons.

The use of planning to strengthen authority against the interests of private individuals will be more difficult.

The distinction between professional advice and political choice will be better understood.

The information will be useful to those who wish to advance community

* For a different perspective on Housing Action Areas see pp. 45–46.

self-help and self-determination as a means of improving the environment.

The distinction between the planning and the financial interests of the authorities will be better understood.[22]

This is a mixed and ambitious list of potential benefits. One could discuss some of them quite critically. But what is important is that they represent an imaginative, positive and active approach to the disclosure of information – a point to which we shall return shortly. The RTPI claim to have been the first of the professions to campaign for freedom of information. In doing so they recognised that legislation requiring public participation in certain areas of planning did not go far enough.

Lessons from Participation in the 70s

In participation exercises there have often been shortcomings beyond the failure to specify objectives. Where the giving of information has gone wrong, over and over again one can attribute the failure to the particular way in which local government officers and professional planners have learnt to work. These are factors to do with the procedures and structure of the organisation and the profession; and they are for that reason likely to influence the implementation of any act dealing with freedom of information.

When information is released, planners generally insist on its 'accuracy' – prompted by professional pride in their product and by concern for their accountability. As we have seen, information is the planner's stock-in-trade. He digests large amounts of it through surveys of different kinds. (And he publishes it. For example, the recent 'reports of survey' for the Ipswich sub-region structure plan on topics such as population and housing were some 700 pages in total, nearly six centimetres in thickness and three kilos in weight.) The plan which he creates is in a sense no more than a bundle of information. It is the officers in other departments who run the schools or produce the houses. It is not surprising if the planner is resistant to his product being published in a digested or summarised form. But this has meant that the content of much publicity is too complex and detailed for most of the public, with topics in which they are very interested buried among technicalities of much less interest.

Planners have tended to assume that it is they who should formulate, write up and publish the information, although they admit to no special skills or training for the task. It is assumed that planners should arrange and man public meetings and exhibitions. But these events might look more genuinely participatory and their content be more intelligible if other members of the community took some responsibility for re-interpreting the available information. Whether a message is attended to, let alone understood, depends a lot on whom it is coming from.

If the disclosure of information is to mean more than its availability, simply, to an élite who have the skills, motivation and opportunity to unravel its technical complexity and sheer bulk, the nature of what is assumed to be 'informative' has to be considered, as well as the form and manner of its availability. Information is only information if it can be used by someone. But it is possible for information which is relevant to someone's interests to be pitched at a level which defeats them. One can well imagine how the National Coal Board's projections in Nottinghamshire could have been disclosed; and how the data would have been of little or no help in enabling miners to appreciate the effects of it all on their lives over the next few decades. The miners should not have to rely on the presence and goodwill of a specialised interpreter of the information. (The National Union of Mineworkers appear to have been a rather sleepy watchdog over Ashfield.)

'Availability', 'disclosure' or 'freedom' of information do not guarantee 'accessibility'. The Sharrow Action Group knew that information was available. It may have been freely available, with no hint of secrecy. But they knew that they lacked the keys to make it accessible. Participation exercises have shown that even apparently energetic methods of publishing information by local government reach only a small fraction of the intended or potentially interested audience. The local authority is an unfamiliar source of information. And local government itself is uneasy about breaking down the barriers between government and the electorate by having one of its officials penetrate community networks and carry information back and forth. (This disquiet has been expressed, for example, in experiments with environmental liaison officers.[23] It was doubted whether someone could work in and for both local government and the community without betraying confidences or being seduced by one party.)

These observations on participation – and they may well extend to disclosure – suggest a need for changes in conventional attitudes, assumptions and ways of working in local government. Simply introducing the 'adequate publicity' of the 1968 Act or a general right to 'freedom of information' cannot cure all ills. Secrecy in local government is a symptom of structural features. A conclusion of research on public participation has been that it was tacked on to the planning process, and that to be really worthwhile it had to become an integrated and necessary part of the process.

An Active Approach to Freedom of Information

To judge by the experiences with participation, a blanket requirement to disclose information would be too passive a step. It would also tend to treat the public as mere recipients, ready to sop up anything put their way. But different people need different information at different times and places. If there is a misfit between needs and information, communication goes awry. An active approach to information would go further than eliminating secrecy: it would involve disclosing the right information to the right people at the right moment.

Mistakes in participation exercises have meant that the public often receive information which is purely technical, or from their viewpoint too partial. Reports of survey and planning proposals are published; but not the rationale for technical decisions, the underlying policy issues, the intended means of implementation, or advice on how the outcomes could be enjoyed by citizens. Other missing items have included 'follow-up' information – successful communication is rarely the one-off process of much participation. Secondary information, about the participation process itself, has been available only from the limited viewpoint of the planners – their time-table, needs and expectations. When people react to proposals, they are not always told of others' contributions. Details of whom has been informed of what, and of whom has responded, may be important in enabling effective participation.

The validity of these criticisms is of course open to debate. They contain much that is ideological. They do not take into account the unpreparedness of the planning profession and of local government machinery for the potential of participation; both are being invited to change radically. Above all, the criticisms go a long way beyond what was, taken literally, an unadventurous, limited piece of enabling legislation. The 1968 Act only requires authorities to give 'adequate publicity' to their reports of survey and planning proposals; and to ensure that people who 'may be expected to desire an opportunity of making representations to the authority with respect to those matters' should be given that opportunity and should have their representations considered. One has to look further to know the spirit behind the Act.

After enactment, planning authorities wanted to know where to look; some were insistent that central government advise them on how to comply with the legislation. It is clear that the same need would follow enactment on freedom of information. For example, the Royal Town Planning Institute has already suggested a principle of discretion for authorities in providing information. They refer to the quantity of information potentially involved; the problems of storage and retrieval; the need to distinguish between important and trivial information; and the need to frustrate people who ask for information purely to delay action. Rather than see these problems lead to a discretionary principle, however, the sensible course would be to advise planners how to deal with them. With regard to storage and retrieval, for example, authorities could both be advised of appropriate techniques and required to put them into practice. The Advisory Council on Public Records could play an important role by instituting its own research, drawing up detailed codes of practice and monitoring progress.

Let us extrapolate from the example of participation. Ten years after an act on freedom of information we would certainly predict the disappearance of any blanket secrecy. More will be known about the inside of planning departments than before, at least by a minority of interested, and probably sophisticated, individuals. In some authorities considerable pains will have been taken to engage in active information disclosure. In a majority, perhaps, a reactive attitude will have ruled, with the onus placed on the public to be aware of what they wish to know and to ask for it. Here and there, where resources are allocated and where officers and councillors are willing to rethink their habits of governing, we shall be able to see what a positive approach to information disclosure could mean. If adult education gives a strong lead to teach people about the informational base of local government and how to use it, we shall see their increased involvement in monitoring and influencing the policies which affect them. The most important gain will be the cure of that distrust which enforced ignorance creates, and a sense in people of their incorporation in government as a simple consequence of it presenting an open face. To achieve this one needs to look beyond enactment.

The key will be the advice and guidance with which legislation is supported.

REFERENCES

1 Ferris, John, 'Participation in Urban Planning: The Barnsbury case'. Occasional Papers on Social Administration, no. 48, G. Bell, 1972.
2 Ministry of Housing and Local Government, *People and Planning*, HMSO, 1969, appendix 10, pp. 70–71.
3 Ferris, John, *op.cit.*, p. 61.
4 *Ibid.*
5 Royal Town Planning Institute, *Draft Policy Statement on Open Government*, September 1979, p. 2.
6 Ferris, John, *op.cit.*, p. 64.
7 Peaden, John, 'A Sheffield Action Group', in Darke, R., and Walker, R, (eds.), *Local Government and the Public*, Leonard Hill, 1977, pp. 143–159.
8 Dennis, Norman, *People and Planning*, Faber and Faber, 1970, and *Public Participation and Planners' Blight*, Faber and Faber, 1972.
9 See especially chapters 13–16 on 'information control'.
10 Royal Town Planning Institute, *op. cit.*
11 Quoted in Wates, Nick, *The Battle for Tolmers Square*, Routledge & Kegan Paul, 1976, p. 9.
12 Quoted *ibid.*, p. 154.
13 Coates, Ken, *Ashfield: What's Going Wrong?* Institute for Workers' Control, Nottingham, 1977.
14 *Ibid.*, p. 28.
15 *Ibid.* p. 9.
16 *Ibid.*, p. 22.
17 *Mansfield Chronicle Advertiser*, quoted *ibid.*, p. 20.
18 Town and Country Planning Act, 1968. This legislation followed a report of the Department of the Environment's Planning Advisory Group.
19 The material in the rest of the chapter is based on Boaden, Noel, Goldsmith, Michael, Hampton, William and Stringer, Peter, *Planning and Participation in Practice*, Pergamon, 1980; and on associated research reports published by the Department of the Environment and Sheffield University.
20 Stringer, Peter, *Tuning in to the Public: Survey before Participation,* Linked Research Project into Public Participation in Structure Planning, Interim Research Paper 14, Sheffield University, 1978.
21 The Pennar example is based on unpublished research material gathered by the author.

22 Royal Town Planning Institute, *op.cit.*, p. 1.
23 For example in, Hampton, William, *Providing the Posh Words . . .*, Department of the Environment, 1978.

Transport 8
Mick Hamer

Much information about our road, rail and bus networks – and the way these are planned and run – is denied to the public. In this chapter, Mick Hamer reviews examples of secrecy in the Department of Transport during recent years, in particular over three crucial transport issues: new road routes, the closure of railway lines, and the weight of heavy lorries. He argues, too, that unnecessary secrecy – for instance over proposed rail cuts in the 1970s – can rebound on civil servants and ministers. His conclusions include a proposal for a cheap and simple means of arranging for public access to information held by the Department of Transport.

Transport Users' Consultative Committees (TUCCs) are quangos. They were set up under the 1947 Transport Act with the principal purpose of safeguarding the interests of travellers on what is now British Rail. In 1962 their terms of reference were narrowed. And when I was appointed to one TUCC in 1976 it was not even up to giving British Rail a nip in the leg.

An enormous range of information on Britain's transport is held by one government department – the Department of Transport. The DTp is responsible for British Rail (although not of course for its day-to-day management), the administration of the transport supplementary grant system, vehicle licensing, ports and docks, the regulation of the road haulage and bus industries, and the trunk road system. Some of these responsibilities, most importantly trunk roads, are exercised by the Welsh Office in Wales and the Scottish Office in Scotland. The nationalised industry boards – for rail, bus and air – and the local authorities – whose transport responsibilities include all non-trunk roads – of course hold their own share of information. And like central government departments they are selective about the information they release. This chapter concentrates on the area I know at first hand, the responsibilities of the Department of Transport for inland surface transport.[1]

The type of information which the Department of Transport possesses ranges from statistics (for example on the age and sex of vehicle drivers and details of bus operations), through technical standards (like those on bridge safety), to financial and policy details. Some of this information is available. Policy white papers are published at intervals by HMSO. The DTp and its research arm – the Transport and Road Research Laboratory – publish research results and other data. But the bulk of the DTp's information is not published.[2]

This unpublished information falls roughly into four classes. The first and largest class is not published in part for the very good reason that publication would be prohibitively expensive. Some of these facts and figures are 'freely' available. Statistics on car registration by companies and private citizens, and how precisely these break down into a variety of categories are one example. There are not many problems getting access to these details, providing the right person is asked. This proviso is important. It assumes the right person can be found – not always easy. Ask the wrong person and the answer may be along the lines of 'I'm afraid we don't have the information in the form you want it.' Which translated is either a simple attempt to fob off or reflects genuine ignorance. Generally, requests for information which is – in theory – freely available only founder because the caller fails to track his way through the bureaucracy: civil servants' reactions should not in such circumstances be regarded as evidence of conspiracy.

The second class of unpublished information is that which the Department of Transport – in common with other government agencies – keeps properly under wraps. This is the information collected from firms and individuals on the understanding that it is given in confidence. This applies, for instance, to the National Travel Survey data, collected periodically, where the DTp will not reveal details about the households that contributed to the Survey. Similar confidentiality applies to the annual Road Goods Survey and to the vehicle licensing details held at Swansea. Clearly, an official right of access to information like this would be a gross infringement of personal liberty. A balance has to be struck between the usefulness of the information on the one hand and confidentiality on the other, and in this area the DTp has, in my view, got the balance about right.

More questionable are the Department of Transport's motives in the third class of unpublished information. The DTp always refuses to give details of reports prior to publication – a not uncommon tactic in many organisations. In government departments, there are two reasons for this kind of embargo.

One is parliamentary privilege. MPs are jealous of their rights. It is ministers who formally present white papers to Parliament. So the release, for instance, of the 1977 Transport Policy white paper to journalists under an embargo – a convention which bars publication until a specified date – but before the white paper was presented to Parliament provoked protests in the House about breach of privilege.[3]

The second reason is the wish to manage publicity – again a common, although more questionable, characteristic of many organisations including government departments. One example was the Minister's announcement of the status and standard of part of the planned Oxford – Birmingham M40 motorway, on the last day that Parliament sat before it rose for Easter 1980.[4] Parliamentary questions with such judicious timing are normally prompted by ministers. In this case, what would have been an important news story and a controversial ministerial decision missed Saturday's papers entirely, made a small appearance in one Sunday paper and featured briefly on Tuesday (there were no papers on Good Friday or Monday bank holiday). Officially, the DTp avers that the timing of this announcement was a 'cock-up' – an excuse that does have a certain ring of truth. The timing of publication can be crucial and postponement can, as I argue below, be damaging to the interests of consumers *and* of the Department. But short-term embargoes like these are not particularly objectionable and are usually only of minor consequence.

The final category of unpublished information, and the one which is of greater interest and importance, is the material which the Department of Transport keeps most closely guarded, or tries to, and which it does not necessarily plan to release at all. Most of this relates to policy, or policy formation.

The Department undoubtedly sees the sensitivity of an issue as a sound and major reason for secrecy. In an internal report on the organisation of the Department's Transport and Road Research Laboratory, Mr Dan Gruffydd Jones, an Environment Department Under-Secretary, wrote:

A particular piece of research will sometimes lead to conclusions which conflict with established or evolving Ministerial policy. Given the tactical nature of Parliamentary politics this conflict can on occasion give rise to some embarrassment . . . embarrassment is best avoided by managing the conflict rather than by seeking to eliminate it . . . a Departmental R & D [Research and Development] establishment cannot expect to be entirely free to publish research conclusions at times of its own choosing. Political or commercial embarrassment can almost always be avoided by discussion beforehand and by sensible timing of publication, and any civil servant engaged in R & D must accept that this is a necessary feature of the environment in which he works.[5]

And a Transport and Road Research Laboratory circular forbidding staff to talk to the press says:

Because of increasing public and political interest in much of our work all staff must always be on their guard against giving to the media views, opinions or additional details on published or unpublished information . . . information officers are more experienced in handling media enquiries which, on occasion, can be very difficult and can easily lead to misquotation with serious consequences . . . initial contact, even if very brief, often stimulates follow-up questions, possibly of a sensitive nature.[6]

Three examples of politically sensitive subjects which the DTp keeps closely guarded are: proposals to build new roads; plans to close railway lines; and schemes to increase the weight of juggernauts. The saga of delay and obfuscation evident in the correspondence between the Welsh Office and a local resident over proposals for the Bangor by-pass (see p. 155) is just one example of official secrecy over road plans. It is arguable that the wealth of examples of Department of Transport secrecy on road routes, rail cuts and juggernauts is a simple reflection of increasing public interest in these issues. And the reasons for secrecy in any particular case are several: the motives of civil servants (and on occasion of their ministers) are sometimes honourable, sometimes distinctly dishonourable, and sometimes a mixture of both.

Results, for instance, must be verified: statistical data is checked and double-checked before it is released, and all the more carefully if it is going to be the subject of critical scrutiny at a public inquiry. There is also the problem of interpretation. Data or facts, and the output of research, as Gruffydd Jones noted, may appear to contradict established policy. On its own, a piece of information may be liable to 'misinterpretation'. This can range from a genuine

The Bangor By-pass:
A Calendar of 'Free' Information

Late 1977	The Welsh Office issues statutory notice of plans for the A55 Bangor by-pass.
5 Dec 1977	Mr Zaba, a local resident, writes to the Welsh Office to ask for more information and a copy of the 1970 traffic census – the main source of the traffic forecasts for the area.
Mid Dec 1977	The Welsh Office replies, threatening to charge for the general information, not mentioning the traffic census.
End Dec 1977	Mr Z writes again to ask for the traffic census.
14 Jan 1978	No reply has come from the Welsh Office. Mr Z writes to the Secretary of State for Wales to ask for the traffic census.
14 Feb 1978	No replies. Mr Z phones the Welsh Office and is told he will have a letter within days.
17 Feb 1978	The Welsh Office replies: the traffic census, it says, was carried out in 1970! And all the factual information was being collated and would be sent 'as soon as it is completed.'
27 Feb 1978	Mr Z writes to ask for the 1970 census, and when will the comprehensive document be ready?
8 Mar 1978	The Welsh Office replies: 'The points which you raise are being considered and a further letter will be sent to you in due course.' Mr Z gets the traffic census from his county council.
3 Apr 1978	Mr Z writes to the Welsh Office to ask for further specific data and – through his MP – to the Secretary of State.
11 Apr 1978	Parliamentary Under Secretary for Wales writes to MP, noting that Mr Z had now obtained the 1970 traffic census *and* offering access to the Welsh Office copy: 'in retrospect it might have been better if [Mr Z] had been offered a photocopy in the first instance. . . .'
6 July 1978	The Welsh Office writes to Mr Z, apologising for the 'inordinate delay' and giving brief and unhelpful replies to his specific queries.
3 Sep 1978	The Welsh Office sends Mr Z some information about the proposed road, including a booklet about public inquiries which says 'more information about the proposals . . . can be obtained from the appropriate office'. Mr Z writes to ask for the comprehensive document promised six months ago.
26 Oct 1978	The Welsh Office replies: 'it is considered that the information you require is contained in the statement . . . which has been sent to you'. Mr Z writes to the Welsh Office, itemising six deficiencies in the information so far supplied.
21 Nov 1978	The public inquiry opens. The information becomes freely available

danger of being taken out of context – an excuse which only really has any force when the background is also secret – to a disagreement within the Department over precisely what the information means.

Furthermore, a civil servant may be reluctant to authorise disclosure of information, more particularly information that affects a sensitive policy area, and even more so to an individual or organisation known to be antagonistic towards Department or government policy. When a civil servant is doubtful whether certain information should be disclosed, the procedure is to refer the decision upwards to a more senior civil servant who may in turn decline to take a decision. Even if the information is finally released, there can be a long delay.

There is some validity in this Civil Service caution. But this should not obscure the principal issue: does it make sense to keep information about transport from the public? Is secrecy desirable?

New Roads

The explanation for secrecy becomes clearer if we look at the way the Department of Transport deals with the public over road building plans. By controlling the quantity, quality and timing of information, it aims to avoid embarrassment for either the Civil Service or the government and to minimise opposition to Department policy.

The DTp fears, for example, that objectors may find grounds for criticising its case for a new road. Consequently it will only release what is usually highly technical information at a very late stage, thus preventing effective scrutiny of Department figures.

Bangor is not an isolated example. Every inquiry that I have been associated with – more than a dozen – has had its quota of complaints about the late production of information. At the inquiry into the M27 Swaythling Link proposal in Southampton, the traffic forecasting evidence was officially made available to objectors on the first day of the inquiry. Some of the main objectors, who had been pressing the Department of the Environment for their evidence, were allowed to inspect it at the DoE's Winchester office. The volume of material was far too much to analyse in one afternoon nor would the DoE allow copies to be taken away. (In this instance, the objectors were as sharp as the DoE. Left alone with the evidence later in the afternoon, they removed and photocopied it and posted it back to the DoE by the last post.[7])

Again, in October 1978 the Department of Transport announced that it was considering building a motorway – the M66 – between Denton and Middleton, and invited public participation to help decide which route the scheme should take. On 25 February 1979 the Greater Manchester Transport Action Group wrote to the DTp asking for details of the traffic forecasts and cost benefit analysis used to justify the scheme. Almost five months later, on 11 July, the DTp replied: it was not possible to provide the information. On 9 August the Action Group wrote again. The reply from the DTp did not come until 16 October: they 'did not feel justified in carrying out a costly special analysis at this early stage.' The cost of the M66 proposal in 1978 was £57 million. And according to the Action Group, the DTp does in fact have the information they want and it could be assembled without much difficulty.

At Winchester in 1976, the M3 Joint Action Group, which was campaigning against a proposed new road, argued for the upgrading of the existing Winchester by-pass as a more acceptable alternative. The Group raised over £40,000 and retained consultants – Associated Planning Consultants. According to a subsequent *Sunday Times* report, the consultants asked

for bore-hole data on subsoils; are told there are none; then that there are but they would be no use to them; then that there is a whole volume they can see; even eleven volumes. This takes two and a half months. The elusive data reveals flaws in the motorway calculations, in particular the deep peat in the water-meadows would add at least £2½ million to the cost.[8]

Even the start of a public inquiry does not necessarily take information out of the Department's protected classification. The inhabitants of one area of north London have had ten years' experience of official stubbornness over details of transport plans for their area. In 1962 Ernest Marples, then Minister of Transport, made the A1 through Hampstead Garden Suburb 'an experimental lorry route' from the newly-built M1 to London docks. This was before the widespread use of containers and the decline of the docks. In 1969, with the 'lorry route' experiment abandoned but a massive flow of heavy lorries established along this alignment, there was a plan to widen this section of the A1 to accommodate a six-lane dual carriageway. The scheme would have cut off a third of Dame Henrietta Barnett's model community from all its facilities – churches, schools, cinemas and shops – and it was opposed by the Hampstead Garden Suburb Lorry Route Joint Action Committee. Following a public inquiry, the scheme was shelved and a firm of consultants – Scott, Wilson, Kirkpatrick and Partners assisted by consultants from Sir Hugh Wilson and Lewis Wormersley – was employed by the Department of the Environment to investigate alternatives.

Come the summer of 1972, Peter Walker, who was then Secretary of State for the Environment, wrote to the Joint Action Committee to say that he expected the consultants' report to be ready by the end of the year. Time passed. And it slowly became clear that the DoE was reluctant to release the report. This, of course, simply served to increase the Joint Action Committee's curiosity about the report's contents. Pressure built up on the government until finally, in 1974, Environment Secretary Anthony Crosland informed the Committee that the consultants' report was to be 'confidential'.

The Joint Action Committee then turned to the Ombudsman, who had already upheld their previous complaint – that the DoE had misled and misinformed objectors about their plans to widen the road. The wheels of bureaucracy grind exceedingly slow. At the beginning of 1977, just as the Ombudsman's investigation was getting under way, the DoE suddenly announced that they had finished considering the consultants' report and that the only scheme acceptable – a tunnel underneath the suburb – was too expensive. The road proposal was therefore to be dropped from the list of road schemes under preparation.

Many objectors believed this to be a tactical withdrawal by the DoE. For at the same time that the Hampstead Garden Suburb route was being abandoned, the DoE was pressing ahead with plans to the north and south of the route, where an inquiry into the Archway Road scheme was actually in progress in 1977.

So the Joint Action Committee took their fight to get the consultants' report before the Archway inquiry. The Archway Road was an extremely controversial scheme. The inspectors conducting the inquiry came under considerable pressure, such that the first inspector had to be replaced and the inquiry re-started under a new one. Undoubtedly this made the second inspector, Ralph Rolph, much more inclined to consider reasoned and reasonable requests favourably. So when Terry Rand, chairman of the Joint Action Committee, argued that the consultants' report was relevant to the Archway scheme, inspector Ralph Rolph agreed with him and directed the Department of Transport to produce the report.

The DTp returned to the inquiry with an *edited* version of the consultants' report. Initially inspector Rolph was inclined to accept this version as adequate. Terry Rand complained that the full version was needed, and accompanied his submission with illustrative quotations. Such was the pressure on the inspector that he became convinced that his own edited version of the report was different to Mr Rand's edited version. (It wasn't.) The inspector claimed he lacked the authority to order the DTp to produce the full report, but, supported by George Stern of Stop the Archway Motorway Plan (STAMP), Mr Rand drew his attention to the Department's *Notes for the Guidance of Panel Inspectors*, which say that inspectors do have the power to direct the DTp to produce evidence. Exasperated, the inspector directed the Department of Transport to produce the consultants' report 'in its entirety'.

On the same day that the Department of Transport was ordered to produce the consultants' report, they were also asked to produce some further traffic figures. When the DTp repeatedly failed to provide the information ordered by the inspector, he adjourned the inquiry until they felt able to comply. Rather than provide the information which would have enabled the inquiry to continue, however, the DTp has permanently abandoned the inquiry and the proposal to widen the Archway Road is, for the moment, in abeyance. At the time of writing the consultants' report has not been published.[9]

What is the motive for the Department's steady resistance to the release of information like this? The north London objectors believe that the consultants' report contains details of plans to widen roads in neighbouring Finchley and that the DTp wanted to get the poorer areas like Archway completed before presenting Finchley with a *fait accompli*. The DTp's argument is that publication of the consultants' report would cause blight. It is an argument that has only limited force. In individual cases blight caused by road plans is relieved by issue of a blight notice which requires the highway authority to buy a house. The publication of various alternative routes would probably force the DTp to buy more houses – against which should be set the profit from re-selling many of them when the route was decided. In physical terms, the publication of more than one route would distribute blight over a wide area instead of concentrating it in a narrow band: to some extent the blight would be less severe but more widespread. The remedy for this problem – an inevitable consequence of road building in urban areas – is not secrecy. It is to pay adequate compensation to households affected by new roads and to ensure that the physical fabric of an area does not decline while alternatives are under consideration.

The Department's furtive tactics in its dealings with the public over road plans have been questioned time and again, and not only in cases involving objectors the DTp might class as destructive – people who would question the very premises on which DTp road planning is based.

In 1975 the Parliamentary Commissioner for Administration (the Ombudsman) was asked to investigate a complaint by Sydney Ostler, a Lincolnshire corn merchant, who had been the victim of secret dealing by the Department. Back in 1972 the DoE published proposals to complete a section of the Boston Inner Relief Road in Lincolnshire. In September 1973 there was a public inquiry into the proposals, but Mr Ostler did not object to the plans because, although the road would pass close to his premises, no land would be required and his business would not be affected. Come December of that year a County Council official, acting for the DoE, approached Mr Ostler and offered to buy part of his land. Only then did he discover it would be required for the new road after all.

What had happened was this. It is standard practice for highway authorities to try to resolve objections prior to a public inquiry. In August and September 1973 a series of secret agreements had been made between the Department of the Environment and three objectors. The DoE had given the objectors written guarantees. The line of the road had been moved. The objectors were mollified – but at Mr Ostler's expense. Although the modification of the scheme was revealed at the public inquiry, no one told him. And there was no reason why he should have been expected to know or to find out.

Once an order has been confirmed by the Secretary of State – as this was after the public inquiry – the 1971 Highways Act only allows six weeks for an objector to ask the courts to intervene before the order is finalised. So although Mr Ostler asked the Court of Appeal to quash the order as soon as he discovered the change in plan, it was too late. Because the originally proposed scheme had been modified, a further compulsory purchase order was necessary for the DoE to acquire Mr Ostler's property. This time the DoE did deign to tell him. And this time Mr Ostler objected. But at a further public inquiry in December 1974 a DoE inspector confirmed the compulsory purchase order, and ruled that whether or not the order was the result of a secret deal was not relevant.

Mr Ostler complained to both the local and Parliamentary Ombudsmen. The local Ombudsman found an irregularity in the evidence of an engineer employed by Boston District Council at the time of the 1973 inquiry. The findings of the Parliamentary Ombudsman, Sir Idwal Pugh – himself a former Permanent Secretary at the DoE – was even more telling; his report said: 'There were serious shortcomings in the way the Department handled the proposals . . . when procedures which have been laid down to ensure fairness and openness are not properly carried out, doubts must remain whether all interests have received fair and equal consideration.'[10]

Another forthright critic of departmental secrecy has been one of the DTp's own inquiry inspectors – Hugh Gardner, a former Ministry of Agriculture civil servant. Commenting on the refusal of the DoE to debate an alternative to the M42 at the Water Orton M42 inquiry which he had conducted, Mr Gardner wrote:

the Department should come prepared to give evidence on the [objectors'] alternative to the M42 which was advanced at the present inquiry. If the Department has a good case, there is everything to be said for stating it in public. If it has not, it is desirable that a better solution to the traffic problems should be found. In the present climate of opinion the 'mother knows best' approach is not generally acceptable. Until the need for the M42 is debated in this way, it will continue to drag on, and time will be wasted not saved.[11]

It is instructive that following this report, Mr Gardner was not appointed to another inquiry for over two years, and then only after the hiatus had been brought to the personal attention of Transport Secretary William Rodgers who sent a note to the DTp civil servant responsible for appointing inspectors.

The Department's secrecy was implicitly criticised, too, in the 1977 Leitch Report.[12] This was the submission of a government-appointed committee of investigation into the methods employed in official traffic forecasting. The DTp ought to be more open in its dealings with the public, was one conclusion of the report. 'So long as Transport 2000 and Friends of the Earth are around,' commented Sir George Leitch at the press conference, 'the DTp won't be accused of being its own worst enemy. But many feel that it is running a close third or fourth.'

Traffic forecasts – a cornerstone of the Department's case for most road proposals – offer one of the sorriest examples of long-running official secrecy on road building and one of the strongest arguments for freedom of information as a means of promoting sound policy-making and economic sense.

The size of a new road depends on the traffic that is predicted to use that road. Thus traffic forecasts have been at the centre of many inquiry arguments. Faced with growing concern about the reliability of the government's traffic forecasts in the seventies the road engineers reacted with a proposal to computerise the forecasts. The new Regional Highway Traffic Model (RHTM) was intended to be able to predict traffic flows on any hypothetical road network for any date in the future. By any standards the RHTM was a vast undertaking. Announcing the project in 1975 John Gilbert, then Minister for Transport, said that the project would require 'a series of roadside and home interviews on a scale never previously attempted.'[13]

From the outset the RHTM was shrouded in secrecy. In mid-1977 Friends of the Earth wrote to the Department of Transport asking for a copy of the specification for the RHTM. Assistant Secretary Maurice Maggs replied:

There is no detailed specification of the Regional Highway Traffic Model as yet. . . . Prior to May '76 a document was prepared which set out the technical and management approach to the development work that might loosely be thought of as a job specification for the regional teams to follow. This document was given a limited circulation on an information basis to County Engineers and Planners with whom the Department liaises and shares data. Only a sufficient number of copies were printed to meet this circulation and we have not seen any need for further printing because the document has served its purpose and takes no account of subsequent work.

The letter was dated, rather unspecifically, 'June 1977'. On 15 April, 1977 – approximately two months prior to this letter – Mr Maggs had written to a number of trade journals as follows:

REGIONAL HIGHWAY TRAFFIC MODEL
Our transport Press Office asked me to let you have a note covering progress on this Project. . . .

Enclosed was an outline of the aims of the model and a progress report. The whole was about a dozen pages long, and could have been easily photocopied.

In June 1978 Transport Secretary Rodgers asked the Standing Advisory Committee on Trunk Road Assessment, chaired by Sir George Leitch, to investigate the RHTM.[14] This second Leitch report concluded that the RHTM was a failure. On its trial run the RHTM had been asked to 'forecast' flows on existing trunk roads. Many of the model's answers were out by a factor of two.

The details of the RHTM's failure were revealed in the *New Scientist* in March 1980.[15] Such was the DTp's embarrassment that the Leitch report was not published until July. Even then a final attempt was made to cover up. The Leitch report was not the subject of a DTp press release – as would normally be the case for reports of this nature. Journalists had to find out that the report had been published. However, just in case, the DTp press office had been thoroughly briefed on how to deal with awkward questions.

Rail Closures

Transport Users' Consultative Committees were established by the 1947 Transport Act. There are regional committees (TUCCs) and a national committee – the Central Transport Consultative Committee (CTCC) based in London. One of their chief tasks over the years has been to investigate proposed rail closures – another sensitive policy area that has been the subject of suppression and secrecy.

Initially the TUCCs were empowered to consider the hardship that would be caused to rail travellers by a closure, taking into account the number of travellers and the economics of running the service. Generally, the TUCCs approved the line closures proposed by the British Transport Commission (this body no longer exists), only occasionally recommending that a line could be run more cheaply instead of being closed.

But in 1957 the TUCC for the south-eastern area strongly criticised the presentation of the technical case for the closure of the Lewes–East Grinstead railway. And again in 1961 the same TUCC, and the Central Transport Consultative Committee which then had to approve the TUCC's advice, recommended against closure of the Westerham branch line in Kent – a recommendation that was turned down by the Minister, Ernest Marples.[16]

These two incidents, coupled with the general restraining influence of the TUCCs on closures and the railways' mounting deficit, contributed to the TUCCs being divested of their right to consider the British Railways Board's financial case for closure (in the 1962 Transport Act). The TUCCs were left in the extraordinary position of only being able to make recommendations on whether a closure would cause hardship or not. (One consequence of the TUCCs' enforced visit to the dentist is that financial results and passenger data on a line which is a candidate for closure are now closely guarded secrets. On what is plainly not a commercial venture – the North Norfolk line – British Rail recently declined to give the *Guardian* details of passenger use on the grounds of – delicious infelicity – 'commercial intelligence'.[17])

The 1962 Transport Act cleared the way for the Beeching round of cuts – already planned by the Ministry of Transport. On 8 October 1959 the Conservative Party had won the general election. Ernest Marples was appointed Minister of Transport. Concerned about the British Transport Commission's rising deficit, he set up a special advisory group of businessmen, under the chairmanship of Sir Ivan Stedeford. It is believed that the group was critical of the Transport Commission's management structure and that it advised surgery for the railways. But the report – although it is now twenty years old – remains a closely guarded secret. The Department of Transport refuses even today to make it public.[18]

While it is not known what the Stedeford committee recommended, it is known that Ernest Marples was very impressed by the views of one of its members – Richard Beeching. In June 1961 Beeching was appointed chairman of the outgoing British Transport Commission. When the 1962 Transport Act came into operation on 1 January 1963 he became chairman of the new British Railways Board, and it was he who drew up a plan – *The Reshaping of British Railways* – for major surgery, which became the blueprint for the rail closures of the late 60s.[19]

The rail closure programme began in earnest after the Labour Party's victory in the 1966 general election, by which time Beeching had resigned. It was, as someone who was a Transport Ministry civil servant said, 'a crude cost cutting exercise'. For each cut, the TUCCs said whether there would, or would not, be hardship. In private the Minister of Transport received his civil servants' advice and they, as might be expected of a Ministry whose expertise was in road building and not running railways, took the view that money must be saved. Although the civil servants' advice was so partisan, and thus newsworthy, it is a sign of attitudes of secrecy that no one asked the Ministry what advice was being given. (Presumably, they wouldn't have been told anyway.)

Two subsequent rail closure plans highlight one of the senseless risks of official secrecy – that it will leave egg all over the faces of officialdom.

In 1972 the DoE civil servants drew up the sixty-one page *Rail Policy Review*. It discussed several closure options, the most drastic of which proposed the closure of 123 out of 200 government-supported services by 1981. This option was disclosed in the *Sunday Times* in October.[20] The reaction of the government followed a well-trodden path. Minister of Transport John Peyton said the plans were just one of a number of options under discussion; nothing had been decided. Less predictable was the over-reaction of the Department of the Environment's security advisers. On 29 November two Scotland Yard detectives called on the offices of the *Railway Gazette* which had given the plan to the *Sunday Times*. They examined the *Gazette*'s files – looking for the original document – but left empty-handed. A week later, the police interviewed the editor of the *Sunday Times* and threatened prosecution under the Official Secrets Act. Eventually the investigation was dropped.[21] So too was the closure plan and instead the 1974 Railways Act laid down a new basis for the support of the passenger rail network.

The most recent passenger closure scare came in November 1979 when the *Guardian* reported an option to close forty-one services.[22] The newspaper report was tactfully timed to come out on the day when Transport Minister Norman Fowler was due to answer oral questions. The *Guardian* report was 'untrue', said the Minister; he saw no case 'for another round of massive cuts in the railways'. He also denied that there had been any 'secret talks'. Next day, the *Guardian* disclosed that the plans were in British Rail's corporate plan, that this had been sent to the Minister, and that there had been talks. Eventually, and paralleling the 1972 disclosure, the Minister wrote to British Rail ruling out any 'substantial' rail closures.

The common thread in the 1972 and 1979 closure scares is that secrecy eventually proved counter-productive. Official secrecy over plans like these – that will affect and worry nearly every railway user – is always a gamble. If maintained, the chances of success for the government are high. If broken, the chance of failure is equally likely.

The Lorry Lobby

The Department of Transport's habit of furtively pushing an unpopular policy option before it has been announced – and the gamble involved in doing so – became all too clear in 1978.

The DTp is notorious for being on the side of heavier lorries. Just how biased it is only became evident when a minute from the head of the DTp's freight directorate, Joseph Peeler, to his immediate boss, Peter Lazarus, was leaked to Transport 2000 (a public transport pressure group). By early November 1978 this minute had featured in every Fleet Street newspaper.[23]

The minute was the freight directorate's response to Transport Secretary William Rodgers' announcement that he was to set up a committee of inquiry to investigate heavy lorries. It was by any standards an extraordinary document. The inquiry was seen as 'a means of getting round the political obstacles to change the lorry weights problem'.

The sort of resolution which Peeler had in mind was also spelt out – 'For the purpose of this note it is assumed that we wish . . . to move, as soon as parliamentary and public opinion will let us, to a maximum gross weight of thirty-eight or forty tons [higher than the existing maximum of thirty-two tons] . . . the establishment of a clear and overwhelming case on balance for heavier lorries is seen as the main end of the inquiry.'

The minute revealed just how close this section of the DTp was to the road haulage lobby and how it would wish to control the timing and content of the inquiry:

An inquiry offers a way of dealing with the political opposition to a more rational position on lorry weights. . . . It should provide a focus for the various road haulage interests to get together, marshall their forces and act cohesively to produce a really good case which should not merely establish the main point at issue but should do good to their now sadly tarnished public image. This would make it easier for the Government to propose legislation . . . in their favour. . . . A wide ranging inquiry could be advantageous presentationally, and less open to accusations of 'rigging' but it would be . . . difficult to keep under control . . . the more the scope of the inquiry is extended the longer it will take and the greater the danger that the main issue will be lost sight of.[24]

Apart from intriguing speculation about which other DTp inquiries have been similarly prejudged, the most significant feature shared by the rail closure leaks and the Peeler leak is that they are both Civil Service advice to ministers on policies which are plainly matters of great public interest – and how to push a policy that has yet to be announced publicly. In this respect they differ from the examples of secrecy surrounding road schemes which is largely a means of implementing announced policies.

The Open Road

The first point to make, in fairness, is that there has been a marked improvement in the Department of Transport's attitude to secrecy during the eight years in which I have had dealings with it. The Department is now much more open that it was. This has largely been a function of change at the top. The almost complete turnover in its top civil servants really dates from Peter Shore who was horrified by their pro-road attitudes. Mr Shore brought in Sir Peter Baldwin from the Treasury and, when the Department of Transport separated from the Environment, Baldwin became the Permanent Secretary. Baldwin's influence has brought the DTp much more into the open.

Also, since Peter Shore held office, the political bosses of transport – Shore was followed by William Rodgers and then Norman Fowler – have fairly positively favoured open government. Two cases illustrate this trend. Peter Shore's consultation document on transport policy[25] brought 1,600 responses from the public and interested bodies. After the resultant white paper had been published in 1977[26] an academic researcher asked the DTp for access to the background material. He was refused on the ground that many of the respondents to the consultation document would not have been told that their submissions might be published. But Sir Arthur Armitage has recently conducted an inquiry into lorries and the environment. This inquiry had, by March 1980, received 1,800 submissions. On 20 March, Sir Arthur wrote to Frank Dobson MP to assure him, 'I intend to make the evidence . . . publicly available. . . . At the very least I will arrange for it to be lodged in some appropriate place where it will be available for inspection.'

However, while there does appear to be greater awareness of the desirability for openness on transport issues at the highest levels in the Department of Transport, this does not always permeate the middle and lower levels of the Civil Service. Old habits die hard. And, privately, senior civil servants will concede that junior staff can be politically naive, and clam up out of fear, rather than out of a positive wish to guard secrets.

Certainly much of the secrecy that surrounds new road schemes is indefensible – even under the present system. There can be no respectable reason for withholding from the public technical information like cost benefit analyses, traffic forecasts and subsoil data. The risk of blight is offered as the major reason for not releasing alternative road proposals at an earlier stage in new road planning. But on closer examination – as I have argued – this too lacks substance. Any positive movement towards open government would undoubtedly help consumers objecting to road schemes to prepare their case.

Part of the reason for the blanket suppression of information on matters like road and lorry schemes must be the pervasive secrecy that envelopes policy-making. It is the most crucial area of government work to which the public has no right of access. Policies gestate in the Department of Transport – as elsewhere – for an unknown length of time. Arguments are put. Alternatives are discussed. The more sensitive the subject the more secret the process. Eventually a consensus view is reached. And only then is there some public manifestation of this process – a green paper, a white paper, or the simple announcement of a decision. Only at this stage, if then, has the public a chance to make its views known.

Information is influence. And the information that lies in the files of the Department is vital to a full understanding of an issue. In the files are facts, opinions, arguments. Even if these are summarised during the compilation of a green paper, there can be no guarantee that the green paper accurately reflects the Department's knowledge nor that nothing of value is left in the files. If that were so there would be no point in official secrecy anyway.

A Filing System for Open Government

So for a full understanding of how policies evolve – which is a prerequisite for influencing those policies – a procedure for public access to various Department of Transport files would need to be worked out. The ideas sketched out below are offered as a stimulus to discussion.

Each division in the Department has its own filing system, kept in a central registry serving that division. Other divisions are kept informed on a 'need to know' basis. The files contain a variety of material, from scrappy notes to considered papers, and originating from anyone from the Permanent Secretary down to an executive officer. Each file is unique. There is no copy (and all hell breaks loose on the rare occasions when one is lost). Papers from one file will of course be duplicated in other related files, some of which may not be held by the same division. If a civil servant wants to minute another about an issue, he will call for the file from the registry. One copy of his minute is appended to the file and copies are sent to those who need to know. The DTp also has a system of loose minutes: a minute is written without first calling for the file but of course a copy is subsequently appended to the appropriate file or files.

Because different divisions of the Department of Transport maintain separate registries – unlike some other ministries which have one central registry of all files, accessible to all within the ministry – there is the possibility that the 'need to know' basis of copying information from one division to another could be abused. There is no evidence that it is. But similar systems have been abused in the past. In the post-nationalisation tussle between the Railway Executive – which operated the railways and broadly favoured steam locomotives – and the British Transport Commission – responsible for general policy and more receptive to a diesel or electric alternative – the Executive kept the BTC at arms length by circulating two sets of minutes. As required, the BTC were sent minutes. But a second set was reserved for internal circulation only.[27] While procrastination raged over alternatives, the Executive launched a major steam locomotive building programme in 1951 which only ended in 1960. It is arguable that secrecy can contribute to huge wasteful blunders like this.

It would be simple and cheap to arrange for public access to a system like that of the Department of Transport. The registries already maintain an index of their own files. These indices could be copied and lodged in a few libraries – the House of Commons Library, the libraries of the Transport Department itself, and the copyright libraries. Copies of the master files – it would obviously be impracticable to arrange for public access to the originals – could be made on demand or made in advance and kept permanently at the DTp, with an extra charge for extra copies. Parts of some files – those with information collected from firms or individuals with a guarantee of confidentiality – would be exempt from public access.

There is a further set of files to which the public would need access if we are to be properly informed of the policy process.

These are the special files made up for a minister prior to a decision being taken. They contain a considered paper on the Department's view – reflecting the discussion that has already been recorded on the divisional files – plus comments by the divisional head's superiors. The Peeler leak came from such a file.

There is no question that opening up the files would have an effect on Departmental practice. All minutes would be written 'with publication in mind'. Civil servants would undoubtedly stop using minutes as a vehicle for conversation, although the mandarin practice of exchanging chatty notes has already waned in favour of the telephone, and a right to access would certainly accelerate this trend. It is unlikely that the files – or their users – would lose anything thereby.

Another effect would be to sound the death knell of the myth that the Department speaks with one voice. Again, this would be no loss. Complete internal agreement on policy issues is rare. The Department performs no useful public service by maintaining the pretence of unanimity and reinforcing that pretence by secretive conduct.

REFERENCES

1 The Department of Transport (DTp) was formed in September 1976 to take responsibility for all the transport matters which had been the province of the Department of the Environment since 1971, and, before that, the Ministry of Transport.

2 Relations between the Department and the outside world are mainly the responsibility of the Information Directorate which organises information services covering advertising campaigns, public relations and publicity, including the issue of official announcements in the form of press notices and handling all enquiries from press, radio and television.

3 *Hansard*, 27 June 1977.

4 *Hansard*, 3 April 1980.

5 Gruffydd Jones D., *Report on the Organisation of DTp Research,* reported in *New Scientist*, 10 April 1980.

6 Transport and Road Research Laboratory circular, February 1980.

7 *Motorway Monthly* (journal of Transport 2000), vol. 1., no. 4, March 1977, p. 3.

8 *Sunday Times*, 12 March 1978.

9 Information supplied by Terry Rand of the Hampstead Garden Suburb Lorry Route Joint Action Committee.

10 Parliamentary Commissioner for Administration, *Third Report for Session 1976–77*, HMSO, case no. C.236/K, paras 16 and 18. See also *Municipal Engineering*, 21 January 1977, p. 80.
11 *M42 Water Orton Inquiry Report*, para. 9.15, available from the Midland Road Construction Unit.
12 The 'Leitch Committee' was originally the Advisory Committee on Trunk Road Assessment. It subsequently became a Standing Advisory Committee. There have been two reports on the Regional Highway Traffic Model; the first appeared in 1977 and the second in 1980.
13 Recorded in *Transport for Society, Proceedings on Conference November 1975*, Institution of Civil Engineers, 1976, pp. 1–2.
14 See 12 above.
15 *New Scientist*, 13 March 1980.
16 St John Thomas, David, *The Rural Transport Problem*, Routledge and Kegan Paul, 1963, pp. 39–40.
17 *Guardian*, 23 May 1980.
18 Private communication from the Department of Transport to the author, 2 June 1980.
19 British Railways Board, *The Reshaping of British Railways*, HMSO, 1963, became better known as the Beeching Report.
20 *Sunday Times*, 8 October 1972.
21 See *The Times* of 2 and 9 December 1972 for accounts of these events. Leslie Huckfield MP tried to put down questions in the House: see *The Times* 12 December 1972.
22 *Guardian*, 29 November 1979.
23 First published in the *Guardian*, 30 October 1978.
24 Quoted from *A Reproduction of the Letter and Memorandum about a Proposed Inquiry into Heavier Lorries from Mr Joseph Peeler to Mr Peter Lazarus*, published by Transport 2000.
25 Department of the Environment, *Transport Policy: A Consultation Document*, HMSO, 1976.
26 Department of Transport, *Transport Policy*, Cmnd 6836, HMSO, 1977.
27 Bonavia, M. R., *The Organisation of British Railways*, Ian Allan, 1971, pp. 53–54.

Product Testing 9

Peter Sand and Joyce Epstein

The right to make an informed choice about the products we buy is a
cornerstone of the consumer movement. On our behalf, government
monitors a large range of consumer goods and services: the toxic content of all brands of cigarettes, for instance, is measured by the Government Chemist; and the faults of every make of car are recorded
through the MoT test. On our behalf, too, government is industry's
largest customer, buying, for example, carpets and detergents and felt
tip pens in bulk, and in the process learning more about comparable
qualities and costs than an individual consumer could ever hope to do.
Yet little of the information collected in this way – and with public
money – is released in a form that helps the individual consumer to
spend his money more wisely. Drawing on experience in the United
States, where the public can get access to the findings of government
product testing, Peter Sand and Joyce Epstein argue that the interests
of UK industry and government, as well as of the individual consumer,
would be better served by the release of government-held information
about the goods on sale in our high street shops.

Government departments and local authorities in the United
Kingdom publish a vast amount of information on products and
services. Each year, data is issued that shows anything from how
many cars fail the MoT test to how many schoolchildren are
infected with vermin. But relatively little of the information made
available by government is of any practical use to the individual,
because most of it is published only in its aggregate form. The
Department of Transport, to take the MoT test example, has been
collecting and publishing statistics on failure rates of passenger
vehicles since 1968, but details of which cars have been found to
have which faults have never been published, valuable though this
information would be to prospective car buyers. Although the
aggregate information – for example, twenty-one percent of cars
failed the test in 1978 because of brake defects – is interesting,
the question of which specific makes of cars failed the tests because

of defective brakes is more than merely interesting: it could be a matter of life and death.

Make-by-make results of annual car tests have been published in other countries. In 1969, ironically, *Motoring Which?* was able to draw attention to the fact that British cars exported to Sweden had a much higher failure rate than average and indicated the parts of individual makes of British cars most prone to defects.[1] *Motoring Which?* recommended that the (then) Ministry of Transport should publish the results of their annual safety tests saying, 'It would be tremendously helpful to car buyers, and should make sure that the manufacturers eliminate common safety faults.' Two years later, *Motoring Which?* reported that the Ministry had rejected this proposal along with others for making the MoT tests more effective[2].

The potential importance to consumers of product information based on tests as an aid to rational (and more economical) buying has been one of the foundations of the consumer movement. As long ago as 1927, Stuart Chase and F. J. Schlink (two of the founders of the organisation that became Consumers' Union in the United States) wrote:

Each year the Government buys some $300,000,000 of supplies and equipment – ranging all the way from thumbtacks to dredging machines; from baseballs to battleships. . . . Skilled chemists, physicists, engineers, research workers, in a hundred fields are passing continually and relentlessly upon the relative quality of the goods which the purchasing agent proposes to buy. . . . For an operating cost of $2,000,000 it is estimated that the Bureau of Standards saves the Government in the neighbourhood of $100,000,000 every year – an investment which nets fiftyfold. Why cannot this technique be extended to aid the consumer at large as it has aided the United States Government?[3]

Perhaps the optimism of the late 20s about the value of product testing has become tempered in the early 80s, but the idea that the government holds product information (or, if it doesn't, that it should!) which could be useful to consumers is quite deeply rooted in the consumer movement. But as we shall see, this valuable product information has proved elusive over the years and in this country remains so.

In the United States there has been a number of cases where consumer organisations have been able to get access to important information under the Freedom of Information legislation. The kind of information of potential interest to consumer organisations varies widely. One important area is that relating to goods and services which are purchased or used by government. Obviously, many of the goods and services used by government fall well outside the domestic consumer market, defence equipment, for example, and industrial machinery, but there is a large area of overlap where government departments buy and test goods which individual consumers may themselves buy, or at least be exposed to in institutional settings.

There are a number of ways in which government purchasing of this kind may be relevant to the consumer interest. Firstly, the results of product testing and use: if, for instance, a particular range of furniture is found unsatisfactory by government, why shouldn't consumers benefit or be protected from buying it, by being informed of the results of the government tests? Secondly, the test methods and specifications used by government departments, who put much effort into ensuring that the test methods they use are sound, are of interest to consumer organisations. It is surely in everyone's interest that test methods and specifications used by government should be widely available. Finally, in principle, information on goods purchased with public funds, tested by public employees at public expense, and used in public departments, ought to be available to benefit the public.

The case in favour of government disclosure of the information which it holds on products and services, then, rests on: the usefulness of the information to consumers and consumer organisations; and the principle of accountability for public spending.

But the experience of anyone who has ever approached the subject has been to run up against the unwillingness of civil servants and public employees to disclose information. This characteristic has been described variously as a 'natural propensity', an 'ingrained conservatism', 'inevitable' and, simply, 'Whitehall habit and practice'. Civil servants may also have specific fears about exposing their work to public scrutiny: the basis for public procurement decisions in supplies departments may appear to be inadequate, subjective or even improper, especially if it hints at the merging of government and industry interests. Industry has always sheltered behind the blanket cover of 'commercial confidentiality', something which has been enthusiastically defended by government. Government often claims that it needs industry cooperation and therefore would not like to do anything which would jeopardise industry goodwill. In 1976, for example, the Department of Employment refused to release Retail Price Index information by type of food shop, because of the 'adverse effect on the cooperation of shops' – presumably of those shops charging higher prices.[4]

Some of the reservations about information disclosure carry some weight. Business has legitimate claims to confidentiality in areas like new product development, marketing plans and so on. But in areas that affect, for instance, personal health and safety – as in the MoT example – the consumer interest surely ought to override any commercial reservations. The withholding of car defects data is not the only example of industrial interests apparently taking precedence over consumer health and safety. Although by the very nature of secrecy, we cannot know what the government knows but is not telling ('The extent of secrecy is itself the ultimate secret')[5], there are known instances where government has withheld product information of potentially vital importance to consumers.

One such case is that of the carbon monoxide (CO) level of cigarettes. Carbon monoxide may aggravate heart disease and cause other health problems. And yet the government has, at the time of writing, refused to publish figures for the various brands of cigarettes, despite the fact that the Department of Health has been testing cigarettes for CO-yield since 1974[6]. The case is similar to that of ten years ago when government refused to publish tar and nicotine levels by brand of cigarette. In 1971, the Consumers' Association published the information despite violent objections by the tobacco industry.[7] The information is now freely available and the health warning on all cigarette packs includes an indication of the tar content. A decade later, the Department claim 'technical difficulties' as the reason why CO levels cannot be published. The Canadian, United States and Swedish governments all publish (or are about to begin to do so) CO-yield data; in Britain, the Consumers' Association and the *Sunday Times* have now published their own CO test results. Since the argument about 'technical difficulties' does not hold, the government is now claiming that the information cannot 'be understood by the average person', and so it must still be withheld.

This 'natural propensity' of government officials to withhold information has a solid basis in the form of the Official Secrets Act which has been described as 'one of the toughest in western democracies'.[8] In practice, as Chapter Two explains, the Official Secrets Act does not often seem to be formally invoked when organisations like the Consumers' Association have sought official information on goods and services. Prosecutions under the Act are rare, but the degree to which it functions, less formally, as a deterrent to the release of information on products and services is a matter for speculation. Section 2 has also been used semi-explicitly as an alibi for refusing to disclose information. In 1964, for example, a typhoid epidemic in Aberdeen caused the government to withdraw from circulation millions of tins of corned beef. When the press tried to get information on where and how the tins were stored, the Ministry of Health refused to answer on the grounds that it was an official secret.

How Freedom of Information Law Works
for Consumers in America

The United States Freedom of Information Act (FOIA), passed in 1966 and amended in 1974 and 1976, directs federal agencies to make available any identifiable agency records to any person, upon request. The FOIA has been used extensively by consumer groups and other public interest organisations to get information, previously unavailable, on consumer products and services.*

Not all of this information has been produced merely for the asking; much was obtained only after lengthy periods of litigation. The government agencies holding the sought-after information can, and often do, refuse to release it if it can be argued that it falls within the scope of one of the nine exempted categories laid down by the Act. Information about consumer products is frequently denied to applicants on the basis of the fourth exemption: if information is a 'trade secret'; if it is financial or commercial, or if it is privileged or confidential, it can be withheld. In the first few years of the FOIA's operation, corporations tended to make broad claims (largely upheld by government) as to the confidentiality of product and business data held by the government. More recently, though, the mere claim of 'confidentiality' by business has not always been sufficient grounds for withholding information. More and more, the concept is being challenged; companies must show that there is a reasonable basis for claiming confidentiality, and that the company in question would suffer substantial harm (not just some injury) if the information were released.

Despite these difficulties, there have been numerous instances since the introduction of a Freedom of Information law in the

*See also pp. 30–34.

States where consumer groups have successfully sought previously unpublished information collected by government agencies. Agencies are not required to keep records of information requests but through cases settled by litigation and through informal surveys[9] a number of examples can be found, including: Consumers' Union won access to the results of comparative tests, conducted by the Veterans' Administration, on hearing aids. This took two years of litigation, because the VA was at first denied access on the grounds of the fourth exemption. Consumers' Union got the Department of Agriculture to release information on violations of minimum standards in the New York City school lunch programme. The Federal Reserve Board released information to Consumers' Union on a survey of bank interest rates on consumer loans. The Center for Auto Safety, a public interest group, got the National Highway Traffic Safety Administration to make public its correspondence with General Motors in relation to an investigation of car safety defects. The Health Research Group, another public interest organisation, obtained test data from the government on food additives (dyes). The Union of Concerned Scientists used the FOIA to gain access to information held by the Nuclear Regulatory Commission on safety problems at a nuclear plant (discovering, among other things, that the government knew about certain problems but had done nothing to correct them). The Environmental Defence Fund obtained government test data on pesticides, as well as data on the toxic effects of asbestos.

The opening of United States government files has not always been so useful. Government's 'natural propensity' for secrecy has stocked their files with a good deal of rubbish. Dresner quotes one source as saying: 'We have received many papers under the FOIA with which we haven't done anything. You think that they are going to be greater than they really are. I have found that when things are secret they become so tantalising that you have to see them. Once you see them, it's ridiculous for them to be called secret.'[10]

Consumer advocates have played a particularly prominent role in the campaign for freedom of information in Canada. The Canadian Access to Information Bill (expected to become law by the Summer of 1982) makes specific reference to the desirability of disclosing information derived from 'product or environmental testing'. Canadian experience provides numerous examples of consumers denied product information that would have been of benefit to them. In the case of children's car seats, for instance, the Consumers' Association of Canada (CAC) believed the Department of Consumer and Corporate Affairs' standards to be unrealistically stringent, but since the government refused to release its test results there was nothing the CAC could really dispute. But when, in 1977, a Canadian government-approved seat failed a United States Consumers' Union test, a public re-examination of car seat standards brought to light a profile of bureaucratic rigidity and even data manipulation over car seat testing.[11]

Public Purchasing

Millions of pounds of taxpayers' money is spent each year buying, testing and using products in various government departments. (Other major purchasing bodies, not reviewed here, include the nationalised industries.) Very often these are the kinds of products in the domestic sector that individual consumers and their organisations might be interested in – cleaning liquids, cars, ballpoint pens, carpets, sheets, chairs, and so on.

The information – both formal and informal – amassed by various government bodies after years and years of procurement experience is of potentially great interest and value to the public. It is, however, largely inaccessible to us. It is the official policy of most government departments not to make information on product testing, test methods or test results publicly available. The main reason given is the necessity to protect commercial confidences. Since no one outside government has access to the protected information, there is no way of judging the validity of this claim.

The Property Services Agency (PSA) is the main procurement agency for national government. Figures for what the PSA sold in 1978/9 to various government departments were[12]:

Fuel	£146.2 million
Furniture	£34.0 million
Furnishings (curtains, carpets, etc)	£28.1 million
Domestic goods, etc	£16.1 million

To put it somewhat more vividly, the PSA bought (in 1975) over sixteen and a half million bars of soap, eight and a half million pieces of crockery and glassware, half a million chairs, two million square metres of carpet and four million litres of detergent.

It is difficult to find out precisely the extent of product testing carried out by the PSA. It appears that there is not a tremendous amount, but exactly which products are tested and in exactly what ways, the PSA does not reveal publicly. It also does not reveal the results of whatever product tests they do carry out.

Consumers' Association made a specific enquiry about carpet buying and carpet testing in 1976. Carpeting often represents a major investment by consumers, and the PSA's experience of those two million square metres in one year might have taught them something consumers would also like to know. However, the PSA adheres to its policy of non-disclosure, referring to unspecified government 'rules' which prevent them from releasing information. Further, they maintain that, '. . . there is little . . . in PSA Supplies' carpet-buying practices useful or . . . relevant, to the solution of the problems faced by the private buyer in looking for a carpet.'[13] Private conditions of use, the Agency claims, are too different from those of public use, and anyway test results are treated as a confidence between the Department and its suppliers. The PSA fears the consequences of 'breaking faith' with trade, if they publish the information they hold on products.

In 1978/79 the PSA spent over £150 millions of public money on supplies. Its concern, though, is with breaking faith with the suppliers, not the public. This attitude is particularly unfortunate in view of the fact that the PSA is in a unique situation to monitor feedback from large numbers of users in some cases, even when there is no product testing in the formal sense. For example, the PSA buys large quantities of branded razor blades, for use in prisons, hospitals, and so on. In one instance, an immediate flood of complaints received by the PSA alerted the Agency to the fact that one particular consignment of blades was defective, causing people to cut themselves. The PSA settled the problem on their own with the supplier, but the existence of the defective blades was never made public. Did blades from the same batch continue to be sold at retail outlets throughout the country? The dispersed distribution would not lead so easily to identification of a defect.

The PSA claim, that since the level of public use is so much heavier than that of domestic use the results of product testing would be of no interest or value to ordinary consumers, is not entirely accurate. In the first place, the PSA carpeting goes into many domestic settings, like married quarters for the armed forces, where carpet wear is comparable. Secondly, while it may be true that the carpeting in a busy public waiting room receives heavier wear than the carpet in Mrs Smith's front lounge, it could still be useful for Mrs Smith to know, in comparative terms, which type of carpeting had the best wearing qualities.

In 1978/79, the Department of Health and Social Security (DHSS) spent £1,144 millions of public money on National Health Service supplies (excluding medicines) but refuses to disclose product information for such items as sheets and mattresses, partly on the grounds that hospital use is so much heavier than domestic use. There is no doubt that hospital bedding receives more wear than in the home. That does not make comparative durability information any less useful. There are suggestions (in the House of Commons eleventh report, 1980, from the Committee of Public Accounts) that important product information, rather than not being relevant, is simply non-existent. The report found that 'management [at the DHSS] lacked the information necessary to develop effective supplies policies, and did not always obtain the best value for money.' When the Consumers' Association sought information on how the DHSS chooses its mattresses, they were told that purchasing was 'evolutionary' and that supplies officers just 'know' what to buy out of long traditions of use.

An important local authority body with purchasing interests is the Local Authorities Management Services and Computer Committee (LAMSAC). One of LAMSAC's functions is to improve purchasing performance in local government. It provides advice about a number of separate product groups, including cleaning materials, stationery, food, furniture, clothing and vehicles. In 1977 local authorities spent £2,000 millions on supplies. From talking to LAMSAC, however, it would appear that testing is not an important aspect of local purchasing. A lot of the information about products held by local authority procurement officers comes through informal exchanges of information, trial and error, etc. and officers (again) 'just know', through experience, which are the 'bad' products – experience which consumers might well like to share. But LAMSAC puts out no information on the performance of the products it buys. Apart from PSA-compiled catalogues of manufacturers' own information about products – some of which are available to local authorities at a small discount – LAMSAC say they have no other product information available for distribution.

The Greater London Council (GLC) is one local authority which conducts formal product testing. The GLC supplies department – with an annual turnover of £176 millions – and the scientific branch, test a wide range of products including branded paints and other building materials, food, educational supplies, detergents, polishes, etc. Their laboratory has £2½ million worth of equipment, and staff receive in salary some £1.4 millions per year in public funds.

The Greater London Council does make available some test information. The *Annual Report* for the Scientific Branch (no longer published), the *Development and Materials* bulletin (published five times a year), and numerous occasional papers present details of test methods and results for a wide range of products, many in the domestic sector. But usually these publications identify brands only as Brand 1, Brand 2, etc. Thus, for example, the 1973 *Annual Report* tells us that the GLC tested eleven brands of hard gloss paint and approved only three of them. It does not reveal which brands of paints were approved and which were rejected. Paints which pass the GLC tests go on their 'Approved List' and are the only paints that can be used by contractors doing work for the GLC. The Approved List is not made public, except to contractors. The reports describe the shortcomings of rejected products but do not identify, for example, which paint was 'Brand 4' – rejected because of 'unsatisfactory exterior durability'; and which was 'Brand 1' – rejected because of 'undue sinkage of all finishing coats into their respective undercoats'. It might be useful for consumers to know which are the less durable, sinking paints but the GLC is not telling, because it would 'prejudice their trading position'. They also insist that since the GLC considerations are so different from those of the ordinary consumer, the GLC test results would be 'absolutely useless' to the public.

The GLC does, in some cases, name specific brands. Some reports identify the brands of products found to be satisfactory, but not the brands found unsatisfactory. Other reports, testing only one brand, may identify its satisfactory and unsatisfactory uses. The GLC is perhaps less secretive than some other official bodies who do product testing but it is selective in what information it releases.

Her Majesty's Stationery Office (HMSO) also does a considerable amount of product testing in its laboratory, but refuses to release test result data at all. HMSO spent about £50 million in 1977/78 on paper, and about £20 million on the purchase and hire of office equipment. Their laboratory tests more items than HMSO buys, many of which are in the domestic sector – pens, paper, pencils, ink, paper clips, rubbers, staplers, rulers, typewriter ribbons, glue, etc. The results of such testing could be useful for ordinary consumers; for example, the brand of ballpoint pen which lasts longest, the best kind of typewriter ribbon, the kinds of glue least likely to cause dermatitis, and so on – all of which examples arise out of HMSO testing programmes. But none of the test results is publicly available.

Government has at times been surprisingly open about concealing product information. In 1978 and 1979, the Price Commission conducted a study of prices of car parts. It collected data from a number of companies. The report of the study was published but with blank spaces where information had been deleted by the Department of Trade. The beginning of the report had a short note saying that 'the Secretary of State has omitted from the report certain findings of fact the publication of which he considers would be against the public interest.' According to one critic, however,

the deletions are only in the *commercial* interest of the big car companies . . . and very much against the *public* interest of ordinary car owners. . . . How can the Government justify censoring, for example . . . the finding that for sparking plugs the replacement equipment price is no less than ten times the original equipment price?. . . Why shouldn't the public be told that for oil filters, the retail mark-up is a huge 150 per cent?. . . Nor can any of this information which has been censored be seriously said to damage commercial interests, since it is all in aggregate form and none of it relates to any individual concern. . . .[14]

There is an openly acknowledged list of subjects on which ministers do not accept Parliamentary Questions. These include, for the Ministry of Agriculture, questions on the day-to-day functioning of the various food marketing boards, the British Sugar Corporation, the Meat and Livestock Commission, and forecasts of changes in food prices; for the Department of Health and Social Security, purchasing contracts in the NHS; for the Department of Trade, the names of companies being investigated under the Companies Act 1967; and almost every department will refuse to supply information on any subject if they deem it too much trouble.

The claim that agencies cannot cope with demands for information cannot be verified. In the United States, the FBI claimed at one point that because of staff shortages, they could not supply certain information requested by a newspaper. The newspaper filed a suit under the FOIA and got a court order for the FBI to supply the information. Overcoming its manpower problems, the

FBI then managed to produce 3,773 pages of documents within thirty days.

Needless government secrecy prevents consumers and the organisations that represent their interests from getting product information that may be of practical benefit to them. It may even at times involve vital questions of health and safety. Apart from the consumer interest, the principle of accountability for the spending of public money is not well served by a policy of secrecy. At a time when the government is making strenuous efforts to cut back on the spending of public money and above all to avoid waste, one would expect, at the very least, that more information would be available as a check on the efficiency of public purchasing.

Freedom of information is not a cure-all. Rates of morbidity are unlikely to drop because the DHSS publishes CO-yields, nor will traffic deaths decrease significantly when the Department of Transport publishes car defect data by make of car. But there can be little justification in keeping this information from those who *are* interested and concerned. A freer exchange of information could lead to improvements in the quality and reliability of goods and perhaps enhance the performance of British industry.

REFERENCES

1 *Motoring Which?*, October 1969.
2 *Motoring Which?*, October 1971.
3 Chase, Stuart and Schlink, F. J., *Your Money's Worth*, Macmillan, 1927.
4 Letter to the authors from the Department of Employment, 26 August 1976.
5 Quoted by Michael, James, in 'The Politics of Secrecy/The Secrecy of Politics', *Social Audit*, vol. 1, no. 1, Summer 1973, p. 55.
6 *Sunday Times*, 22 June 1980.
7 *Which?*, September 1971.
8 Christoph, James B., 'Administrative Secrecy in Britain: A Comparative View', *Public Administrative Review*, January/February 1976, p. 26.
9 Dresner, Stewart, *Open Government: Lessons from America*. Outer Circle Policy Unit, 1980, see especially Chapter Five.
10 A journalist on the *Los Angeles Times*, quoted Dresner, *ibid.*, p. 73.

11 Correspondence between Mr John Blakney, Consumers' Association of Canada, and the editors.
12 Property Services Agency, *Annual Report 1978/79*.
13 Letter to Consumers' Association from the Assistant Controller of the Property Services Agency, August 1976.
14 Michael Meacher MP in a letter to the *Guardian*, 31 October 1979.

Welfare Benefits 10
Melanie Phillips

The administration of welfare benefits is a huge undertaking and millions of consumers – parents, widows, the disabled, the sick, the unemployed, pregnant women, the elderly – depend on its efficiency and fairness. Yet official secrecy has, over the years, prevented informed debate and scrutiny of this crucial public service. And the obscurity of many benefits' forms and leaflets and the failure of DHSS officers to inform people fully about their rights inevitably contribute to the shortfall in the numbers of people who claim the benefits to which they are entitled. Here Melanie Phillips looks at the allegedly 'open' review of the supplementary benefits system, at the notorious A Code and its successors, and at some samples of official gobbledegook in information leaflets for claimants.

In the last official handbook published before the supplementary benefits scheme was changed, David Donnison, chairman of the Supplementary Benefits Commission, wrote: 'No other public service offers a fuller explanation of what it does and how it works.'[1] This apparent truth begged many questions. For although the area of social security benefits probably pumps out more official information than any other section of government, it has attracted at the same time the most acrimonious criticism about its secrecy and failure to divulge information to the public.

The criticism directed at the Department of Health and Social Security has been, perhaps, even more bitter than other complaints about secrecy in government. For, every year, hundreds of millions of pounds of social security benefits remain unclaimed by people who are legitimately entitled to them. It is default on a scale far larger than the estimated fraud and abuse of the system which the present government has undertaken to eradicate. There are thought to be many reasons for this take-up failure – among them the stigma and shame of depending on the welfare state, a desire for independence, a feeling that the amount of money involved is not worth the bother of claiming. But public ignorance also makes a significant contribution to this failure – ignorance of a complicated system, administered through several levels of law, policy and interpretation which may or may not be open to public scrutiny.

The means-tested supplementary benefits scheme has attracted most such criticism, although national insurance benefits have had their share as well. But the supplementary benefits scheme is notoriously complicated, and although the changes brought about by the Social Security Act 1980 were designed to simplify it, the new scheme appears to be just as hard to understand. Indeed, some welfare rights workers have complained that the system remains just as complex as before, but because all the rules have been changed, the painstaking progress made in unravelling its previous complexities has been wasted. The mixture of complication and secrecy proves a lethal cocktail for claimants who are unwilling or unable to press for their rights. In 1978, nine percent of the population depended on supplementary benefits – a proportion that is expected to rise as a result of the cutbacks in national insurance benefits and the rise in unemployment. That nine percent depends on a subsistence level of income, originally designed as the 'safety net' to catch the few who fell through Beveridge's national insurance scheme. For those millions who now depend on it, knowledge about their rights can mean the ability to survive from day to day.

Changes in Policy and Administration

During the last few years, the supplementary benefits scheme has slowly been opened up to greater scrutiny as the result of intense and sustained pressure. Welfare rights groups have played a considerable part in this, but it would be wrong to underestimate the part played by the Supplementary Benefits Commission (SBC) itself. A quango that disappeared in the 1980 changes, it was reviled by many claimants who saw it as 'the enemy'. Indeed, one could cite several examples of its refusal to challenge the *status quo*, particularly its defence of the secrecy shrouding the A Code, the confidential guidance to social security officials issued under the previous scheme. But at the same time it did make valiant efforts to improve the standard of its leaflets; its handbooks, the official guides to claimants, gradually contained more and more information; and it called repeatedly for more and better publicity to encourage take-up.

With the demise of the Commission, a fifth column exerting pressure, admittedly limited, on the claimant's behalf has now disappeared. Instead of the discretion it employed in administering the scheme, there is now a formalised set of rules enshrined in law. Apart from the Secretary of State, the key person is the Chief Supplementary Benefits Officer (CSBO), a civil servant whose role is closely modelled on the Chief National Insurance Officer. It is still too early to tell whether the CSBO will use his position to press for more openness, disclosure and reform, or whether he will simply administer the scheme according to his own interpretation of the rules of the game.

Government policy on openness about benefits underwent some remarkable changes under the former Social Services Secretary, Patrick Jenkin, between 1979 and 1981. There was not so much a U-turn as an S-bend; first there was a commitment, then the government reneged upon it, then it changed its mind again. The new scheme replaces a system built upon discretionary interpretation of law and policy by one founded upon legally enforceable rights that diminishes the element of discretion. In making such a change, without increasing the total amount of money funding supplementary benefits, the government admitted an element of 'rough justice' as a result of which some claimants would become better off and some would lose out. As a *quid pro quo* for this unsatisfactory state of affairs the government said originally that all the rules and regulations of the new scheme would be published. There would, it was understood, be no more A Code – the unpublished guidance to social security officials the secrecy of which had caused so much controversy. However, the government then appeared to change its mind. Mr Jenkin told the Opposition social services spokesman, Stanley Orme, that the procedural guidance under the new system, and the CSBO's own guidance to officials, would not be made public. As Mr Orme said: 'The A Code is dead; long live the A Code.'

At the end of 1980, however, to many people's surprise, part of the Chief Supplementary Benefits Officer's guidance was published, and the Department of Health and Social Security announced that other parts of his guidance, plus the relevant sections of the S Manual – the rewritten A Code – would also be released. Subsequently, it announced that the whole of the S Manual, subject to various changes and deletions, would be published, probably by the end of 1981. Mr Jenkin announced this as part of his Department's 'campaign' on open government. But it seemed likely that the manual's emasculation would make it such a tame document that the DHSS would have nothing to lose by publishing it; the contentious sections would be incorporated into other social security guidance which would remain secret.

The 'Open' Reviews of Supplementary Benefits

Such an ambiguous attitude towards open government was, perhaps, unsurprising in the Department that had produced the *Supplementary Benefits Review*.[2] This recommended the re-organisation of the scheme, and was an unprecedented example of open government – although, in the light of subsequent developments, one that was capable of bearing the most cynical interpretation. The review by the Department of Health and Social Security team was published in July 1978, along with more than forty background papers. The review team then embarked on a programme of more than a hundred meetings with staff, members of supplementary benefit appeal tribunals, claimants, pressure groups, academics, local authority representatives and other interested members of the public. More than one thousand written comments were also analysed by the team. Department civil servants lost no opportunity to emphasise how impressed they were with their own commitment to open government, demonstrated by this huge and time-consuming exercise. The Supplementary Benefits Commission was also pleased. In its annual report for 1978, it commented: 'This was an unprecedented exercise in the field of social policy-making with which we were greatly impressed, both because of the openness of the discussions and because of the intense interest of the many thousands of caring and committed people who took part.'[3]

However, some of those caring and committed thousands were less enchanted by the exercise. Some claimants' groups felt that some public meetings were insufficiently advertised; although some meetings were thrown open to everyone, others were not and there were suspicions even at that stage that the consultation was only a cosmetic procedure. It was acknowledged that the review team went through the evidence with a fine toothcomb, but there was considerable disillusionment when the major criticisms, on which most critics were agreed, were totally disregarded. These criticisms were that the proposed simplification could not be done without additional expenditure, since otherwise it would cause considerable hardship; and that the review had failed to consider the most intractable and fundamental problem in the scheme, that far too many people were forced to depend on it. After being invited to make their vociferous condemnation of these apparent defects, it seemed to some outrageous that the government then proceeded to change the law so that even more people would be forced onto supplementary benefit, and that no extra money was to be provided.

Did this mean, then, that the exercise in open government was a waste of time? Most welfare campaigners think not, on the grounds that it stimulated debate on a difficult subject, made more people aware of what was going on and more prepared to scrutinise the small print in the final legislation. And some of the original review proposals were dropped after public outcry. For example, the review proposed the introduction of a short-term scheme for the first eight or twelve weeks on benefit – a greatly simplified scheme, with one standard rate of benefit and no exceptional needs payments. The resulting uproar over the hardship this would have caused led to some rapid back-pedalling on the proposal. Yet Ruth Lister, director of the Child Poverty Action Group, was cynical about even this. Such an extreme proposal could have been included, she suggested, simply to be dropped – to demonstrate the flexibility of government and its willingness to take note of informed criticism.[4] It is not possible to prove or disprove this somewhat Machiavellian thesis. Nor can we know whether the open nature of the review might have produced a different outcome had the Labour party remained in power after the 1979 election. Tony Lynes, a former adviser to the Department of Health and Social Security during the last Labour government, thought that public reaction and its reflection in the Labour party would have made it politically impossible for Labour ministers to have changed the scheme without a commitment to additional expenditure. Any extra money would have been limited, but it would have been provided as a direct result of the public debate. In his opinion, the openness of the review constituted a significant victory for the DHSS (and notably for the SBC) over the Treasury, which is generally implacably opposed to such public debate on the grounds that it raises people's expectations and creates politically irresistible public pressure for more government expenditure.[5] In the event, the Treasury line of nil expenditure did win – but whether this was because of the election of a Conservative government committed to expenditure cuts, or whether it would have won anyway, must remain a moot point.

However limited it was, that exercise in open government is now bathed in a nostalgic glow. For since then social security policy making has retired further from the public gaze. The review had a second stage, with many more subjects listed for study. Hardly any of these papers have been published. They would be of little interest to the average citizen, perhaps, but would be of considerable use to the many caring and committed thousands who participated in the first stage and who fuel informed debate and influence government policy. It is hard to see precisely why there should be so much reluctance to publish these documents. One reason may be that they refer to areas of acrimony between different government departments – over the unified housing benefit, for example – and publication might be held to prejudice the process of barter between them. The attitude of the staff side should also not be ignored. Before the Supplementary Benefits Commission was wound up, its inspectors used to produce reports which would have been of considerable public interest had they been released. The inspectorate is a small group of middle grade officers which is used as the eyes and ears of the new Social Security Advisory Committee and was formerly used by the Supplementary Benefits Commission, looking at particular aspects of benefits, reading case papers and talking to staff in local offices. Although one or two of their reports were summarised in public in the days of the Commission, most remained confidential briefings to Commission members. The argument for confidentiality rested on the assumption that people expected their remarks to be treated in confidence, and that if this was not so the inspectors would have failed to achieve any staff cooperation. This argument is still used to justify the withholding of information that is in the public interest. It would surely not be too difficult to introduce suitable safeguards to ensure that individuals are not recognised in the reports.

How Discussion is Stifled

An incident in July 1980 illustrated the Department's sensitivity when such information happens to be disclosed.[6] A young DHSS civil servant, seconded for six months to an inner-city social security office, wrote an internal report on his time there. This report pulled no punches. The official said that because of the intense pressure of work, claimants were often treated somewhat brusquely and that the guidance from head office was sometimes ignored. In fact, he said, the social security scheme being operated by this local office was significantly different from the scheme that senior civil servants fondly imagined was in operation. It was 'similar in the main details, of course, but harsher in tone, lacking in refinement and infected with inconsistency and error.'

This report was unusual, not only because few civil servants gain such invaluable grass-roots experience but because even fewer are renowned for their frank and direct prose style. The report was by no means unsympathetic to this local office; it made clear that many of the errors being made – even some of the punitive attitudes – were due to chronic understaffing and lack of training. But when the report was leaked to *New Society*, there was a tremendous row, mainly because the civil servant and the local office were identified. Some of the publicity it received in the popular press over-simplified and distorted the conclusions, portraying the local staff in the worst possible light. This was indefensible. It was argued that as a result of the leak, it would be impossible to persuade local offices to cooperate with similar projects in future. This is surely a feeble argument. The report was valuable because its conclusions applied more broadly than to one office and as such shed an important light on social security policy. It is directly in the public interest for such information to be known outside Whitehall.

Other, more crucial, policy material has been hidden. When the 1980 Social Security Act changing the supplementary benefit scheme was introduced in Parliament, it was immediately clear that MPs would be incapable of informed debate without the detailed regulations. These were to flesh out the operation of the new law and would contain the detailed instructions about specific benefits – legally binding regulations that replaced the old discretionary policies. They were not to be published, however, until long after the Bill passed through its Commons scrutiny. The Department of Health and Social Security published a general summary of the regulations, but this was plainly unsatisfactory. MPs protested that they were unable to perform their duty in scrutinising the new law in detail, but to no avail. When the regulations were finally published, they were presented to Parliament *en bloc* and had to be voted upon in their entirety, so there was no way in which individual regulations could effectively be challenged in the Commons.

Statistical information on social security is getting progressively harder to obtain. During 1979, the Department of Health and

Social Security revealed that it would no longer publish every year its breakdown of statistics in the *Family Expenditure Survey* – another government economy measure.[7] This detailed information was crucial in setting out the extent of poverty in the country. It enabled campaigners, including MPs, to be specific in their suggestions for improving benefits. But now this breakdown is to be published only every two years. The Supplementary Benefits Commission itself realised the general value of information to policy making, particularly when it came to improving take-up. In a discussion paper published in 1978, it said, 'We ourselves have been concerned about the robustness of the statistical material and the lack of detailed information about the differences in the circumstances and take-up rates for various groups of claimants. We consider that reliable information is a prerequisite for effective action to improve take-up of supplementary benefit.'[8]

The A Code

Before the scheme was changed, the A Code came to achieve an almost symbolic significance, both as a symbol of closed government and as an indicator of the government's lack of sincerity towards the poor. Its mystique was undoubtedly heightened immeasurably by its secrecy. It was a huge and constantly expanding loose-leaf system of unpublished interpretation and guidance to social security staff, setting out SBC policy and how precisely this was to be put into practice – details, in general, that were not available in the official handbooks or the leaflets. Since it is thought that some of the equivalent information in the new system is still to remain unpublished, it is worth looking in some detail at the A Code controversy.

Constant leaks of the Code irritated the DHSS and the SBC. In its 1978 Report, the Commission wrote that a great deal of 'nonsense' had been talked about the Code.

The A Code is invariably referred to by the press as the 'secret' Code, with the implication that here is something pretty sinister; and in general the suggestion is scarcely veiled that it probably contains all sorts of dodges for doing claimants out of their rights. In fact of course the bulk of the Code is accounted for by the need, in a scheme dealing with the whole population, to cover the vast range of situations that arise and the variety of resources they will have. In addition staff have to be instructed on procedure – filling in control documents, issuing payable orders, reviewing claims to take account of changes of circumstances, etc – and this necessarily takes up much space. It would be a fraud on the public to publish such a document in the sense that publication is usually meant; certainly nobody would wish to buy it. This is not just because of its dullness or because the economic price would be so high. Like the internal instructions of any large organisation, the A Code has to be amended frequently and any edition would soon become out of date. On the other hand, for our part as the Commission, we have – subject to holding back such material as might weaken defences against fraud and abuse – no particular objection to the A Code's being made publicly available save that doing so pays tribute rather to the totem than the reality of open government. The responsibility for deciding this matter rests, however, with ministers.[9]

This churlish passage provides an insight into the contradictory and evasive Civil Service attitude towards publishing information about social security. It suggested that publication of the Code was irrelevant to claimants' needs. This, actually, was not true; but if it were true, there would be even less reason to protect it from public scrutiny. If it was considered necessary information for those officials administering benefits and deciding how much money people should be paid, then it was equally necessary for those claimants to have access to that information. It was true that it was huge and needed constant up-dating. But then this was equally true of the volumes of supplementary benefit regulations and national insurance benefit regulations that were available at larger public libraries and sometimes in social security offices. The A Code could have been made public in the same way.

As for the attempt to shuffle off responsibility onto ministers, it is amusing to note the reaction of Stanley Orme, then the Social Security Minister and previously a noted champion of open government, when the *Guardian* obtained a copy of the A Code and published extracts from it.[10] Mr Orme chose the novel approach of denying that the document was secret. He wrote to the paper: 'The A Code must be the most open "secret" there is. First, the rules about entitlement to supplementary benefit are already widely published in the Department's leaflets, available from any of our local offices, and in detail in the Supplementary Benefits Handbook, available from any Government bookshop. Second, the instructions in the A Code are a mixture of those known benefit rules and advice to officials on how to handle claims. . . .'[11]

Accordingly, the *Guardian* tested the 'openness' of the secret by formally requesting a copy of the Code from the DHSS as well as copies of some of the many other secret social security codes.

The paper was not surprised when all these requests were turned down on the basis that the documents were all covered by the Official Secrets Act. The A Code had, in fact, been leaked in parts to the press on a number of occasions; several welfare rights groups had also obtained copies which they found invaluable in advising claimants. But those civil servants who had made the Code available in this way, and those welfare rights workers and journalists who had disseminated the information in it, were all breaking the law. That there were no prosecutions under the Official Secrets Act was simply a matter of government policy.

So how important to claimants was the A Code – and, by extension, how important is the new S Manual? The A Code's subtle nuances of interpretation presented an overall picture of suspicious and rather insensitive bureaucracy, despite the considerable space devoted in it to telling officials to behave in a courteous and sympathetic manner towards claimants marked by misfortune. Read from cover to cover – not a pastime one would recommend – it revealed a ready suspicion of strikers and cohabiting couples. It also revealed that the DHSS was advising officials not to draw claimants' attention towards various benefit openings, but only to respond if asked.

Under social security law, only the man of an unmarried couple living together as man and wife is normally entitled to supplementary benefit; if he is in full-time work, he and his cohabitee are excluded from benefit. The copy of the A Code obtained by the *Guardian* pointed out that 'fine judgement' was required to decide whether a couple were living together as man and wife if they denied that this was the case. The Code guided officials through this sensitive area by instructing them to conduct discreet inquiries by specially trained 'nominated officers', with special investigators for the difficult cases in which the house had to be watched:

The nominated officer should conduct a full and sympathetic discussion with the woman of the whole situation. He should attempt to obtain answers to as many as possible of the questions contained in form A6 (LT) but he should be careful not to let the claimant see these questions, nor should he give the impression that he is completing a questionnaire. Questions concerning a sexual relationship and sleeping arrangements should not be asked directly and answers can only be obtained if the claimant (or man) volunteers the information.

In view of this emphasis on discretion, with instructions forbidding 'surreptitious attempts to view bedrooms', the Code then read rather strangely:

Evening visits, if necessary, should only be made on the authority of the HEO (Higher Executive Officer). Before authorising an evening visit, the HEO should be satisfied that, in the circumstances of the case, such a visit should not be likely to arouse justifiable public criticism. The HEO should also consider whether known factors of the case suggest that the nominated officer should be accompanied; if so, the second officer (preferably a woman if the nominated officer is a man) should take no part in the interview apart from the normal courtesies.

The guidance went on to say that in some cases claimants might not even know they *were* living together as man and wife: 'The growth of such a relationship may be so gradual that the parties do not completely appreciate that the relationship is no different from that of man and wife.'

The Code contained harsh guidance on benefits for strikers' families. Although the law states that strikers are entitled to no benefit for themselves, they are entitled to claim it for their dependants. But the guidance meant that such families could face eviction.

Cases where eviction is impending because of rent arrears which have accrued before the dispute should not automatically be considered under A3060 (payment of benefit to meet debts). If there are dependant children or the claimant is old or severely disabled and urgent measures are needed to stave off eviction, payment should be kept to the minimum and the claimant should be advised to come to some arrangement with his landlord to pay the balance off when back in work.

If the claimant insisted that the payment was not enough to meet exceptional expenses or avoid eviction he would be issued with the relevant claim form. But it would be endorsed: 'The SBC do not consider that a payment for urgent need is appropriate.'

Such examples demonstrate how the law, itself approved by Parliament and subject to democratic scrutiny, can be operated in ways which at the very least are questionable and to which some members of the public might well object. Yet no questions can be asked about such administration if guidance like this remains undisclosed. Such secrecy could, conversely, work against the claimant's interest if he failed to realise how far the Code actually protected his rights and how social security officials were ignoring the guidelines it laid down. There was an example of this in 1976 when Jo Tunnard, then a worker in the Child Poverty Action Group's citizens' rights office, stumbled across A Code instructions on mortgage interest.[12] The Code revealed that separated wives claiming supplementary benefit were entitled to a mortgage interest allowance even if the mortgage was not in their name – an enlightened policy designed to alleviate the hardship of mortgage worries at a time of emotional crisis. Yet many women had been refused this help, despite the policy instructions of which they and their solicitors had been ignorant, and in some cases women had lost their homes through financial hardship. If the Code had been publicly available, this would have been far less likely to happen.

Keeping Claimants in the Dark

Interestingly, the last official handbook published by the Supplementary Benefits Commission went further than any previous SBC handbook in including information that had previously been restricted to the Code. There were various possible explanations for this progress: that the Commission had finally been won over to the cause of freedom of information; that it had been embarrassed into doing so by the pressure of repeated disclosure; that as the scheme was shortly going to change it had little to lose by publishing information that would shortly be out of date; or that it was putting down a marker, to try to ensure a more open approach when the new scheme came into operation.

For the new scheme has the potential to restrict the claimant's knowledge of his rights as much as the old. The predominantly discretionary policies of the Supplementary Benefits Commission have, it is true, been enshrined in legally binding regulations, so in theory the scheme should have become clearer and more open. But in practice this seems not to be the case. From 1972, supplementary benefit regulations were published in a loose-leaf volume known as the Yellow Book. Before the scheme changed, these largely contained administrative rules or regulations about the machinery of making payments. Under the new system, most of the regulations relate to the benefits themselves and so there are many more of them. A complete set including all the amending supplements costs more than £20, and requires a trained mind to penetrate it. It is hardly the sort of reference that the average claimant would peruse, and the cost might even discourage a claimant's adviser.

Yet the regulations are at least available for public scrutiny. They are as important as the regulations relating to national insurance benefits, published in equivalent volumes known as the Brown Books. But these have created their own problems. The Disability Alliance said that one of the biggest problems at appeals was that the claimant did not know what kind of information was required from him or her and what would be considered irrelevant. With national insurance benefits, it was simply a case of finding the argument that fitted the relevant rule, unlike the old supplementary benefit appeals where the element of discretion meant that the case had to include a presentation of the home circumstances. With a national insurance benefit such as mobility allowance, said one Alliance worker, people would present social factors which to them were highly relevant reasons for wanting the benefit but which were, in official eyes, totally beside the point. She said,

It's about whether you can put one foot in front of the other; it's medical evidence they want, and social factors will simply irritate the tribunal. Another common complaint is that if someone is in bed and breakfast lodging before being rehoused, the local social security office has a ceiling above which it won't pay charges; the argument that the claimant can't afford to pay is not the argument they want. You've got to get the patter, know how to respond to them. Welfare rights officers need courses to teach them how to do this. National insurance benefits catch people out, and so you've got to get hold of the Brown Book and then find your way around it. If you find one in a local social security office, you find yourself closeted in a little room with a civil servant breathing down your neck, which can be very intimidating. They can't say they haven't published the information, but everything militates against the consumer being able to use it. To claimants, the staff are the enemy and vice versa. Claimants know that if they make a fuss the staff can hit them back through the use of discretion.[13]

Even though this discretion has now been reduced, there is still a considerable amount of fine judgement involved. Apart from the regulations, the public has access to the supplementary benefits handbook, which is essentially a popular version of the regulations. The S Manual, the procedural guide, is apparently to be published, but the Chief Supplementary Benefits Officer's guidance on interpretation of the regulations and of the considerable body of case law that will build up from appeals will not be published in full. The CSBO's guidance is, in fact, more important than the S Manual because his interpretations will have a direct bearing upon the benefits people get. The parallel is the confidential guidance produced by his 'twin', the Chief National Insurance Officer. Nick Warren, a solicitor formerly with the Family Rights Group, said that the publicity over the A Code had obscured the fact that important secret codes also operated within the national insurance system. Because these had never been disclosed, it was impossible to estimate exactly how important they were. But it would be useful to know, for example, how an insurance officer interpreted the extremely vague regulations on mobility allowance where there was considerable room for fine tuning.[14]

It is probably no coincidence that the promised publication of the S Manual should come at a time when the changing emphasis of social security policy makes it less important than it was. The government's drive against benefit fraud has directed the whole thrust of social security administration away from helping to meet need and towards a systematic weeding out of 'abuses'. It is a fair bet that anything relating to fraud will not be published in the S Manual, and the various fraud codes of guidance will remain secret. It could be argued that this is only right; to divulge such information would surely hamper fraud detection work. But behind this discreet umbrella shelter disturbing policy developments of which the public should be aware but which have been revealed only because they have been 'leaked'.

Early in 1981, *New Society* carried details of some of these developments, publishing extracts from the confidential DHSS *Fraud Investigators' Guide* and other documents.[15] These revealed that policy was shifting away from bringing fraud charges to trial; benefit was being stopped on the basis of evidence that would not have stood up in court. One such internal document said: 'In the past, as many cases as possible were pursued to prosecution but, in future, while the deterrent effect of successful prosecutions will continue to be borne in mind, the cessation of a claim might be regarded in appropriate cases as the most cost effective way of dealing with the matter.'

This point was amplified further by a DHSS letter passed to the Child Poverty Action Group, which said of the teams of special investigators on anti-fraud drives: 'In some instances the cases were submitted for prosecution and in others, where sufficient evidence for prosecution was not available, benefit was withdrawn.'

The *New Society* article also revealed that where an official decided that a case was 'not suitable' for prosecution, he was advised to interview the suspect. 'He may give you sufficient information to justify withdrawing (or reducing) his benefit. Or he may decide to withdraw his claim.' Despite a caveat warning officials to avoid anything that could lay them open to accusations of pressurising claimants, it is not hard to see how such guidance could lead to precisely that kind of pressure.

Another leak, this time to the *Sunday Times*, revealed confidential instructions to officials to probe the sex lives of unmarried mothers claiming benefit.[16] In this last case, the government acted promptly to review such instructions. All these examples, however, revealed policies which ran counter to natural justice or common decency and which would never have been known had they not leaked out.

The highly complex, legalistic new supplementary benefit system will probably be even less accessible to the public than a system based largely on discretion. There is now even more need for highly trained welfare rights officers, but with present government policy on public expenditure there is hardly any likelihood of an increase in their numbers. And they are few and far between. Only about twenty-five local authorities have their own welfare rights service, almost all of them urban areas controlled by Labour. Most of these have only one or two workers, and in many cases they simply advise other professionals such as social workers and are not directly accessible to the public. There is also voluntary sector provision – citizens' advice bureaux, for example, but these vary greatly in expertise.

The lack of specific advice on benefits operates against claimants at all stages of the claiming process. But perhaps the biggest problem arises right at the beginning, before they even claim. It is a circular problem: that to find out about their right to a benefit, they have to ask about it, but in order to ask they have to know about it in the first place. There are many grouses about the attitude of social security officials who, it is said, tend to make it difficult for claimaints to discover which benefits they can claim. One often-cited example is the B1 form. When people sign on for unemployment benefit, they may be entitled to supplementary benefit instead or in addition. This, however, has to be claimed on a separate form – a B1 – but these forms are not issued automatically. Indeed, officials are instructed not to give BIs to people unless they ask for them specifically, or if they look as if they need supplementary benefit. One man who was helped by the Disability Alliance suffered from multiple sclerosis. He inquired whether he was eligible for supplementary benefit, but was told he did not qualify as he had too much money in savings. So he left the office empty-handed and tried to manage. It was only when he read an article in *Woman* magazine that he realised there were numerous benefits which he could claim. Overnight, his income doubled. This, said the Alliance, illustrated the point that the Department of Health and Social Security was oriented towards the benefit rather than the consumer. Counter staff were allocated to specific benefits and did not know about the rest. If they decided that a claimant was not entitled to one benefit, they would not inquire further and discover what he could claim. There was also the difficulty of a high turnover of counter staff, with very young clerks who might be ignorant, uninterested or even hostile to the claimants. And the long queues in local offices hardly created a favourable atmosphere for long and searching discussions.[17]

Ironically, the situation seems to have got even worse now that the scheme has been 'simplified'. The Child Poverty Action Group's citizens' rights office, in the first few months of the new scheme, was reporting that counter staff were inadequately trained and were in many cases ignorant of the new regulations. They were tending to use the S Manual and not the regulations themselves; this led to mistakes, which would be rectified once the rights workers referred officials to the relevant regulation. It soon became apparent that the familiar pattern was repeating itself; persistent or better informed claimants were getting more from the system than claimants who simply believed what their local offices told them.

There have been some spectacular demonstrations of the extent of ignorance among claimants about their rights. In 1978 Strathclyde Regional Council published the result of a project it carried out in a centre for physically disabled people in Scotland.[18] This consisted of assessing the entitlement to benefit of seventy-two members of the centre and their families, followed by help with their claims. The results showed a previous massive shortfall in take-up; at the end of the project, the group were more than £12,000 per year better off in annual income. Yet these were all 'professional claimants' – people generally dependent on state benefits for most of their lives.

The team discovered poor overall knowledge of benefits, very poor knowledge of supplementary benefit discretionary areas, little knowledge and some confusion about appeals and uncertainty about how their weekly benefit totals were made up. As a whole, the group had heard of less than half the benefits mentioned to them. Only one in four knew about attendance allowance reviews and appeals, and only two in ten knew about national insurance appeals. Apart from such ignorance, and the everpresent problem of stigma, the schemes were so complex that the disabled people had a hard task working out which benefits to claim. Would they be better off on supplementary benefit rather than invalidity benefit, for example, or on non-contributory invalidity pension rather than supplementary benefit? And so on.

The staff are traditionally regarded as the claimants' enemy, with punitive attitudes towards many groups of claimants, particularly the unemployed or strikers. But trade union officials representing the staff display concern that, particularly at a time of expenditure cutbacks, they are unable to identify need and fulfil the 'welfare' part of their role. A spokesman for the Society of Civil and Public Servants said that claimants often failed to put down all the relevant information on their claim form. They were frightened of getting things wrong because they were put off by the forms themselves, or they were afraid of being classified as scroungers by appearing to complain about all their domestic circumstances. The cutbacks in social security staff and the rise in the number of claimants meant drastic cuts in home visiting which was essential to discover such details. A Department of Health and Social Security national survey – itself never published – had shown that between ten and fifteen per cent of social security payments were incorrect because of the lack of home visits. Said a spokesman:

You get a man with six kids who is on the dole. He reports to you that he has increased his family. You assume that this is correct. But what you don't know is that the child has some disability and the family needs extra heating in the house, or has to maintain a constant temperature. He doesn't tell you that because he doesn't know he has to tell you. Suddenly, he asks for help with a fuel bill; there's been a threat of disconnection. You visit, and only then find out about the infirm child – and that the house is damp, and that the wife is incapable of managing money.

The vast majority of supplementary benefit interviews are not detailed enough. Officers don't have sufficient knowledge of the system to ask the right questions. They ask the obvious; they should go deeper. After working on it for about three years, the officer should have a fair knowledge, but what tends to happen is that officers get put into these situations after six months.[19]

Claimants' groups remain unconvinced that the majority of officials are motivated by such enlightened concern for the welfare of claimants – concern which appears to increase in direct proportion to the seniority of trade union officials or civil servants themselves. But official attitudes are by no means the only stumbling block. Social security leaflets are another area of concern, both because of their unavailability and their incomprehensibility. There are enormous numbers of leaflets, published about every conceivable benefit. But it is a rare social security office where a potential claimant will find a comprehensive set prominently displayed; and post offices, and then only main post offices, are only obliged to have four leaflets on permanent display. Geoff Fimister, senior welfare rights officer in Newcastle, said that official concern with better publicity seemed to ebb and flow.[20] There had traditionally been a couldn't-care-less attitude which resulted in minimum publicity; then the 1970s saw a move towards a genuine attempt to improve the quality and quantity of leaflets, particularly on supplementary benefit; now publicity was again being downgraded, with leaflets becoming harder to find and the move towards better design petering out. Renewal of leaflets remained, in a changing field, inadequate. Regrettable lapses of time occurred between renewals: a leaflet on unemployment benefit, renewed in May 1980, was last printed in August 1978; a leaflet on attendance allowance, also renewed in May 1980, had last been updated in December 1975.

Having successfully overcome the hurdles of (a) knowing about the benefit in order to know about the benefit and (b) finding the relevant leaflet, claimants may then find themselves completely baffled by what they contain. A leaflet on maternity allowance, for example, was acknowledged in at least one case by the National Insurance Commissioner to be incomprehensible. Late claims may not generally be backdated 'unless you have a good reason for not having claimed earlier.' In this particular case, a woman argued that among the good reasons for her late claim was

the fact that she had misunderstood the contribution conditions
for entitlement set out in a DHSS leaflet.

The relevant section of the most recent version of the maternity
benefits leaflet says:

The 2 contribution conditions which you must meet in order to get
maternity allowance take account of whether you claim before or after
your baby is born. They are based on the *relevant time* which is the
Sunday of the 11th week before the week in which your baby is: **expected**,
if you claim *before* your baby is born; **born**, if you claim *after* your baby
is born.

It then spells out the conditions:

First condition: Before the relevant time you must have paid Class 1
(employee's) contributions on earnings of at least 25 times the lower
weekly earnings limit or equivalent Class 2 (self-employed) contributions
in any one tax year. Each Class 2 contribution you have paid counts as
a Class 1 contribution on earnings at the lower earnings limit. You may
also meet this condition if you have: paid at least 26 flat-rate Class 1 or
Class 2 contributions before 6 April 1975; *or* paid Class 1 contributions
on earnings well above the lower earnings limit even though your employment did not last for 25 weeks; *or* only recently started paying
contributions; *or* stopped receiving a widow's or widowed mother's allowance for any reason other than your re-marriage or because you are living
with a man as his wife.
Second condition: You must have paid or been credited with Class 1
contributions on earnings of at least 50 times the lower weekly earnings
limit or equivalent Class 2 (self-employed) contributions (see first condition) in the tax year relevant to your claim.[21]

And so on. Small wonder that the National Insurance Commissioner declared: 'Quite frankly, I do not find the pamphlet easy
to understand in relation to contribution conditions. Bearing in
mind all the facts of this case, I come to the conclusion that the
misinterpretation of the contribution condition was a mistake that
any person not skilled in social security law would have made.'

Another woman complained to the Equal Opportunities Commission that she had not realised how inflexible was the eighteen
weeks' period for the allowance. 'After having, (I thought) made
sense of the leaflets issued by the DHSS, I believed I would be
entitled to 18 weeks' maternity allowance regardless of when I
gave up work. . . . As far as I can see, there was nothing to say
that I had to give up work 11 weeks before the birth to get my
full 18 weeks' allowance! However, when I received my allowance

book I found that I had only been awarded 11 weeks' allowance. . . .'[22]

To be fair, the Department of Health and Social Security has made an effort in recent years to render its forms and leaflets intelligible to the ordinary claimant, particularly those on supplementary benefit. For example it commissioned the Salford Form Market – an advice centre on official forms and leaflets for the public – to redesign six or seven forms. The Form Market, an experimental project, concluded:

> There has been no major effort to write official prose in language which is understandable to the majority of the population, including those people often described as semi-literate. The related problems of semi-literacy and the complexity of official messages hit hardest at people who are already socially disadvantaged. Often for them the ability to read something successfully can be a matter of survival. Twenty-five percent of all adults have a reading age below fourteen. Most forms and leaflets require a reading age above fourteen, many well above.[23]

One reason for the unintelligibility of leaflets is the tension within the Department of Health and Social Security between the information and policy-making divisions, with information generally losing out because so much importance is attached to getting the law right. To a certain extent complexity is inevitable, if the law is itself complicated. But at the same time, if the DHSS sought the advice of enough experts on communications the leaflets would undoubtedly be clearer. They need to be written by people who are adept at making complicated ideas understandable to the general public. Whatever their merits may be, civil servants do not usually boast this particular expertise. The fact that the Department does not generally seek this advice provides its own comment on the government's willingness to improve take-up. If it really wanted more people to claim their rights, it would be advertising benefits on television and in newspapers and magazines. The usual official response to such a suggestion is that social security offices would then be swamped by inquiries from people who were not entitled to these benefits; the staff would be engulfed and the public would be disappointed. The answer to this would be to ensure that the advertising was clear, and to increase the staff. It was, after all, in Beveridge's original plan that local offices should contain advice bureaux where members of the public could find out 'not only about the official provision for social security, but about all the other organisations – official, semi-official and voluntary, central or local – which may be able to help' them in their difficulties.[24]

The whole issue of social security information ultimately boils down to whether such benefits are seen as people's rights, or as up-dated poor law handouts. At present, they tend to be seen as the latter, both by claimants and by officials. Claimants feel ashamed to ask for them; officials do little to discourage that shame. Access to information about benefits, from the highest levels of government policy down to the humblest leaflet, amounts to an obstacle course, with hurdles supplied variously by the Official Secrets Act, Civil Service parsimony, prejudice against supposed work-shyness, and bureaucratic bungling – refereed by politicians of both parties who are indifferent to the needs of the poor. The right of access to all this information, with the onus upon government to disclose it promptly, fully and accurately and so that people can understand it, can only be granted when claiming benefit is itself perceived as a democratic right.

REFERENCES

1 *Supplementary Benefits Handbook; A Guide to Claimants' Rights*, Supplementary Benefits Administration Papers 2, revised November 1979, HMSO, p. 13.
2 *Social Assistance: A Review of the Supplementary Benefits Scheme in Great Britain*, Department of Health and Social Security, July 1978.
3 *Supplementary Benefits Commission Annual Report 1978*, Cmnd 7725, HMSO, p. 12.
4 Interview with the author.
5 Interview with the author.
6 *New Society*, 10 July 1980.
7 *Guardian*, 22 October 1979.
8 *Take-up of Supplementary Benefits*, Supplementary Benefits Administration Papers 7, HMSO, 1978, p. 1.
9 *Supplementary Benefits Commission Annual Report 1978, op.cit.*, p. 59.
10 *Guardian*, 4 January 1979.
11 *Guardian*, 5 January 1979.
12 Tunnard, Jo, *No Father, No Home?*, Poverty Pamphlet 28, Child Poverty Action Group, 1976. See especially the conclusions and recommendations contained in chapter IV.
13 Interview with the author.
14 Interview with the author.

15 *New Society*, 22 January 1981.
16 *Sunday Times*, 22 March 1981.
17 Interview with the author.
18 Casserly, John and Clark, Bill, *A Welfare Rights Approach to the Chronically Sick and Disabled*, Strathclyde Regional Council, March 1978.
19 Interview with the author.
20 Interview with the author.
21 *Maternity Benefits*, National Insurance Leaflet NI.17A, Department of Health and Social Security, September 1979.
22 *I Want a Baby . . . but What about my Job?* Equal Opportunities Commission, March 1979.
23 Quoted in Vernon, Tom, *Gobbledegook: A Critical Review of Official Forms and Leaflets – and How to Improve Them*, National Consumer Council, 1980, p. 46.
24 *Social Insurance and Allied Services*, Cmnd 6404, HMSO, 1942, para. 397. Quoted in National Consumer Council, *The Fourth Right of Citizenship*, NCC, p. 7.

Energy

11

Frances Williams

Decisions about energy – ranging from a household's choice of heating system to national plans for the development of nuclear power – ought to rest on full information about relative costs, efficiency, and safety. But government and the nationalised energy industries are parsimonious and selective with the information they release, argues Frances Williams, while the consumer watchdog bodies for gas, electricity and coal can do little to improve the situation.

Decisions about the supply of energy and its use have a fundamental impact on every aspect of people's lives, from the air they breathe to the goods they buy. The crucial strategic decisions are taken largely by central government and the nationalised energy industries. And these institutions have a virtual monopoly over the information necessary for those decisions. They can and do use their monopoly to dictate the terms of energy debate by selective release of information or to prevent informed debate altogether by keeping information to themselves.

Government and the nationalised energy industries also use the information they hold to influence the decisions individuals make on energy use, from insulating the loft or changing the heating system from oil to gas, to buying a more economical car. And two of the industries – electricity and gas – impinge on people's lives in a personal way, through their direct involvement in supplying fuel to the home.

Consumers   and consumer organisations – have three distinct reasons for wanting information on energy: first, to contribute to the formulation of energy policy, and to do this they need information to help them understand and analyse present circumstances and the consequences and implications of policy options for the future; secondly, to monitor the effects and impact of current policies on consumers and the extent to which the energy industries are meeting the needs and interests of their customers;

thirdly – a point not explored in detail in this chapter but nevertheless an important one – to enable individuals to take sensible decisions in their own best interests (for example, on what heating system to install), and to assert their rights and obtain proper redress if they have a complaint or grievance.

Without information those on the outside of the decision-making machinery are at a serious disadvantage. And so, it can be argued, are the decision-makers themselves. Inbreeding of intellectual arguments is likely to lead to bad decisions. As the Council for Science and Society has put it 'pluralistic channels of analysis, information, advice and opinion, are the only safeguards against rationalised follies.'[1]

This chapter concentrates on problems of access to information held by central government and the nationalised energy industries. But the oil multi-nationals also exert powerful influence and pressure on national and international energy policy. These companies operate mainly in the private domain and are exempt from any continuing public scrutiny of their activities, although from time to time oil companies are the subject of investigations under competition legislation.[2] Access to information held by private companies raises some difficult issues which are outside this book's terms of reference. But consumers' basic interests in disclosure of information are no different in relation to the major private oil companies than they are to the nationalised energy industries.

The Institutional Framework

Primary responsibility for the government's energy policy rests with the Department of Energy, but a number of other departments have substantial energy interests – notably the Department of the Environment, the Department of Transport, the Department of Industry and, above all, the Treasury. Since autumn 1979 each of these departments has been 'shadowed' by a parliamentary select committee. These shadow committees superseded most of the pre-existing select committees, two of which – on science and technology and on the nationalised industries – had conducted a number of enquiries on or relevant to energy issues. The Department of Energy is the sponsoring department for the nationalised energy industries – the electricity supply industry (including the nuclear industry), the gas and coal industries and the British National Oil Corporation (BNOC).

The electricity supply industry in England and Wales comprises the Central Electricity Generating Board (CEGB), which is responsible for the generation and transmission of electricity; twelve autonomous area boards which distribute electricity to consumers; and the Electricity Council which acts as a forum to bring together the generating and distributing sides of the industry. The CEGB also has close relations with the Atomic Energy Authority, which is responsible for research and development into nuclear energy, and with British Nuclear Fuels, a publicly owned limited company which makes and reprocesses nuclear fuel. The Scottish electricity industry is organised on an integrated basis, with the South of Scotland Electricity Board and the North of Scotland Hydro-Electric Board responsible for both generation and distribution. Their sponsoring department is the Scottish Office.

The British Gas Corporation is an integrated industry responsible for the supply and distribution of gas throughout Britain. The task of distributing gas to consumers is devolved to its twelve regions.

The National Coal Board is responsible for mining and extracting coal in Britain – but it has only a small share of the retail market. The retail coal trade is almost entirely in private hands.

The British National Oil Corporation implements government measures for state participation in the development of UK oil resources. It has major interests in the exploration and operation of most of the North Sea oil fields in production or under development, participates in all the commercial fields and is also a major trader in petroleum. The BNOC advises the Secretary of State on oil matters and undertakes activities on behalf of the government including management of the state's land pipelines and storage sites; in mid-1981 its structure and powers were under review.

The electricity, gas and coal industries each have some form of statutory consumer representation, though with different functions, rights and responsibilities. There is no consumer watchdog to monitor the activities of either the oil or the nuclear industries.

Each area electricity board (and the two Scottish boards) has a consultative council with a statutory duty to represent the interests of consumers to the board in relation to its plans and operations. The board in its turn must inform the council of its 'general plans and arrangements' for exercising and performing its statutory functions.[3]

In addition the chairmen of consultative councils sit on the area electricity boards as *ex officio* part-time members.

The CEGB and Electricity Council have no statutory consumer representation. But in November 1976 the Electricity Consumers' Council was set up on a non-statutory basis to represent consumers in policy making at national level. The Labour government intended the Council to become statutory when proposals to unify the electricity industry in England and Wales were implemented – but these proposals were abandoned by the present Conservative government.

The British Gas Corporation is obliged by law to inform the National Gas Consumers' Council of its 'general plans and arrangements' for exercising and performing its functions in relation to the supply of gas.[4] The national Council, and twelve regional consumer councils, are charged with considering the interests of gas consumers and representing them to the British Gas Corporation.

The Domestic Coal Consumers' Council has a duty to consider 'any matter affecting the sale or supply . . . of coal, coke or manufactured fuel for domestic purposes'[5]; but the National Coal Board is under no obligation to provide the Council with information, nor to consult it in any particular way.

Government and the Energy Industries

A considerable amount of information passes from nationalised industries to their sponsor departments – including corporate plans, investment programmes, proposals for major investment projects, and regular reports on plans and progress. The extent to which government departments choose to intervene in industry decisions as a consequence of this information varies widely, and there have been continuing wrangles between the two sides about the appropriate role of government, and how much information is necessary to fulfil that role. Strictly speaking, nationalised industries are under a statutory obligation to supply any information required by the sponsoring minister. In practice there have been occasions when information requested has been refused.[6]

In general, civil servants are heavily dependent on the information given to them by the industries, which will necessarily be selective and may not always be objective. Nor are government departments at all times kept up to date by the industries. This caused some embarrassment when a substantial downward revision of electricity demand forecasts, announced by the CEGB in February 1980 soon after the government had given the green light for an expanded nuclear power programme, obliged the

Prime Minister to ask the Central Policy Review Staff to re-assess whether the two earliest nuclear stations should go ahead (it said they should).

Some of the information supplied to government by the energy industries may be published in government statistics, in their annual reports and accounts or as evidence to a select committee – but most remains buried in government files. A great deal is supplied, as a matter of convention, in confidence – even though it may not be in any way sensitive. For example, the Department of Energy has refused to provide even the Department of the Environment with its estimates of long-run marginal costs for fuel, on the grounds that the estimates contain 'elements of fuel industry commercial information' and to pass them to another department would be a breach of confidentiality. This means that the two departments are basing policy on different pricing assumptions.

Parliament

Ministers are technically accountable to Parliament for the workings of their own departments and for certain aspects of the operation of the nationalised industries sponsored by them. Parliamentary questions on day-to-day management matters are disallowed (subject to ministerial discretion) but otherwise ministers can be questioned on their statutory responsibilities towards the industries, information about the industry in general and matters of public importance. Of course this does not mean that the requested information is always forthcoming.

The other major channel for information about government energy policy and the operations of the fuel industries is through the parliamentary select committee system. Select committees can take evidence from any source and have very considerable powers to order the production of papers by private bodies or individuals, so long as these are relevant to their work. Their powers encompass nationalised industries but not government departments headed by a Secretary of State (which includes all five departments with major energy interests). In practice, the formal powers of select committees are rarely invoked and a great deal of information is obtained voluntarily from government departments, nationalised industries and other bodies.

However 'the Government has expressed reluctance to provide evidence which involves, for instance, matters of national security, the affairs of private individuals or bodies, information given to

them in confidence, matters which are the subject of sensitive
negotiation between governments and details of future legislative
proposals.[7]

It is difficult to quarrel with governments' reluctance to release,
say, details of the private affairs of individuals or genuine matters
of national security. But 'information given in confidence' may
cover instances where there was no need for the government to
guarantee confidentiality and where the information is of public
interest. This includes many of the details supplied to them by the
nationalised industries. Further, in the interests of preserving the
'collective responsibility of ministers', civil servants are instructed
not to give information on advice to ministers by officials, or
interdepartmental or ministerial consultations, about the level at
which decisions are taken, nor about the methods used to review
government policy (such as whether the Central Policy Review
Staff was called in).

The notion of the collective responsibility of ministers can be
pushed a little too far. The Select Committee on Procedure has
pointed out that if select committees were consistently refused
information on departmental or inter-departmental organisation
this could prevent them from adequately scrutinising the administration and expenditure of government departments.[8]

Witnesses to select committees may also ask for a private hearing of evidence and indicate those parts of the evidence which
they would prefer not to be published. These requests are normally acceded to. (For example, a 1978 select committee enquiry
accepted in confidence BNOC's five-year plan, an analysis of the
electricity supply industry's capital expenditure estimates used for
the government's public expenditure white paper, and the National Coal Board's five-year plan.)[9] Otherwise the reports of, and
evidence to, select committees are published in full.

Select committee reports and evidence furnish a great deal of
interesting and useful information, much of which would otherwise remain unpublished.[10] But select committees are understaffed
and do not always have the resources to ensure that the right
questions are asked to obtain the maximum amount of useful
information, nor to prevent the concealment of information by
skilful witnesses.

It is worth noting too that the powerful Public Accounts Committee, which is served by the Comptroller and Auditor General
and his staff, does not have access to nationalised industry
accounts because these are audited not by the Comptroller but by

private auditors. This is a particularly severe handicap in the case of the BNOC, which acts to a large extent as an executor of government policy.[11]

Competition Agencies

Nationalised energy industries may on occasion come up for scrutiny under competition legislation. In the past the Price Commission has looked at gas and electricity prices and the profit margins of coal merchants,[12] while the Monopolies and Mergers Commission has investigated connection charges for gas and electricity and the retail showrooms operated by British Gas.[13]

The 1980 Competition Act, which abolished the Price Commission, gives the Monopolies and Mergers Commission new powers to enquire into the efficiency and costs of the service provided by a public corporation, or the possible abuse of a monopoly situation by it. The CEGB was the first energy industry to be examined under these new powers (the report was published in 1981). The Act also provides for the Office of Fair Trading (OFT) to undertake investigations, at the request of the Secretary of State, into prices of 'major public concern' including those of nationalised industries. The reports of OFT investigations need not be published.

The Monopolies and Mergers Commission and the Office of Fair Trading can require an industry to provide any information which is relevant to the enquiry (as could the Price Commission). For publication, however, the Commission is asked to exclude 'so far as that is practicable' information about the private affairs of individuals or matters relating to a particular company 'where publication of that matter would or might seriously and prejudicially affect [their] interests'. In relation to companies (and individuals in the Price Commission legislation) these matters can be included in the report if they are necessary 'for the purposes of the report'.[14] Both the Price Commission and the Monopolies and Mergers Commission have been careful not to disclose confidential evidence 'unless it is essential for proper understanding of the issues'.

Information regarded by most companies, including nationalised industries, as 'sensitive' includes detailed figures on turnover and profit margins (for example, in relation to specific goods), information on wage costs and manning levels which could antagonise trade unions, and details of future plans or projections. The area electricity boards were particularly sensitive about Price

Commission requests to show returns on contracting and servicing separately. Contracting was generally profitable while servicing operated at a loss. Boards were thus open to criticism on a number of counts: private operators might allege unfair competition on servicing, whereas other critics might see the same figures as a sign of inefficiency.

The Secretary of State has additional powers to exclude from copies of the final report matters the publication of which he considers would be against the public interest. A glance through recent Price Commission and Monopolies and Mergers Commission reports suggests that these powers are used, following representations by the companies involved, to overrule Commission decisions to publish 'sensitive' information.

Consumer Councils

The area electricity boards and the British Gas Corporation (but not the National Coal Board) have a statutory duty to provide information to their consumer councils. But, 'in practice, some [electricity] boards interpret the duty freely, generously, and on a regular basis: but others do so narrowly, grudgingly and only in response to specific requests from the area council.'[15] A report by the National Consumer Council in 1976 noted that, in spite of the consultative councils' chairmen being members of the area electricity boards, the flow of information was not uniform.[16]

In 1980 the Public Interest Research Centre examined the usefulness of some of the regular information provided to electricity consultative councils. The Centre found that as well as some useful information the reports often provided a great deal of inessential or irrelevant details in copious quantity (like the numbers of staff receiving safe driving awards). Essential information was omitted and little was said about expected future developments and trends. The Centre also noted that boards tended to provide more, and more specific, information where this reflected credit on their operations, whereas otherwise the opposite was true – such as, 'fewer complaints were received than in the previous year and it is pleasing to report that seventy-three complimentary letters were received.'[17]

Information Supplied on a Confidential Basis A further difficulty experienced by consumer councils is that much of the information provided by the boards is supplied on a confidential basis.

It is quite common . . . to find that some information, when it is supplied, is accompanied by the declaration that it must be regarded as off the record – which means, in effect, that it is given on condition that the council shall not use it to support any case it might wish to make publicly in opposition to the board.[18]

Information on gas supplied regularly on a confidential basis includes: background information relating to proposed price increases; statistics on accidental deaths from gas poisoning and deaths from gas explosions; target standards of service to domestic gas consumers (but not on how performance measures up to these standards); information from British Gas' national defects monitoring service for gas appliances; certain information on potential and actual disconnections and references of consumers in difficulty to the Department of Health and Social Security and local authority social services departments.

The supply of information on a confidential basis hampers the ability of consumer councils to represent consumers' interests effectively. They are denied the opportunity to put their case to a wider audience and to enlist the help of other organisations, the public and the press. They cannot fully account for their policies and activities to their constituency – the customers whose interests they are there to serve. And, most seriously, they may feel obliged to tone down or suppress criticism of board policies and practices in order to safeguard the trickle of information from the industry. The ability to supply information on a confidential basis as it pleases can be a powerful weapon in the hands of an industry which intends to keep a consumer council quiescent.

There are undeniably some kinds of information which consumer councils need to enable them to consider consumers' interests but which are better kept out of the public domain. This would include information which is genuinely 'commercially sensitive' – that is, which could be used to advantage by a competitor or customer company, such as plans to raise prices and sales, and those under discussion with trade unions, such as pit closures. But there is no such justification for much of the information currently provided to consumer councils on a confidential only basis. Even where information is genuinely confidential consumer councils should be entrusted with the details if they are relevant to consumers' interests. They should not get the information orally 'off the record' – as the Domestic Coal Consumer Council (DCCC) does with pit closures – or have sight of papers which must then be committed to memory – as happened with a report on the London Electricity Board's future sales and contracting policies.

Chairmen of consultative councils who sit on the area electricity boards may experience particularly acute difficulties with the status of the information they receive as board members. This was one reason why the Chairman of the DCCC averred that he would rather not be a member of the National Coal Board: 'to what extent could I take to my Council confidential matters that have been told me as a member of the Board but were not for public consumption?'. On the other hand the Scottish electricity consultative councils said that 'there has never been any difficulty in asking the Boards for further information to which Chairmen as Board members are already legally entitled.'[19]

On balance, the consensus of opinion favours the informational advantages of having a consumer council chairman on the board of the industry. The Select Committee on Nationalised Industries concurred with the view of the Labour government, the National Consumer Council and the energy consumer councils (with the exception of coal) that: 'An important element in the provision of information to consumer councils is the extension of Board membership. Your Committee believe that a voice for consumers on the Board is valuable, but that a representative has ears as well.'[20]

Refusal to Supply Information   Despite heavy reliance on confidentiality, the energy industries also refuse a number of specific requests for information from consumer councils, on the grounds that the data is not available or would be too costly to collect and analyse, that the request is for 'management information' which is no concern of the consumer council, or that 'sensitive' areas – especially labour relations – are involved. These grounds were all used by the London Electricity Board (LEB) when it refused to provide the Consultative Council (LECC) with twelve indicators of performance and standards of service (such as the percentage of servicing appointments kept and the average number of reads per meter reader) it had requested.[21]

In April 1980 the LECC asked the LEB to disclose to it new written instructions issued the previous December to clarify the role of disconnection staff, and also any verbal, managerial or other guidelines related to them. The Council were concerned that the new instructions which made it clear that disconnectors were not expected to act as cash collectors or settlement negotiators, could put them in technical breach of the code of practice on disconnections. This code aims to protect households in hardship from having their electricity or gas supplies cut off. The Board refused to supply the information.

In June the LECC was alarmed to discover that domestic disconnections by the LEB in the first quarter of 1980 were more than treble the number for the same quarter in 1979. Over the year 1979/80 LEB disconnection figures, in absolute numbers and as a proportion of domestic credit consumers, were a great deal higher than those of other boards.

These figures clearly reflected LEB's stated policy of getting tough with debtors in autumn 1979.[22] The Council again asked the Board for full disclosure of the written instructions to disconnectors, this time on a confidential basis. The LEB did not reply. In September 1980, in the face of the Board's refusal for the third time to disclose the instructions, the Council agreed that the Chairman should ask for the instructions to be disclosed to himself in his capacity as a member of the Board. At the time of writing, the Chairman had not made this request. But it is not at all clear, even if the information were given to him, whether he could pass that information on to the Council to which it had previously been refused.

Why has the LEB refused to disclose its instructions to disconnectors? According to one member of the LECC, the Board refused on the grounds 'that it was unwilling to risk consumers flourishing the disconnectors' instructions in their faces.'[23] This fear, however groundless, that consumers may exploit knowledge of the Board's operating instructions or management guidelines runs consistently behind many of the LEB's refusals to provide what it calls 'management information', even on a confidential basis. But the fact is that operating practice often impinges on or grows out of the implementation of policy and is thus of legitimate interest to consumer councils.

The LECC has also recently sought information, without success, on the range of reconnection fees charged by each district of the Board, because it was concerned that fees seemed to vary more widely than cost differences alone would justify. One report had quoted reconnection fees plus security deposits ranging from £10 to over £100.[24] The Council also asked to be involved in the work of an LEB internal working party which it had heard was reviewing policy on reconnection fees, to which it received the reply that 'Whether or not there is an LEB Working Party on reconnection fees is an internal matter for the Board and no concern of the Council.'[25]

The LEB's almost pathological dislike of publicity is reflected in its 1979/80 annual report where, in a very defensive review of the year, it says: 'An unfortunate result of the extensive use of the media by the Consultative Council and the welfare organisations to voice criticisms of the Board . . . has been to encourage a hostile attitude towards the Board by a small section of its customers. . . .'[26]

Information not Known to Exist   Consumer councils have problems of another kind. They are not always made aware of information collected by the industries of interest to them.

In early 1980, following press reports of a number of deaths in the south west and Wales from carbon monoxide poisoning connected with the use of solid fuel heating, the Domestic Coal Consumers' Council discovered that the National Coal Board had for some time been collecting statistics on such deaths. The Board had never drawn the attention of the DCCC to the matter, though it was of obvious consumer concern.

The DCCC then mounted a publicity effort in the autumn to persuade people to observe basic safety precautions. Neither the National Coal Board nor the Solid Fuel Advisory Service had made any special efforts themselves to publicise safety precautions prior to the increase in deaths. The Board have now said that they will notify the DCCC of deaths from carbon monoxide poisoning involving solid fuel.

Relationships with Outside Organisations and the Public   The energy consumer councils may open their meetings to the press and public if they wish, and may release documents such as council papers. They are under no obligation to do so.

In practice, most of the electricity consultative council and regional gas consumer council meetings are open to the press and their papers may be made available. The LECC sends the press agenda papers, minutes and, with the agreement of the Chairman, supporting papers. Some regional gas consumer councils lodge their minutes in local libraries. (Meetings and papers of district committees are strictly confidential because the complaints and problems of named individuals are discussed.)

Meetings of the DCCC, National Gas Consumers' Council and Electricity Consumers' Council are held in private and papers are normally confidential (though ECC minutes are publicly available).

All the consumer councils produce annual reports describing their work over the year, and commenting on aspects of industry policy and practice. The gas and electricity consumer councils also include analyses of complaints. But, with few exceptions, the annual reports do not contain information about the industries' work that is not readily available elsewhere.

The consumer councils also publish some information for the general public – for example, on gas safety or how to cope with high electricity bills – and the Electricity Consumers' Council in particular puts out a number of research reports and policy papers for information and discussion.

Consumer councils may, however, face difficulties in publishing work which is critical of the industry. The Levin report is a case in point. In 1979 Dr Peter Levin, a member of LECC, spent six days at one of LEB's district offices, with the Board's agreement to look at the operation of the code of practice on disconnections and the fuel direct scheme (whereby people on supplementary benefit pay for electricity and gas through deductions at source from their weekly benefit). The first draft of the report was discussed with LEB officers and with staff of the DHSS and the Supplementary Benefits Commission (SBC). Dr Levin then rewrote the report and submitted it to the LECC in January 1980. At its meeting in February the LECC endorsed the report and its recommendations and decided that formal responses should be sought from the LEB, SBC and the Department of Health and Social Security before considering further action, including publication.

The report had some criticism to make of the LEB's and the Department of Health and Social Security's procedures for handling debtors – but it showed an appreciation of the difficulties involved and made a number of detailed and constructive suggestions for improvement. The Chairman of the Supplementary Benefits Commission, which also came in for criticism, wrote: 'All in all I think this is a very fair report . . . the results and recommendations have been extremely useful. . . . I believe that the report's generally constructive tone would be widely welcomed.'[27] The Parliamentary Under-Secretary of State at the Department of Health and Social Security, Mrs Lynda Chalker MP, wrote that 'I would see no objection to the publication of this report.'[28]

In April, however, the Council voted eleven to three not to publish the report nor the responses to it, after the LEB representatives had made it clear that publication would make the Board even less willing to cooperate with the Council than it had been in the past.

Convinced that the LEB was ignoring the most important lessons from his study and that as a result consumers in hardship were suffering needlessly, Dr Levin decided to publish the report independently.[29] In his introduction he says he felt obliged to do so because the LEB had 'largely failed to respond' to a confidential report. Following this, the Council decided to write to the Minister of State for Consumer Affairs about the whole episode, saying that it had demonstrated yet again the clear necessity for consumer bodies in the nationalised industries to be given stronger executive powers and a statutory right of access to information, so that they could do their job with maximum effectiveness and public credibility.

Consumer councils themselves vary a good deal in their openness with public and press, the extent to which they publish their work and the trouble they take to help outside organisations which may be seeking information about industry activities. Some consumer councils are regrettably very reluctant to assist or provide information to outside groups.

On occasion the very existence of consumer councils severely restricts access to information by others. The case history on page 221 catalogues the typical experience of a pressure group (National Right to Fuel Campaign) seeking certain detailed information on policy towards electricity disconnections so that its workers could advise clients accordingly.

Government Information to the Public

Published Information

Information on energy published by government includes: regular statistics on energy production, consumption and sales; fuel prices; type of heating installed in new council homes and numbers of homes insulated under government schemes; household spending on fuel; heating additions and lump sum payments for heating for those on supplementary benefit;[30] white papers, such as that on the nationalised industries, and consultation documents, including one on energy policy generally and others on specific aspects of policy such as energy labelling;[31] background papers and reports of working parties, such as reports by the Advisory Council on Energy Conservation, the Marshall Report on combined heat and power and a report on energy forecasting methodologies:[32] research reports such as those produced by the Energy Technology Support Unit, the Building Research Establishment or outside

**The Electricity Council and
its Consumers: A Calendar of Secrecy**

1 The pressure group writes to each of the twelve area boards of
the Electricity Council requesting information.

2 The boards reply that, because the group has written to them
all, a single reply for the whole industry will be prepared by
the Electricity Council.

3 The Electricity Council writes to say that the policy details are
a matter for the boards (*note*: this is why the group wrote to
them in the first place), but that all boards do their best to
ensure that disconnections policy is applied fairly and
compassionately, etc, etc.

4 The group writes again to the twelve area boards for the
information, explaining that the Electricity Council's reply is
too general.

5 The boards reply that the information requested is given to the
area consultative councils. The group must write to them for it.

6 The group writes to the twelve area consultative councils
requesting the information.

7 The consultative councils respond variously: some give the
information requested; some demand to know what the
information is to be used for, necessitating more
correspondence; some fail to reply.

8 Over a year later the group has received some information.
But it is incomplete, not comparable between area boards and
out of date. The original purpose in requesting the information
has been overtaken by events. The person trying to get the
information, wholly frustrated, has given up.

consultants;[33] information aimed at the general public, including
advice on energy conservation, comparative heating costs, the
petrol consumption of new cars and a guide for landlords and
tenants on reselling electricity.

While Tony Benn was Secretary of State the Department of
Energy acquired a good reputation for broadening the range of
information published.* Of particular interest was the series of

* The Select Committee on Science and Technology, in its report on the SGHWR
programme, drew attention to the willingness of Mr Benn and his department to
publish policy documents. 'As a result we – and, indeed, the scientific and technical
Press – have found ourselves in the rather unusual position of being able to monitor
the progress of a major policy review without being hindered by the secrecy surrounding much government policy-making.'[34]

Energy Commission papers started in October 1977, which included discussions of various aspects of policy (energy pricing, depletion policy and so on) not only from the Department but also from other Commission participants such as the fuel industry chairmen, trade union leaders and consumer representatives (comprising the chairmen of the three national energy consumer councils).

The Energy Commission was disbanded by David Howell, the Secretary of State for Energy, in July 1979. A valuable source of information for consumer organisations and the public was lost as a consequence.

Refusals to Publish Information

It is a convention that ministers share collective responsibility for government decisions and as a result governments normally refuse to make public advice to ministers by officials, inter-departmental correspondence on policy and so on – though background papers may be published. This convention makes it difficult for outsiders to know what decisions are being taken when, on what basis and by whom, and effectively prevents them from intervening in any part of the internal policy process.

In March 1980 an inter-departmental working party was set up to study ways of helping the old and disabled make more efficient use of energy.[35] In July 1980 it apparently recommended a major programme to insulate and draught-proof the homes of elderly people using job creation programmes, at a cost of £25 million a year.[36] This approach was rejected by the government and the working party was asked to go away and come up with a less expensive recommendation. But the original options considered by the working party will not be made available for public discussion.

Also in March 1980 documents leaked from the Department of Energy revealed that there were differences of view between the Departments of Energy and Environment on the level of loft insulation to be specified in the building regulations for new housing. A Department of Energy memorandum stated that 'The Department of the Environment has recently put out a consultative document which suggests a lower level of loft insulation in domestic buildings than we consider desirable or cost effective.'[37] Yet the bases of the arguments for a lower or higher level of loft insulation were not aired in public.

Governments have also been known to suppress research reports where the results or the recommendations could be politically embarrassing. The following example relates to a report on energy conservation prepared by a government research agency. This agency, according to one report, 'has a great reputation for its scientific publications not least because they are so clearly impartial. It is indeed a firm principle that results should be published honestly and that there should never be any suggestion either that they should be suppressed when inconvenient or that they should be amended in any way.'

The research project in question started in 1978, and the draft report was circulated to various officials for comment in mid-1979, prior to its planned publication. It immediately ran into trouble. One senior official wrote back:

. . . a decision on publication needs to take into account three possible risks of embarrassment to Ministers and/or the Department: (a) Over the figures or methods of calculation . . . (b) That any of the material could be used to criticise the previous policies or Government expenditure. (c) In the other direction, that the material could be used to increase public pressure for new policies or additional public expenditure. Quite apart from these issues, there seems to us to be a risk . . . that the report could be misunderstood or misinterpreted and used in this way as a means of pressurising Ministers into misguided or premature decisions. If the report is to be published, it will be necessary to include a suitable caveat.

Despite the fact that the policy division mainly concerned did not believe that publication of the report would lead either to undue pressure on ministers or to adverse criticism of past or present policies, other officials continued to hold up publication of the report while making a continual stream of minor technical and presentational comments. In the course of the exchanges, the same senior official wrote revealing: 'While I share your assumption that research reports should *normally* be published, this is surely not invariably the case. There can on rare occasions be good reason either for suppressing publication altogether, or for judicious editing.'

In June 1980 the report was still held up by lack of agreement over the detail, and at the time of writing (October 1980) it is being completely redrafted as a technical and 'policy-free' paper. It is not certain even that this version will be published, and it is unlikely to have as wide an appeal as the original report, which was intended 'to be of assistance to all those interested in the general debate about the allocation of national resources to energy conservation.' This would naturally include consumers and their organisations. Moreover, the technical content of the report may now be significantly out of date.

A similar reluctance on the part of civil servants to sanction published material which could lead to pressure for changed policies or criticism of existing ones was revealed by the *Sunday Times* on 16 March 1980. The story concerned attempts by officials to dissuade Michael Meacher, then Parliamentary Under-Secretary of State at the Department of Health and Social Security, from using evidence from surveys in reply to a Parliamentary question tabled in January 1976 on the incidence of hypothermia (dangerously low body temperatures).

The reply as drafted gave the number of deaths each year attributable solely or mainly to hypothermia: 1970 – sixteen, 1971 – fifteen, 1972 – twenty-one, 1973 – twenty-two, 1974 – seventeen. Michael Meacher pointed out that these official figures for death from hypothermia were minute compared with those suggested in independent research studies. In particular, a national study carried out by Fox and others of a thousand old people in 1972 found that one half per cent of the sample had dangerously low body temperatures in the morning (though these had risen by the evening), equivalent to perhaps 45,000 in the population as a whole.[38]

Opposing the use of this data one official wrote that if the reply suggested a high incidence of hypothermia, then: 'The danger in this is that our reply might be used to bring pressure on the government to divert scarce resources from other purposes to prevention of hypothermia. . . .'

Later the same official wrote:

We felt that in this politically sensitive area it was of great importance not to be issuing information which may be misleading and which could certainly be used against the government. It is almost certain that any reply which suggested that large numbers of old people might be suffering from hypothermia would be used to bring pressure on the government to improve heating provision for old people in some way.

The matter was passed further up the Ministry and Mr Meacher was overruled. The final reply was that the Minister was unable to make an estimate on the incidence of hypothermia because medical evidence was inconclusive; and that the only firm information available came from death certificates. The figures given earlier were then quoted.

An investigation of heating for the elderly was carried out for the Department of the Environment (DoE) by the Research Institute for Consumer Affairs (RICA). The homes of thirty elderly people were given basic insulation and draught proofing, and some were given extra or replacement heating appliances. The RICA monitored the effects on fuel consumption, comfort and costs of these thermal improvements over the winter 1976–77.

RICA's report, entitled 'Thermal Improvements in Old People's Dwellings', was submitted to the DoE in July 1977. A year later, in July 1978, the DoE published a revised version under the title 'An Exploratory Project on Heating for the Elderly'. This report, unlike that of RICA, contains no recommendations. Moreover, the RICA report listed all the available recommendations and requirements on desirable temperature levels in the homes of elderly people. The DoE report omits these. It fails to mention even the Department's own requirement that heating systems in new housing for the elderly should be capable of achieving design temperatures of 21 degrees Centigrade (and 18 degrees Centigrade in all other new housing).

'Massaged' Information

Governments can also disguise – or 'massage' – information in order to present a partial picture which suits their book but can be misleading.

In April 1980 John Moore MP, Parliamentary Under-Secretary at the Department of Energy, retaliated against suggestions that the government was not doing enough on energy conservation. He said that over £200 million of private money had been spent in the previous year on home insulation 'of one sort or another'. In fact this figure includes £150 million spent on double glazing which is one of the least effective energy-saving measures. Very little by way of energy saving will have resulted from this expenditure. (Incidentally, it is not possible to ask a Parliamentary question to bring out the facts on private spending on insulation because it is not a ministerial responsibility.)[39]

Nationalised Industry Information to the Public

Published Information

All the nationalised energy industries publish annual reports and accounts, which contain much useful information about financial performance, the industries' activities, employment and labour productivity, and the like. But the reports contain very little information on the standards of service to customers and value for money provided by the industries.

The electricity supply industry publishes its medium-term development plan which is widely circulated. But the National Coal Board's medium-term development plan is confidential and so is the corporate plan of the British Gas Corporation. Both of these are submitted to the Secretary of State for Energy and used internally. They are not shown to the consumer councils. A short summary was included in BGC's annual report 1979–80 but the NCB's annual report simply mentioned the plan's existence and general objective.

All the industries publish research reports or articles about their research[40] but many reports remain unpublished. The Public Interest Research Centre compiled a list of confidential research reports by the Electricity Council, a number of which could well be of interest to consumer organisations and the public. They included reports on the performance of warm air heating systems, the domestic appliance market, and the reliability of supplies to consumers.[41] But the consumer councils do not get these reports as of right, though they may be made available on a confidential basis on request.

Finally, the industries publish information aimed at the general public, such as advice on energy conservation and the running costs of appliances, easy ways to pay, the code of practice on disconnections, principles for domestic appliance servicing by electricity boards, how to read the meter and so on.

Information not Published

The industries do not publish certain kinds of information. These include information classed as 'management' information (such as LEB's instructions to disconnectors), 'sensitive' information (such as indicators for productivity of meter readers) and 'commercial' information (such as details of individual industrial and commercial contracts). And some kinds of information seem to remain unpublished simply because the industries want to keep them under wraps.

The Central Electricity Generating Board does not provide, for example, details of the costs of increasing planning margins (that is, the additional capacity required to ensure that peak demand can normally be met.)[42] It is thus difficult for outsiders to judge whether the best trade-off is being made between additional cost (which can be very substantial) and increased security of supply. Similarly, the CEGB does not give a breakdown of the reasons for supply failure (strikes, plant failure, etc) which would have a bearing on the appropriate size of the planning margin.

In the mid-1970s a number of consumer organisations and the Select Committee on Nationalised Industries called for an investigation of the potential role of self-cancelling token meters in place of coin slot meters for gas and electricity. The Select Committee said that 'we would join NCC [the National Consumer Council] in wishing to see, at the least, a considered evaluation of the proposal made publicly available.'[43]

The Electricity Council undertook small-scale field trials of token meters in 1977, together with some survey work. In May 1980 it produced a six-page report on their possible use[44] which concluded that they had a very limited and specialised role to play. This report was not published, though it was sent to consumer councils, and it did not contain sufficient information – about the conduct of the field trials and their results, about the technical options and their costs – for outsiders to come to an independent judgement about the potential for token-operated prepayment meters.

Although there has been some advance in accountability on the safety aspects of nuclear power, 'the economics of nuclear power decisions over the past two decades have not been exposed to the same scrutiny and discussion – mainly because the information has not been made available.'[45] In a study of nuclear power decissions[42] Professor Roger Williams concluded that better accountability of the whole policy system, and especially of the Atomic Energy Authority (AEA), would have contributed to better decisions. Instead secrecy was built into the system from the start and became an obsession. In addition the AEA itself enjoyed a near monopoly of technical information and its recommendations were rarely questioned by government, least of all in public.

One might have thought that, faced with matters which they could not really be expected to understand, decision-makers would have sought safety in opening out policy arguments so that outsiders might identify weaknesses insiders were either not qualified to assess or which they were prevented from even acknowledging because of institutional affiliations. Instead, on grounds of commercial security or constitutional propriety, the arguments were repeatedly closed up.[46]

The CEGB has recently introduced a new argument into the

discussion of nuclear power, called 'net effective system savings'. It argues that even without future growth in electricity demand new nuclear power stations are worth building because they would be more cost effective and cheaper to run than existing coal or oil-fired stations. These costings are disputed[47] but it is difficult to make independent estimates without access to the relevant information and assumptions used. Although the CEGB do publish some cost figures[48], they are not sufficiently detailed to enable outsiders to make their own calculations.

A prominent concern of consumer and welfare organisations for some time has been the plight of households who remain disconnected for long periods – over a month, say. Some information on the duration of disconnections was given to the Select Committee on Nationalised Industries in 1976. At that time the British Gas Corporation said that they had only recently begun to collect statistics on the subject, while the Electricity Council's figures were imprecise and included vacant premises, holiday properties and so on.[49]

In July 1978, following pressure from a member of the consultative council, the South Eastern Electricity Board (SEEboard) agreed to collect some information on long-term disconnections by sampling households when reconnected. SEEboard pleaded that looking at the records of *all* disconnected households to obtain more accurate information would involve a disproportionate amount of work, and this was accepted by the majority of consultative council members.

When an independent long-term review on the code of practice on disconnections was set up in early 1979, the gas and electricity industries were put under more pressure to provide figures on long-term disconnections for the review. It later became known (though the consumer councils were not informed) that electricity boards were collecting detailed information to send to the Electricity Council, and statistics for 1978–79 for each board were finally published early in 1980.[50] The Department of Energy said then that it did not receive information from British Gas Corporation on the periods of disconnection.

The figures for electricity were not originally collected on an entirely comparable basis. Some boards based them on reconnections; others looked at the records of households currently disconnected. They are now all prepared by seeing for how long reconnected consumers were disconnected. This seems likely to understate the true incidence of long-term disconnections, since families who remain disconnected, some permanently, are not counted. The understatement will be most serious when, as during 1980, the numbers disconnected are rising.

Reports by British Gas investigators into the causes of gas explosions are confidential. This means that a) people seeking redress from the Corporation for injury or damage caused by explosions are disadvantaged because it is difficult for them to challenge the Corporation's account of what caused the explosions and b) consumer organisations cannot judge whether or not the Corporation is doing all it should to prevent such explosions.

Following four severe gas explosions in the Christmas holiday 1976, the Secretary of State for Energy and the Chairman of the British Gas Corporation commissioned a report on the causes of these and other explosions to consider whether safety procedures and so on could be improved. The report (the King Report) made a number of recommendations and observations.[51] One was that there should be an official source of information on incident statistics, which would classify and correlate details and issue regular reports: 'It was a severe setback to discover that the statistical record was very poor and that it was impossible to collect reliable data on gas explosions for more than the last few years and that even here only British Gas had adequate information.' There are still no independent sources of information on gas explosions. The National Gas Consumers' Council is sent statistics by the British Gas Corporation – on a confidential basis only – but no details are given about causes.

British Gas do not reveal figures for compensation paid to members of the public following gas explosions. When the British Safety Council asked for this information they were told first that that total amount paid out was not available because the sums were not collated centrally. On writing to the regions the Council was then told that replies were being prepared centrally and finally that 'such information is confidential between the regions and the parties concerned.'[52]

The Corporation withholds its internal reports on gas explosions on the grounds that they are privileged documents prepared for the Corporation's regional solicitor so that he can advise on BGC's legal rights and liabilities. British Gas claims that facts are made available to a coroner's inquest if there is a fatality and that it does give information and help in non-fatal accidents to those affected and those acting for them. In addition, gas engineers from the Department of Energy carry out independent investigations into gas explosions where they consider that desirable. 'They are willing to give interested parties the facts contained in their reports'[53] – but presumably not the reports themselves.

Two recent court cases however cast some doubt on whether British Gas can reasonably withhold investigation reports on the grounds of legal privilege. In the first case, Waugh v. British Railways Board, the House of Lords held that

The public interest was, on balance, best served by rigidly confining within narrow limits the privilege of lawfully withholding material or evidence relevant to litigation. Accordingly, a document was only to be accorded privilege from production on the ground of legal professional privilege if the dominant purpose for which it was prepared was that of submitting it to a legal advisor for advice and use in litigation.[54]

In the case of the internal enquiry report on a fatal accident which was the subject of the appeal, the House of Lords held that use for possible litigation was only one of the purposes for which the report was prepared. The other was to establish the cause of the accident so that appropriate safety measures could be taken:

Since the purpose of preparing the internal enquiry report for advice and use in anticipated litigation was merely one of the purposes and not the dominant purpose for which it was prepared, the board's claim of privilege failed and the report would have to be disclosed.

Thus someone affected by an accident who wishes to sue British Gas for compensation must bring an action seeking discovery of the internal report. The action would have to contend that obtaining legal advice was not the *dominant* purpose of the report. In the opinion of Lord Edmund-Davies 'the test of dominance will, as I think, be difficult to satisfy when enquiries are instituted and reports produced automatically whenever any mishap occurs, whatever its nature, its gravity, or even its triviality.' This is certainly the case with the Corporation's internal enquiry reports, which are made routinely whenever a gas explosion occurs.

The second case concerns the *Sunday Times'* fight in 1972 to publish documents and information on thalidomide, at a time when the manufacturers, Distillers, were being sued for compensation by the parents of children born with thalidomide deformities. An injunction to prevent publication was upheld by the House of Lords on the grounds that it was wrong to prejudge the issues in pending proceedings. But in April 1979 the European

Court of Human Rights ruled that, while the mass media should not exceed limits necessary to the proper administration of justice, it was incumbent on them to impart information on matters of public interest, including those before the courts. The public had a right to such information.

The nationalised industries, like the government, are sometimes guilty of massaging information to suit themselves. In particular, their accounting policies have come in for criticism from various sources.[55]

The Price Commission criticised the treatment of depreciation by the South of Scotland Electricity Board and the British Gas Corporation.[56] It also ticked off the SSEB for not fully disclosing contingency provisions – which might otherwise conceal inefficiencies in estimating or in actual performance – and for its treatment of interest paid on loans for power stations under construction, which had a substantial impact on the prices charged to consumers. The Monopolies and Mergers Commission criticised the way the British Gas Corporation allocated its costs to gas appliance marketing.

The effect of these accounting deficiencies is to reduce the value of the existing information published by the industries, and to increase the difficulties experienced by consumer organisations and others in monitoring financial performance.

Conclusions

This chapter has tried to give some impression of the very great difficulties faced by outside organisations, and individual consumers, in obtaining information from government and from the nationalised energy industries on policy, on performance and on customer rights. Even where information is not refused outright, inordinate delays, the release of partial information, the passing of responsibility for providing information from one organisation to another, all serve to obscure activities and policy from the public gaze.

Of course certain types of information may be genuinely sensitive or private – the debt records of named individuals, say, redundancy plans not yet announced, or details of private contracts. But the information requested by consumers and their organisations (and refused by government and the industries) is very rarely of this kind.

Rather, government and the industries have sought to protect themselves from bother, criticism, embarrassment or scrutiny.

And where organisations have been given limited statutory rights, as consumer councils have, the industries still try to ensure nevertheless that the councils remain dependent on their good will – so that the receipt of information becomes a privilege granted in return for good behaviour.

Both governments and nationalised industries tend to assume that they know best what is good for society and that demands for information from the public distract them, with deleterious effects on efficiency, from the task in hand. This view is highly undemocratic; and it is wrong.

REFERENCES

1 Council for Science and Society, *Deciding about Energy Policy*, CSS, 1979.
2 Price Commission, *BP Oil Ltd – Oil and Petroleum products*, HC 87, HMSO, 1979 and *Esso Petroleum Company Ltd – Oil and Petroleum Products*, HC 88, HMSO, 1979; Monopolies and Mergers Commission, *Petrol: A Report on the Supply of Petrol in the United Kingdom by Wholesale*, Cmnd 7433, HMSO, 1979.
3 Electricity Act 1947, section 7 (5).
4 Gas Act 1972, section 10 (2).
5 Coal Industry Nationalisation Act 1946, section 4.
6 National Economic Development Office, *A Study of UK Nationalised Industries*, Appendix volume, NEDO, 1976, p. 91.
7 First report from Select Committee on Procedure, *Report and Minutes of Proceedings*, volume 1, HC 588 – 1, HMSO, 1978, para. 7.8.
8 Select Committee on Procedure, *op. cit.*, para. 7.15.
9 Select Committee on Nationalised Industries, *Reports and Accounts of the Energy Industries*, HC 583, HMSO, July 1978, pp. 59, 67, 102.
10 *Ibid.*; Select Committee on Nationalised Industries, *Gas and Electricity Prices*, HC 353, HMSO, 1976; Select Committee on Nationalised Industries, *Consumers and the Nationalised Industries: Pre-Legislative Hearings*, HC 334, HMSO, 1979; Select Committee on Science and Technology, *SGHWR Programme*, HC 623, HMSO, 1976.
11 Public Accounts Committee, *British National Oil Corporation*, HC 621, HMSO, 1978.
12 Price Commission, *Area Electricity Boards – Electricity Prices and Certain Allied Charges*, HC 132, HMSO, 1979; *British Gas Corporation – Gas Prices and Allied Charges*, HC 165, HMSO, 1979; *Margins of Coal Merchants in West Wales*, HC 214, HMSO, 1978.

13 Monopolies Commission, *Connection Charges for Electricity and Gas*, Cmnd 5036, HMSO, 1972.

14 Fair Trading Act 1973, section 82(1); Price Commission Act 1977, section 6(8).

15 Letter from Mr Don King, then Chairman of the London Electricity Consultative Council, to Mrs Sally Oppenheim MP, Minister of State for Consumer Affairs, 4 March 1980.

16 National Consumer Council, *Consumers and the Nationalised Industries*, HMSO, 1976, p. 56.

17 Medawar, C., 'Measuring and Improving the Performance of the London Electricity Board', in *Consumers of Power*, Social Audit Ltd, 1980, p. 15.

18 King to Oppenheim, *op. cit.*

19 Select Committee on Nationalised Industries (1979), *op.cit.*, p. 49, para 163.

20 *Ibid.*, p. xiv, para 19.

21 Medawar, C., *op.cit.*, pp. 34–38, 42.

22 See, for example, *Financial Times*, 11 September 1979.

23 Levin, P., *In Debt to the LEB*, Child Poverty Action Group, 1980.

24 *Roof*, July/August 1980.

25 Letter dated 20 August 1980 from the Secretary of LEB to the Secretary of LECC.

26 London Electricity Board, *Annual Report and Accounts*, 1979–80, p. 1.

27 Letter dated 31 March 1980 from the Chairman of the Supplementary Benefits Commission to the Chairman of LECC.

28 Letter dated 28 March 1980 from Mrs Chalker to the Chairman of LECC.

29 Levin P., *op. cit.*

30 See *Digest of UK Energy Statistics* (HMSO, annual); *Energy Trends* (Department of Energy, monthly); *Housing and Construction Statistics* (HMSO, quarterly); *Family Expenditure Survey* (HMSO, annual); *Family Expenditure Survey: Expenditure on Fuels* (Department of Energy, annual): *Social Security Statistics* (HMSO, annual): Supplementary Benefits Commission *Annual Report* (HMSO, annual).

31 *The Nationalised Industries*, Cmnd 7131, HMSO, 1978; *Energy Policy: A Consultative Document*, Cmnd 7101, HMSO, 1978; *Energy Consumption Labelling of Household Appliances: A Consultative Document*, Department of Energy, 1980.

32 Advisory Council on Energy Conservation, *Report to the Secretary of State for Energy*, Energy paper 40, HMSO, 1979; *Combined Heat and Electrical Power Generation in the United Kingdom*, Energy paper 35, HMSO, 1979; *Energy Forecasting Methodology*, Energy paper 29, HMSO, 1978.

33 Such as *Energy Conservation: A Study of Energy Consumption in*

Buildings and Possible Means of Saving Energy in Housing.
Building Research Establishment Current Paper 56/75, 1975;
Consumers' Association, *Energy Efficiency Labelling*, Department
of Energy, 1978.

34 Select Committee on Science and Technology, *op.cit.*, para. 6.

35 *Hansard*, 27 March 1980, col. 1662.

36 *Sunday Express*, 3 August 1980.

37 *Observer*, 30 March 1980.

38 Wicks, M., *Old and Cold: Hypothermia and Social Policy*,
Heinemann, 1978, p. 160.

39 Private communication from John Cartwright MP, 2 July 1980.

40 For example, the Electricity Council has published research reports
on *The Economics of Improved Thermal Insulation* (1975), *Ranking
Energy Saving Ideas* (1978) and *Designs for Low Energy Houses*
(1976). The CEGB publishes a journal, *CEGB Research*, as does
the British Gas Corporation, the *Watson House Bulletin*.

41 Medawar, C., *op.cit.*

42 Memorandum by the Electricity Consumers' Council relating to the
Monopolies and Mergers Commission investigation into the
efficiency and costs of the Central Electricity Generating Board, to
be published.

43 Select Committee on Nationalised Industries (1976), *op.cit.*,
para. 81.

44 Electricity Council, Report on the possible use of token-operated
prepayment meters, May 1980.

45 *Financial Times*, 28 August 1980.

46 Williams, R., *The Nuclear Power Decisions*, Croom Helm, 1980.

47 See *Guardian*, 24 September 1980.

48 For example, Central Electricity Generating Board, *Costs of
Producing Electricity*, CEGB, 1980.

49 Select Committee on Nationalised Industries (1976), *op.cit.*,
appendices 31 and 32.

50 *Hansard*, 3 March 1980, col. 14, written answers.

51 King, P. J., *Summary of the King Report*, November 1977,
reproduced in Chick, L., and Farrar, A., *Report to MPs on Gas
Explosions*, British Safety Council, February 1980.

52 Chick L., and Farrar, A., *op.cit.*

53 Memorandum from Department of Energy, July 1980.

54 Waugh v. British Railways Board, *AELR*, 7 August 1979, p. 1169.

55 Consumers' Association, *Nationalised Industry Accounting Policies*,
December 1979.

56 Price Commission, *British Gas Corporation – Gas Prices and Allied
Charges op.cit; South of Scotland Electricity Board – Price Increases
in the Supply of Electricity*, HC 535, HMSO, 1978.

Appendix
Restrictive UK Legislation on the Disclosure of Information

Section 2 of the Official Secrets Act 1911, because of its all-embracing character, is by far the most important single piece of legislation on official information. However, there are many other statutes which contain provisions for making the disclosure of information a criminal offence; unlike Section 2, each is concerned with a specific kind of information.

The complete list of eighty-nine statutes, given below, was provided by the Minister of State at the Home Office on 10 March 1980 in reply to a Parliamentary Question:

Census Act 1920, section 8(2)
Coal Act 1938, section 53
Essential Commodity Reserves Act 1938, section 1(3)
Population (Statistics) Act 1938, section 4(2)
War Damage Act 1943, section 118
Water Act 1945, section 48
Water (Scotland) Act 1946, section 72(6)
Atomic Energy Act 1946, sections 11 & 13
Coal Industry Nationalisation Act 1946, sections 56 & 57
Agriculture Act 1947, section 81
Cotton (Centralised Buying) Act 1947, section 23(2)
Industrial Organisation and Development Act 1947, section 5
Statistics of Trade Act 1947, section 9
Civil Defence Act 1948, section 4(4)
Cotton Spinning (Re-equipment Subsidy) Act 1948, section 4
Monopolies and Restrictive Practices (Inquiry and Control) Act 1948, section 17
Radioactive Substances Act 1948, section 7
Prevention of Damage by Pests Act 1949, section 22(5)
Food and Drugs Act 1955, sections 5(3) & 100(5)
Army Act 1955, section 60
Air Force Act 1955, section 60
Food and Drugs (Scotland) Act 1956, sections 5 & 36

Clean Air Act 1956, section 26
Naval Discipline Act 1957, section 34
Cinematograph Films Act 1957, section 5
Agricultural Marketing Act 1958, section 47
Offices Act 1960, section 9
Radioactive Substances Act 1960, section 13(3)
Flood Prevention (Scotland) Act 1961, section 34
Covent Garden Market Act 1961, section 32
Factories Act 1961, section 154
Public Health Act 1961, section 68
Rivers (Prevention of Pollution) Act 1961, section 12
Offices, Shops and Railway Premises Act 1963, section 59
Water Resources Act 1963, section 112
Weights and Measures Act 1963, section 48
Agriculture and Horticulture Act 1964, section 13
Harbours Act 1964, section 46
Industrial Training Act 1964, section 6
Cereals Marketing Act 1965, section 17
Gas Act 1965, Schedule 6, paragraph 9
Highlands and Islands Development (Scotland) Act 1965,
   section 12
Rivers (Prevention of Pollution) (Scotland) Act 1965, section 11
Abortion Act 1967, section 2(1)
Agriculture Act 1967, sections 24 and 55
Companies Act 1967, section 111
Iron and Steel Act 1967, section 43
Legal Aid (Scotland) Act 1967, section 18(2) & (4)
Medicines Act 1968, section 118
Sewerage (Scotland) Act 1968, section 50
Trade Descriptions Act 1968, section 28
Post Office Act 1969, section 65
Transport (London) Act 1969, section 36
Agriculture Act 1970, sections 21, 83 & 108
Sea Fish Industry Act 1970, sections 14(1) & 42
Civil Aviation Act 1971, section 36, as amended by the Civil
   Aviation Act 1978, Schedule 1, paragraph 6(9)
Fire Precautions Act 1971, section 21
Highways Act 1971, section 67(4)
Town and Country Planning Act 1971, section 281(3)
Legal Advice and Assistance Act 1972, section 6(1)
European Communities Act 1972, section 11(2)
Harbours (Loans) Act 1972, section 2

Town and Country Planning (Scotland) Act 1972, section 266
Employment Agencies Act 1973, section 9
Counter-Inflation Act 1973, Schedule 4, paragraph 4 as
    amended by Price Commission Act 1977, Schedule 2,
    paragraph 9
Fair Trading Act 1973, section 133
Consumer Credit Act 1974, section 174
Merchant Shipping Act 1974, section 14(8) as amended by
    Merchant Shipping Act 1979, section 40(1)(b)
Slaughterhouses Act 1974, section 20(4)
Control of Pollution Act 1974, section 94
Legal Aid Act 1974, section 22
Rehabilitation of Offenders Act 1974, section 9
Health and Safety at Work etc Act 1974, section 28
Biological Standards Act 1975, section 5
Sex Discrimination Act 1975, section 61(2)
Supply Powers Act 1975, sections 5 & 6
Iron and Steel Act 1975, section 33
Industry Act 1975, section 33
Race Relations Act 1976, section 52(2)
Energy Act 1976, section 18(2) and Schedule 2, paragraph 7
Restrictive Trade Practices Act 1976, section 41(3)
Rent (Agriculture) Act 1976, section 30
Aircraft and Shipbuilding Industries Act 1977, section 52
Consumer Safety Act 1978, section 4(3)
Transport Act 1978, section 11(2)
Estate Agents Act 1979, section 10
Weights and Measures Act 1979, section 12
Agricultural Statistics Act 1979, sections 3 & 4
Banking Act 1979, sections 19 & 20

Thirty-one of these statutes have been enacted since the Franks
Committee first catalogued supplementary statutory provisions in
Appendix V of its report. Further additions to this list of restrictive
statutes were made between March 1980 and June 1981: the Competition Act 1980; the Industry Act 1980 which repealed section
33 of the Industry Act 1975; the Water (Scotland) Act 1980 which
repealed the provision in section 72 of the now wholly repealed
Water (Scotland) Act 1946; and the Civil Aviation Act 1980 which
amended the provisions of section 36 of the Civil Aviation Act
1971.
    Many of these statutes, which are of varying character, are

entirely unobjectionable. Some, for example the Army Act 1955, deal with security matters; others, for example the Rehabilitation of Offenders Act 1974, protect personal privacy. Another group of statutes, for example the Clean Air Act 1956, generally makes it an offence to disclose information obtained by an Inspector from a visit to industrial premises with regard to any manufacturing process or trade secret unless disclosure is in the performance of his duties. A further category, for example the Restrictive Trade Practices Act 1976, generally restricts the disclosure of information which undertakings are required to provide unless with the consent of the person carrying on the undertaking. The last two categories of statutes both raise difficult questions about the nature of commercial confidentiality and the countervailing claims of public interest.*

* See particularly Chapter Six.

Select Bibliography

The bibliography is divided into four categories: general books; general pamphlets and articles; official publications; and draft legislation and miscellaneous.

General Books

Jonathan Aitken, *Officially Secret*, Weidenfeld & Nicolson, 1971.
Leslie Chapman, *Your Disobedient Servant*, Penguin, 1979.
Itzhak Galnoor, *Government Secrecy in Democracies*, Harper Colophon, 1977.
Peter Kellner and Lord Crowther-Hunt, *The Civil Servants: An Enquiry into Britain's Ruling Class*, Macdonald, 1980.
David Leigh, *The Frontiers of Secrecy: Closed Government in Britain*, Junction Books, 1980.
James Michael, *Open and Closed Government in Britain*, Penguin (forthcoming).
Donald Rowat (ed.), *Administrative Secrecy in Developed Countries*, Macmillan, 1979.
David Williams, *Not in the Public Interest*, Hutchinson, 1965.

General Pamphlets and Articles

Trevor Barnes, *Open up! Britain and Freedom of Information in the 1980s*, Fabian Tract no. 467, Fabian Society, 1980.
Tony Benn, *The Right to Know* (text of a lecture to the 1978 annual meeting of the British Association for the Advancement of Science), Institute for Workers' Control, 1978.
William Birtles, 'Big Brother Knows Best: The Franks Report on Section 2 of the Official Secrets Act', *Public Law*, Summer 1973.
James Cornford, 'The Right to Know Secrets', *The Listener*, 31 August 1978.
Lord Croham (Sir Douglas Allen), 'Is Nothing Secret?', *The Listener*, 7 September 1978.
Harold Evans, 'The Half-free Press', in *The Freedom of the Press*, Granada Guildhall Lectures 1974, Hart-Davis, MacGibbon, 1974.
Freedom of Information Campaign, *Secrecy, or the Right to Know?*, the Library Association, 1980.

Patricia Hewitt, *Privacy: the Information Gatherers*, National Council for Civil Liberties, 1977.
JUSTICE, *Freedom of Information* (Chairman of Committee Anthony Lincoln Q.C.), 1978.
Arthur Lewis MP, 'Freedom of Information', *Contemporary Review*, vol. 231, no. 1338, July 1977.
Charles Medawar, *Parliamentary Questions – and Answers*, Social Audit Ltd, 1980.
Charles Medawar, *A Public Right to Know*, Aslib (Association of Librarians Proceedings), 28(2), February 1976.
James Michael, *The Politics of Secrecy: the Case for a Freedom of Information Law*, National Council for Civil Liberties, 1979.
James Michael, 'The Secrecy of Politics', *Social Audit*, vol. 1, no. 1, summer 1973.
Outer Circle Policy Unit,* *An Official Information Act*, 1977.
Tom Riley and Karen Hansen (eds.), *A Review of Freedom of Information Around the World*, International Freedom of Information Commission, 1980.
Scottish Consumer Council, *Rare Access: a Report on Access to Information in Scotland* (provisional title), SCC., Spring 1982.
Ronald Wraith, *Open Government: The British Interpretation,* Royal Institute of Public Administration, 1977.

Official Publications

Civil Service Department, *Disclosure of Official Information: A Report on Overseas Practice*, HMSO, 1979.
Home Office, *Departmental Committee on Section 2 of the Official Secrets Act 1977* (Chairman: Lord Franks), 4 vols., Cmnd 5104, HMSO, 1972.
Home Office, *Reform of Section 2 of the Official Secrets Act 1911*, Cmnd 7285, HMSO, 1978.
Home Office, *Report of the Committee on Data Protection* (Chairman: Sir Norman Lindop), Cmnd 7341, HMSO, 1978.
Lord Chancellor's Department, *Modern Public Records: Selection and Access*, (Chairman: Sir Duncan Wilson), Cmnd 8204, HMSO, 1981.
Lord Privy Seal, *Open Government*, Cmnd 7520, HMSO, 1979.
Prime Minister, *The Civil Service* (Chairman: Lord Fulton), 5 vols., HMSO, 1968.
Prime Minister, *Information and the Public Interest*, Cmnd 4089, HMSO, 1969.

Draft Legislation and Miscellaneous

All Party Committee for Freedom of Information, *A Freedom of Information and Privacy Act for the United Kingdom*, 1976.

Virginia Beardshaw, *Conscientious Objectors at Work*, Social Audit Ltd, 1981.

Civil Service College, *Open Government: Summary of the Proceedings of a Seminar on Open Government Held at the Civil Service College on 13–15 November 1978*, C.S.C. Working Paper No. 6, Sunningdale: Civil Service College, 1979.

Stewart Dresner, *Open Government: Lessons from America*, Outer Circle Policy Unit*, 1980.

Lord Franks, *Disclosure and the Law*, text of an Address given to a seminar on open government held at the Civil Service College 13–15 November 1978, C.S.C. Working Paper No. 5, Sunningdale, Civil Service College, 1979.

Itzhak Galnoor, *Administrative Secrecy in Democracies*, paper given to the International Political Science Association, 1972.

Peter Hennessy and Colin Bennett, *Consumer's Guide to Open Government: Techniques for Penetrating Whitehall*, Outer Circle Policy Unit*, 1980.

Joseph Jacob, 'Discovery and Public Interest', *Public Law*, summer 1976.

Joseph Jacob, 'Some Reflections on Governmental Secrecy', *Public Law*, spring 1974.

The Labour Party, *Statements to Annual Conference by the National Executive Committee*, 1978. (Includes the text of the NEC's Freedom of Information Bill.)

The Law Society, *Official Information: Reform of Section 2 of the Official Secrets Act 1911; and Availability of Official Information to Members of the Public*, Memorandum by the Council's Law Reform Committee, 1979.

The Liberal Party, *Public Access to Official Information: A Liberal Proposal for Legislation*, 1978.

Outer Circle Policy Unit*, *Official Information Bill*, 1978. (This was the basis for Private Member's Bills presented to the House of Commons by Clement Freud MP, Frank Hooley MP and others.)

E. J. Razzell, *Open Government: An Analytical Framework*, Civil Service College, C.S.C. Working Paper no. 8, 1979.

---

* The Outer Circle Policy Unit has now closed. Items published by them can be obtained from: the Bookshop, 9 Poland Street, London W.1.

Index

110; and pesticide research 114; and
traffic forecasts 163
New Society, and social security report
191, 198, 199
Norway, freedom of information 28;
school records 87
nuclear energy *see also* energy 210, 211;
economic aspects 228; independent
scrutiny of, (USA) 118, 227; and
Official Secrets Act 119; suppression
of information 119–21
Nuclear Installations Inspectorate 120

Office of Fair Trading 213
official information, definition and
scope of 5
Official Secrets Act (1911) *see also*
Section 1; Section 2; and consumer
information 175, 176; function of 5;
history 4–15; and local government
15–19; and welfare benefits 194
ombudsman, the 14, 29, 158, 160, 161;
Australia 36; Canada 37, 38; local
government 16, 64, 65, 78, 79
open government 1, 10, 13, 14, 50, 62,
129, 130, 137, 193; green paper on
11, 13; and housing 42, 44, 53, 63–5;
and social welfare 187, 188
Open University, research into personal
files 63
Organisation of Economic Cooperation
and Development, education report
69, 70
Orme, Stanley 187, 193
Ostler, Sidney 160, 161

Parliament, and provision of
information 211, 212; select
committees 211, 212
Peaden, John 131, 132
Peeler, Joseph 166, 170
personal data 16; and housing authority
63–5; and Privacy Act (1974) (USA)
30, 33; rights of individual 17, 28;
statistics for, (USA) 33; in Sweden 34
pesticides 112–16, 121; banned, export
of 115, 116; biased research 114; data
evaluation 115; data (USA) 114;
regulation of 113; and wildlife 113
Pesticides Safety Precautions Scheme
96, 113, 115, 116
Peyton, John 165
Pile, William 70

Pincher, Chapman 119
planning 127–49; Barnsbury, case study
129–31; collection of information 141,
142; commercial confidentiality 135–
41; Millfield, case study 133, 134,
146; misunderstandings 133–5;
Nottinghamshire, case study 137–41;
and public participation 128, 129,
199, 141–9; secrecy 127–32, 138–40;
Sharrow, case study 131, 132, 146;
structure plans 137, 139, 145;
Tolmers Square, case study 135–7
pollution *see also* environmental
information; air 106–9; Alkali
Inspectorate 102–6; control of 98–
101; legal aspects 96, 97, 99, 110;
nuclear energy 118–21; and partiality
109; pesticides 112–16; protection of
interests 95–101, 107, 116; provision
of information 98, 107–9; river 96,
109–12; role of local government
106–12; Royal Commission on
Environmental Pollution 97, 98, 101;
secrecy 100, 101, 111, 112, 121, 122
Post Office, consumer council 23; status
under Official Secrets Act 21
Post Office Users' National Council 23,
24
pressure groups *see also* individual
groups; 7, 29, 32, 101, 135, 186, 188
Price Commission 182, 213, 214, 231
Privacy Act (1974) (USA) 30, 33
product testing 172–83; and consumer
interests 172–4; and consumer
movement (USA) 173, 176, 177, 182;
disclosure of information 174, 175,
182; cigarettes 175
Property Services Agency 127; product
purchasing and testing 178, 179
Protection of Official Information Bill
12
Public Accounts Committee 212, 213
Public Bodies (Admission to Meetings)
Act (1960) 16, 75
Public Health Act (1936), and access to
information 15, 16; and air pollution
95, 96, 107
Public Interest Research Centre 22, 226
public participation 141–9; benefits of
143–5; lessons from the 70s 145–7;
surveys 142, 143
*Public Participation and Planners'
Blight* 133